THE
POWER
OF THE
PENTAGON

CONGRESSIONAL QUARTERLY
1735 K STREET, N.W., WASHINGTON, D.C.

Congressional Quarterly Inc.

Congressional Quarterly Inc., an editorial research service and publishing company, serves clients in the fields of news, education, business and government. It combines specific coverage of Congress, government and politics by Congressional Quarterly with the more general subject range of an affiliated service, Editorial Research Reports.

Congressional Quarterly was founded in 1945 by Nelson and Henrietta Poynter. Its basic periodical publication was and still is the CQ *Weekly Report,* mailed to clients every Saturday. A cumulative index is published quarterly.

The CQ *Almanac,* a compendium of legislation for one session of Congress, is published every spring. *Congress and the Nation* is published every four years as a record of government for one presidential term.

Congressional Quarterly also publishes paperback books on public affairs. These include the twice-yearly *Guide to Current American Government* and such recent titles as *Candidates '72, Dollar Politics* and *China and U.S. Foreign Policy.*

CQ Direct Research is a consulting service which performs contract research and maintains a reference library and query desk for the convenience of clients.

Editorial Research Reports covers subjects beyond the specialized scope of Congressional Quarterly. It publishes reference material on foreign affairs, business, education, cultural affairs, national security, science and other topics of news interest. Service to clients includes a 6,000-word report four times a month bound and indexed semi-annually. Editorial Research Reports publishes paperback books in its fields of coverage. Founded in 1923, the service merged with Congressional Quarterly in 1956.

The Power of the Pentagon was organized by defense writer Jack McWethy, who was the principal contributor to the book.

Thomas J. Arrandale wrote the chapters on the Foreign Relations and Foreign Affairs Committees and on war powers. Other contributors: Robert A. Barnes, Janice L. Goldstein, Martha Gottron, Peter A. Harkness, Margaret Thompson, Stanley L. Williams. Cover design was by Art Director Howard Chapman.

Book Service Editor: Robert A. Diamond

Library of Congress Catalog No. 72-84270
International Standard Book No. 0-87187-034-7

Copyright 1972 by Congressional Quarterly Inc.
1735 K Street, N.W., Washington, D.C. 20006

TABLE OF CONTENTS

No power on earth is stronger than the United States of America today. None will be stronger than the United States of America in the future.

—President Richard M. Nixon, June 1, 1972, to a joint session of Congress on return from the Moscow summit

America must never become a second rate nation. As one who has tasted the bitter fruits of our weakness before Pearl Harbor, 1941, I give you my sacred pledge that if I become President of the United States, America will keep its defenses alert and fully sufficient to meet any danger.

—Senator George McGovern, July 14, 1972, acceptance speech to the Democratic National Convention

INTRODUCTION

The national commitment to a large and expensive peacetime military establishment is a comparatively recent phenomenon in American history. The Defense Department is only 25 years old and owes its creation to a shift in attitudes toward military preparedness caused by the rude awakening of Pearl Harbor and the experiences of World War II. *(Defense Department history p. 103)*

In April 1917, at the outbreak of World War I, the War Department had 2,816 employees in Washington, D.C. One year later the department's personnel had risen to 37,400 working in temporary buildings located on the mall between the Capitol and the Washington Monument. By 1922, the manpower level had dropped back to 4,900 and the temporary buildings were torn down.

The employment experience of World War I was recalled in July 1941, six months before Pearl Harbor, when the House of Representatives was considering funding the construction of a permanent office building (the Pentagon) for 40,000 employees of the burgeoning War Department. One member declared: "We do not want a militaristic nation in the future and therefore we do not need the largest office building in the world for our War Department." *(p. 104)*

By 1972, the Defense Department had long since expanded beyond the confines of the Pentagon. It occupies 22 percent of federal government office space with its 160,000 employees in metropolitan Washington, and it has placed before Congress a request for an additional office building in the Washington area.

Changing attitudes toward military preparedness were dramatically illustrated by the career of William Mitchell, an army officer who as an early proponent of air power predicted in the 1920s that aviation would be decisive in the next war. In 1924, Mitchell said that the Japanese would begin the war with an aerial bombardment of U.S. military installations in Hawaii.

Court-martialed and found guilty of insubordination in 1925 following his public criticism of the defense policies of his superiors, Mitchell resigned from the army in 1926 and launched a career of writing and advocacy for an independent air force. He died in 1936, shortly after the House of Representatives refused to reinstate him to the list of retired army officers.

During World War II, Mitchell's predictions swept the country with the force of scientific discoveries. In 1945 he was posthumously awarded the Congressional Medal of Honor and promoted to the rank of major general; his life became the subject of a popular film in which he was portrayed by Hollywood idol Gary Cooper. These were symbolic gestures of a nation which was well on its way to setting national defense among its highest priorities.

The hostile environment of the cold war clinched the nation's commitment to defense. The first National Security Act, which set up the National Military Establishment, was signed in July 1947—four months after President Truman had announced a policy of military and economic support for "free peoples...resisting attempted subjugation by armed minorities or by outside pressures" —the Truman doctrine. The 1949 amendment to the act, which renamed the new agency the Defense Department, was signed in August, one month after the President had signed ratification of the North Atlantic Treaty and at a time when Chiang Kai-shek's forces were fleeing mainland China for Formosa.

The new designation, the Department of "Defense" was significant. The "War" Department, almost by definition, was an institution which had limited functions in times of peace. The Department of "Defense" symbolized eternal vigilance.

Ambiguities of Power

Americans have grown accustomed to hearing their leaders reassure them that theirs is the most powerful nation on the earth. There is nothing unusual in the assertions of military power which appear on the facing page. President Johnson, challenged on his Vietnam policy, proclaimed: "We are the number one nation and we are going to stay the number one nation." Similar statements may be found in the public oratory of every President since the end of World War II.

But what does it mean to be "number one"—to be the most powerful nation on earth? More specifically, what is meant by the power of the Pentagon and what role does Congress play in its creation and control?

1

The "number one nation" no longer possesses—as it did during World War II—the will or capacity to bring military adversaries to their knees. In an era of limited wars, the avoidance of defeat and the search for an honorable settlement have become substitutes for victory and unconditional surrender. When President Nixon announced the U.S. offensive into Cambodia in April 1970, he said his action was necessary to prevent "the first defeat" in the nation's "proud 190-year history." The "world's most powerful nation" could not risk exposing itself to the world as a "pitiful, helpless giant," he declared.

Turning from limited war to nuclear deterrence, it is probably true, as candidate McGovern has said in defense of his own proposals to cut military spending, that the United States has the power to maintain "more than ten times the number (of nuclear weapons) required to destroy every significant target in both the Soviet Union and the People's Republic of China." It is less clear that such power guarantees that the nuclear holocaust will not occur. The security provided by nuclear arms was questioned by military hero Dwight D. Eisenhower in an article written after he left the presidency.

> No matter how much we spend for arms, there is no safety in arms alone.... I have had a varied experience over a lifetime, and if I have learned anything, it is that there is no way in which a country can satisfy the craving for absolute security—but it can bankrupt itself, morally and economically, in attempting to reach that illusory goal through arms alone.

Power to Spend. Eisenhower's reference to the level of defense spending focuses on the least ambiguous meaning of U.S. military power. The Pentagon has spent $1.2-trillion since the end of World War II, an amount that far exceeds the defense spending of any other country in the world. The U.S. defense budget is larger than the combined defense budgets of all communist nations.[1]

As a percentage of the federal budget, defense spending has been dropping—from 85 percent in 1945 to 59 percent in 1960 and to a projected 32 percent in the fiscal 1973 budget sent to Congress in January. But the $83.4-billion requested for new spending authority for defense is the largest single item in the budget. The figure is seven times greater than the budget request for education and manpower programs, four times higher than the request for health programs, seven times the request for transportation and commerce and 35 times larger than the request for natural resources and environmental protection programs. The power of the Pentagon should therefore be understood in part as an ability to acquire substantial portions of the nation's resources for military purposes.

Future Spending. The Nixon administration has initiated a number of policies which have led some members of Congress to believe that it should be possible to reduce defense spending in the 1970s.

Direct U.S. involvement in the Vietnam war has been reduced and with it the level of spending on the war—down from over $20-billion yearly during the height of Johnson administration involvement to a projected

$3.5-billion for fiscal 1973. The President has proclaimed a policy of reduced military involvement around the globe—the Nixon doctrine. And the strategic arms limitation negotiations with the Soviet Union have led to the signing of two accords—a treaty limiting to two the number of U.S. and Soviet antiballistic missile sites and an interim agreement limiting the quantity of offensive missiles each side could maintain.

Paradoxically, none of these promising developments will prevent a rising level of defense spending throughout the 1970s. The savings from Vietnam have already been absorbed by inflation and by large payroll increases designed to pave the way for an all-volunteer army.

Spending on strategic weapons is expected to rise. The interim agreement on offensive missiles does not restrict qualitative improvements, and the administration's "bargaining chip" diplomacy calls for the development of more advanced weaponry. Defense Secretary Melvin R. Laird told Congress in June 1972 that modernization of offensive strategic weapons would provide an incentive to the Soviet Union for the next phase of arms limitations talks and a hedge if the talks failed.

The net effect of these upward pressures on the defense budget—together with probable cost overruns, further salary increases and expected proposals for other new weapons systems—could push defense spending to an annual level of $100-billion by fiscal 1972.[2]

Congressional Control

An important corollary of the elevation of defense to the highest of national priorities has been the Defense Department's comparative autonomy from congressional supervision and scrutiny. Congressional critics of defense policy have chided themselves for what they regard as their own failure to exercise their constitutional responsibilities. Sen. J. W. Fulbright (D Ark.) has said:

> I must confess that I have not really exerted myself as much as I might have in an effort to control the military. Actually I have been under a feeling that it was useless and utterly futile, that nothing could be done, for example, to cut an appropriation for the Defense Department no matter what I did. This is something that started with World War II. The Congress simply does not review or investigate or exercise control over defense spending.[3]

The Power of the Pentagon examines congressional-military relations as they are developing in the early 1970s. It begins with a close look at the key congressional committees having responsibility for defense policy and explains how these bodies control and are controlled by the military. Part II turns to morale problems in the military—problems which Congress has approached somewhat indirectly through military pay raises and a number of inconclusive investigations. *(p. 21)*

The case studies in Part III illustrate Congress' role in the major defense policy decisions of recent years. By and large, the studies demonstrate that although Congress is subjecting defense programs to more debate and scrutiny than in the past, the Pentagon can still count on congressional approval for its most important programs. *(p. 39)*

Robert A. Diamond
Book Service Editor
July 1972

---

1 *The Military Balance 1971-72*, International Institute for Strategic Studies, 1971.
2 *Setting National Priorities: the Fiscal 1973 Budget*, Brookings Institution, 1972, p.81.
3 Quoted in *The Military Establishment*, Harper & Row 1971, p. 53.

ARMED SERVICES COMMITTEES: ADVOCATES OR OVERSEERS?

Rep. Otis G. Pike (D N.Y.) told Congressional Quarterly: "The House Armed Services Committee doesn't control the Pentagon; the Pentagon controls the House Armed Services Committee."

Rep. F. Edward Hebert (D La.), chairman of the committee, replied in a separate interview: "Now that is the type of irresponsible statements that are made without being documented. That statement is so foolish it answers itself."

"I'd like to see somebody document that," Hebert challenged. "Why, I'm the last man in the world the military wants to get into a fight with. They don't want any confrontation with me, believe me. That accusation is absolutely wrong."

Hebert went on to say: "I intend to build the strongest military we can get. Money is no question. The yardstick should be necessity, not money.

"Now we have some people (on the committee) who disagree with me a great deal whom I respect a great deal. Now you take Pike. Pike is very articulate, very smart and you know that I disagree with him on plenty of things, but I certainly have the greatest admiration for him."

The divergent views expressed by Pike and Hebert represent what many, both in and out of Congress, feel about the roles of the House and Senate Armed Services Committees in overseeing Defense Department spending for weapons and research and development.

Though the committees chop money from the Pentagon's requests each year, critics—including one member of Congress who once worked at the Pentagon—contend that the military budget is padded in anticipation of the cuts.

And once the committees have finished working on the annual procurement authorization bill—a $21.3-billion measure in fiscal 1972—it has been a rare phenomenon when the dollar value of the bill was changed by amendment on the floor.

Three times in the 11 years that the committee has had this type of authorizing power has the Senate overridden opposition by the Armed Services Committee chairman and changed the dollar total of the bill reported from committee. On one other occasion, the Senate changed the total with the agreement of the committee chairman.

The House Armed Services Committee has what might be regarded as a perfect record. Not once in 11 years has the dollar value of the procurement authorization bill been altered on the House floor over the objections of the committee chairman.

"That's right," said Chairman Hebert. "The power is awesome."

John C. Stennis (D Miss.), chairman of the Senate Armed Services Committee, warned the Defense Department in February that his committee would be tightening its oversight role.

The authorization bill sets the appropriations limit each year for military spending on research and development and the purchase of all weapons systems plus manpower levels for the active armed forces and the reserves.

Building Power

The Armed Services Committees were formed as a consolidation of the Military Affairs and Naval Affairs Committees by the Legislative Reorganization Act of 1946. As a result of the act, the number of standing committees in the Senate was reduced from 33 to 16 and duties of the 48 standing committees in the House were consolidated in 18 committees.

In some cases the committee reorganizations resulted in a substantial consolidation of power. For the newly formed Armed Services Committees, however, the power to enforce committee decisions was limited. The Appropriations Committees were responsible for scrutinizing the "line items" in the military budget, not the Armed Services Committees. Not until late in the 1950s did the Armed Services Committees make a bid to exercise more authority.

Where the Armed Services Committees then exercised power was in military organization, policy and the authorization and procurement of manpower through the draft. The committees reviewed plans for developing new weapon systems, but it was the Appropriations Committees which both authorized and appropriated funds for specific military programs. The Appropriations Committees were sensitive to recommendations by the Armed Services Committees, but acceptance of them was not guaranteed by law.

Housing and Construction. One problem which occupied the Armed Services Committees was providing adequate housing for military personnel. Two programs originating in the Senate committee were adopted. They provided both committees with their first substantial authorizing powers.

The Wherry plan, named after Sen. Kenneth S. Wherry (R Neb. 1943-1951), allowed private developers to build and operate military family housing. In exchange, the government leased to developers the land and guaranteed mortgages and a reasonable rental income. The program was enacted in 1949 (PL 81-211).

The Capehart program, named after Sen. Homer E. Capehart (R Ind. 1945-1963), provided that private contractors would build military family housing with private financing. The facility was to be operated and amortized by the military with appropriated funds. The Capehart program (PL 84-345) was adopted in 1955.

Through the housing construction measures, the Armed Services Committees began authorizing limits for appropriations. Although the committees' authorizing powers later were expanded to include almost all types of military construction, ranging from housing to missile test sites, the total still amounted to less than 5 percent of the defense budget.

Procurement and Research. The Armed Services Committees in 1959 attached to their military construction authorization bill a rider which would greatly expand the committees' role in overseeing military spending. The rider required the Armed Services Committees to authorize limits on appropriations used to purchase aircraft, missiles and ships. This was a major breakthrough for the committees, giving them the power to authorize appropriations for approximately 15 percent of the Defense Department's annual expenditures. Prior to this time the committee authorized funds for procurement, not by specific programs, but as bulk figures.

In 1959, as the Armed Services Committees moved to acquire greater power, Richard B. Russell (D Ga. 1933-1971) was chairman of the Senate Armed Services Committee and Lyndon B. Johnson (D Texas Senate 1949-1961) was the third-ranking Democrat. Rep. Carl Vinson (D Ga. 1914-1965) was chairman of the House Armed Services Committee and L. Mendel Rivers (D S.C. 1941-1970), who succeeded Vinson as chairman, was the fourth-ranking Democrat.

The 1959 rider to PL 86-149 went into effect during consideration of the fiscal 1962 budget request. In calendar year 1962 the committees again expanded their authorizing function of appropriations. In PL 87-436 the Armed Services Committees were given the power to authorize limits on appropriations for research, development, testing and evaluation (RDT&E) associated with aircraft, missiles and ships. The following year, 1963, the committees took over the authorizing function for all RDT&E conducted by the Defense Department (PL 88-174).

In subsequent years the Armed Services Committees assumed an increasingly active role in examining the Pentagon's budget request. Accompanying the more active role has been expanded authority. Of the $70.5-billion appropriated in fiscal 1972 for the Defense Department, 33 percent ($23.3-billion) received prior authorization from bills originating in the Armed Services Committees.

By the end of 1971 the Armed Services Committees were originating legislation which authorized appropriations for all RDT&E, for the procurement of all weapons and weapon systems, tracked vehicles and torpedoes, for active duty personnel salaries and almost all construction.

Until authorizing measures from the Armed Services Committees are passed by Congress and signed by the President, no Defense Department appropriation bill can be adopted by the House or Senate. And once the authorizing measure has been signed into law, its limits cannot be exceeded by the appropriations bill.

In addition to authorizing appropriations for the Pentagon, the Armed Services Committees are responsible for setting manpower limits and salaries for the active armed forces and the reserves.

The Armed Services Committees do not authorize annual funds for operation and maintenance of the armed forces ($20.2-billion in fiscal 1972), for retired military personnel benefits and pensions ($3.7-billion in fiscal 1972) or for active duty military personnel benefits and salaries ($21-billion in fiscal 1972). The three categories of spending are carried annually only in the appropriations bill.

PX Systems. Another realm of military finance which the Armed Services Committees have had little to do with has been the on-base clubs and open messes as well as the entire commissary or post exchange (PX) system. These operations fall into the category of non-appropriated fund activity. Congress does not appropriate the funds to maintain the facilities. The clubs and commissaries provide self-generating revenues which are returned to the activities from which they came.

While non-appropriated fund activities were not created by statute, both Congress and the courts have recognized and approved of their existence.

The Senate Government Operations Permanent Investigating Subcommittee issued a final report Nov. 2, 1971, on military non-appropriated fund activity after an investigation of more than two years. The subcommittee found that "corruption, criminality and moral compromise were common to the operations of these non-appropriated fund activities."

The House and Senate Armed Services Committees which have undefined authority over these activities did not participate in the investigation. The House Armed Services Committee announced in November 1971 that it had established its own subcommittee to look into the situation. According to Hebert, the subcommittee's first job was to find out just how much authority the Armed Services Committee has over the operations of non-appropriated fund activities.

Support or Control

Critics and supporters of the Armed Services Committees agreed that the committees act as both advocate and overseer of the armed forces. They differ on the degree that advocacy and oversight have been exercised.

"L. Mendel Rivers (former Armed Services Committee chairman), and to a lesser extent Eddie Hebert, saw the function of the Armed Services Committee as being that of the only advocate which the military has in Congress," Pike said. "They have tended in my opinion, and this is much less true in the case of Eddie, to defend the military against all critics."

Samuel S. Stratton (D N.Y.), sixth-ranking member of the 39-man House Armed Services Committee, said: "I think the Armed Services Committee is an advocate for the military in the sense that most of us recognize that the military is an important part of any free society.

"As Mr. Rivers used to say, 'If you don't have a friend on this committee, you don't have a friend anywhere.' I think we want to keep the armed services strong," Stratton said.

Les Aspin (D Wis.), a youthful (33) committee member and one of its most severe critics, said: "The Armed Services Committee looks on its role as the protector of the uniformed military officer. The committee thinks its role is to find out what the military wants and then try to get it for them.

"The majority of the committee," Aspin said, "are constantly looking for things that the services want and the civilians (in the Pentagon and the administration) have rejected. And then we go and put it back in the budget."

The committee should be an advocate of the budget on which it finally decides, Aspin conceded, but the committee must first vigorously scrutinize that budget. "Take it another way," he said. "If the Armed Services Committee isn't looking out for the taxpayer, then who the hell is? Nobody on the floor of the House is going to be able to push through an amendment to an Armed Services Committee bill and God knows, we've tried."

Hebert said that the committee was not an advocate for the military. "That is absolutely wrong. There is a typical example of irresponsibility in negative statements. A typical example."

"Yes, I'm a friend of the military," Hebert said, "but I'll take them to the woodshed and spank them any time."

Stennis, Hebert's counterpart in the Senate, took a similar position. "I'm not anti-military, but we can do better. One way to improve the military is to put them on their mettle and make them justify what they are doing."

"We put that budget through a fine toothed comb," Stennis said. "Every weapon system ought to justify itself on the facts."

Sen. Richard S. Schweiker (R Pa.), who has served on both the House and Senate Armed Services Committees, said that the Senate committee has too often acted as an advocate for the military.

"The Senate Armed Services Committee, however, is less of an advocate for the military than the House committee is," Schweiker said. "That's a small differentiation, but there is some difference."

"There's a growing gap," Schweiker said, "between the military community and the public. And, if we had done our work as an overseer, we would have narrowed the gap by now."

Why the Support. Why do the recommendations of the Armed Services Committees carry such weight in Congress? Chairman Hebert said it was because of the respect that members have for the Armed Services Committee. "It is the job of the committee to know what's going on in the military and the House knows that," Hebert said.

Aspin cited several factors: "The weapon systems are complicated, people don't like to vote against defense measures, and there's always that lurking fear that there's some secret classified document which shows that this thing is really necessary and not just the pet project of some general."

The military's ability "through sheer resources to get their point of view out" also has aided the committee in collecting support among members of Congress, Aspin said. "You can't pick up a newspaper without reading that some admiral said that the Soviet Navy is threatening us in some way."

"I'll tell you why they support us," Hebert said. "We're about at parity with the Russians now. If we stop now where we are, we will lose parity and become inferior.... In war they don't pay off for second place. There's no exacta or daily double. There's one bet and you've got to have the winner."

Role of Chairman. Both Stennis and Hebert were praised by committee members for the way they run their committees, but they were accused of being tied too closely to military interests.

Because the House has been less able to amend bills which originate in his committee, Hebert operated from the stronger power base. Moreover, Hebert had a

Military Spending by States

The Department of Defense spent about three times more money than any other federal agency in fiscal 1970 and 1971. *(Chart p. 105)*

In 21 states Pentagon spending ranked above outlays from any other federal source in fiscal 1971. In 18 states, the Department of Health, Education and Welfare ranked as the top federal agency in spending. In the other 11 states, top federal agency spenders were the Agriculture Department and the Atomic Energy Commission.

Sixty-nine percent of the members serving on the Senate Armed Services Committee represented states for which Defense Department outlays ranked as the state's number one source of federal expenditures during fiscal 1971. That was 11 members of the 16-member total.

Sixty-four percent of the members serving on the House Armed Services Committee represented districts for which Defense Department outlays ranked as the top source of federal spending in fiscal 1971. That was 25 of the 39-member total.

Prime Contracts. Each year the Defense Department breaks down by state the money flowing into the states as a result of major contracts.

Mississippi, represented by Sen. John C. Stennis (D), chairman of the Armed Services Committee, had substantial increases in its share of the prime defense contract dollar. From fiscal 1962 when Mississippi ranked as the 34th largest recipient of defense contract money, the state moved up to the 17th position in fiscal 1971. Mississippi ranked 29th in population by the 1970 census.

Louisiana, home state of Rep. F. Edward Hebert (D), chairman of the House Armed Services Committee, remained at about the same position during the years 1962-1971. In fiscal 1971, Louisiana ranked as the 26th largest recipient of contract money. The state was the 20th largest in population.

Virginia, which has one senator and two members of the House serving on Armed Services Committees, had a dramatic rise in defense contract dollars. In fiscal 1962 Virginia ranked as the 17th largest recipient of prime contract money and in fiscal 1971 the state had moved to the number four position. Virginia was the 14th largest state in population according to the 1970 census.

Georgia, which at one time had chairmen of both the House and Senate Armed Services Committees, increased its share of prime contract dollars over the decade during which both men served as committee chairmen. In fiscal 1962, when Sen. Richard B. Russell (D Ga. 1933-1971) and Rep. Carl Vinson (D Ga. 1914-1965) were committee chairmen, Georgia ranked as the 19th largest recipient of prime contract money. In fiscal 1970 the state ranked as the 9th largest prime contract recipient and the following year it dropped to the 13th position. It was the 15th largest state by population.

California, New York and Texas were largest recipients of prime contract money in fiscal 1971.

larger proportion of supporting committee votes than does Stennis.

The Senate demonstrated increasing interest in scrutinizing the work of its committee and had in the years 1967-71 years held up key legislation. There was little support for a parallel movement in the House.

"It's really hard to object to anything Hebert does on procedural grounds," said Aspin. "He's very fair. Of course he can afford to be because he's got the votes. Only five of us oppose him on most things in committee." They are Aspin, Pike, Michael Harrington (D Mass.), Lucien N. Nedzi (D Mich.) and Robert L. Leggett (D Calif.).

"Nobody on that committee can say they have any favoritism," Hebert said. "I frankly think without modesty which is not one of my virtues—modesty is definitely not one of my virtues. I think that committee is conducted with full decorum, in a high level. We have a couple of laughs, but hell, you've got to have a laugh sometimes."

"Stennis is always facing a problem that Hebert never faces—the possibility that there are amendments that could take something out of his bill," Aspin said. "I can't remember the last time in the House that Hebert lost an amendment."

The Senate committee has been more analytical and critical of defense matters than has the House committee, Aspin said. He conceded, however, that the Senate committee's increased scrutiny was probably a direct reflection of the Senate's rising reluctance to accept without questioning what the committee had recommended.

Even Hebert admitted that Stennis faced a tougher fight in the Senate than he did in the House. "I think Stennis has got a much tougher job than I have. Now why's that so? You'll have to ask somebody else."

Hebert continued: "Now John's a gentleman. I've told John many times. 'Now John, I wish you weren't such a gentleman. I'd rather you were a no-good son-of-a-bitch. Then I could do business with you much better.' But you know how courtly he is and how nice he is."

Balanced Committee

"The problem as I see it," said Pike, "lies in the fact that none of the committees in Congress is representative of Congress. I think that Congress is representative of the American people, but none of the committees is representative of Congress.

"Take the Judiciary Committee, for example. It's just loaded with guys who are lawyers bucking to be judges. And so the law, the judges and judiciary system can do no wrong in the eyes of the Judiciary Committee."

Aspin cited examples of how amendments he has offered in committee get 10-percent support from the 39 members. "But on the floor, that same amendment will get 25 or 30 percent," he said.

Hebert's response to criticism about the committee's makeup was: "All I can say is look at the record. You can't beat the vote, can you?"

The record shows the House has supported the recommendations of the Armed Services Committee on all issues. On controversial issues, however, the voting margin has been closer on the floor than in committee.

The Senate Armed Services Committee, according to two of its more critical members, was undergoing a change during the years 1969-71.

Stuart Symington (D Mo.), ranking Democrat next to Stennis on the Senate committee, told Congressional Quarterly that an increasing number of senators were "feeling their way into a group that says we have to have a better concept of priorities incident to our increasingly limited resources."

"More than ever before in the years that I've been around here," Symington said, "people—liberals and conservatives—are apprehensive about the future viability of the economy and the soundness of the currency." This kind of apprehension, he said, is having a direct effect on the way the Senate Armed Services Committee and the Senate in general looks at the defense budget.

Asked why he thought the House committee generally reported larger defense authorization bills than did the Senate Armed Services Committee, Symington said: "The only reason there could be for it would be that the House committee was more amenable to the wishes of the Pentagon." (The House committee has averaged $464-million more in authorization bills than the Senate committee.)

Industry in District. "It's a natural thing when people come to Congress," Aspin said, "they want to get on a committee that can help the district they represent."

Sixty-four percent of House Armed Services Committee (25 of 39 members) represent districts for which Defense Department outlays ranked as the top source of federal spending in fiscal 1971. On the Senate committee 69 percent of the members come from states for which Pentagon spending ranked as the top federal source of income in fiscal 1971. *(Box p. 5)*

Symington, in an *Atlantic* magazine interview with Flora Lewis, told of visits he made to the home state of the late Mendel Rivers, former House Armed Services Committee chairman. "You go down to Charleston, South Carolina, and you can't turn around without seeing a Mendel this and Mendel Rivers that....

"They (members of Congress) can go to the source of authority and make a trade," Symington continued. "But I'm not saying Mendel ever voted for something he didn't think was right for our security.... He was sincere about it. If I had come up that way in the Congress and not gone through the Pentagon, I might have felt exactly the same way he did." (Symington became the first secretary of the Air Force in 1947.)

Hebert, Rivers' successor, said: "I told them (defense industry and Pentagon) as soon as I took office (as chairman), 'don't you put anything in there because I'm chairman.'"

"It is wrong if those installations are put in because those members are on the committee," Hebert said. "Realistically, and without indicating anybody does this, you've got to take our system of government into play and look at the reality of it. A man is elected from a district by a majority of the people. And if he does not give the majority of the people what they want, he is not going back. I don't believe that philosophy, but it is a fact of life.

"And why pick on the Armed Services Committee?" asked Hebert. "You take the areas where they have the so-called social problems—welfare and food stamps—

well, those members go back and give them the welfare and give the food stamps and give them all the things the majority wanted for nothing and they vote for him. So why pick on our committee?"

Stennis told Congressional Quarterly that his chairmanship of the Armed Services Committee has "had very little effect" on Mississippi's growing defense industry. "I want to help (Mississippi) in a legitimate way, of course," he said. The state has been undergoing a general industrialization process, he said, and part of that has been defense industry.

Old Pentagon Hands. Aspin, who once served as an economic adviser to former Defense Secretary Robert S. McNamara, said: "We used to think of the House Armed Services Committee as the ones we could count on to carry water for us." The Senate committee, Aspin said, generally caused the Pentagon more problems than did the House.

Symington said that part of the game at the Pentagon was vying for funds with the other branches of the military. One of Symington's first jobs as Air Force secretary was "to get as much of the pie as I could for the Air Force because I believe in air power....Everybody fights for their own team; you can't blame them for trying."

"The Armed Services Committees were the jury before which you had to make your case," Symington said.

One member of Congress who asked not to be named told Congressional Quarterly that he once sat in on sessions with leading military budget planners in which they were trying to estimate how much extra they should add to their budget request in anticipation of Congress' annual trimming.

Investigating Subcommittees. Both Armed Services Committees have investigating subcommittees. The Senate Preparedness Investigating Subcommittee, however, has not conducted a full-fledged inquiry—including hearings by the subcommittee and research by the staff—since 1968, according to one staff member who has been with the subcommittee for more than seven years.

"We still occupy the same suite of offices," the staff member said, "but we don't do much anymore.... There's been an emphasis away from using the subcommittee."

The Senate investigating subcommittee staff has been allowed to shrink by attrition and staff people have been used increasingly for the work of three other subcommittees: Ad Hoc Subcommittee on Research and Development, Ad Hoc Subcommittee on Tactical Air Power and the Special Subcommittee studying close air support aircraft.

"There is no investigating subcommittee now on the Senate Armed Services Committee," Symington said. "The Senate Preparedness subcommittee just doesn't investigate anything anymore." Symington was the ranking Democrat on the subcommittee and Stennis was chairman.

Schweiker, also a member of the subcommittee, was asked what happened to it. His response: "Look who's chairman."

The House Armed Services Special Subcommittee on Armed Services Investigating issued four reports during 1971 on the basis of investigations. The subcommittee reported findings on the crash of an F-14 jet aircraft, on faulty generators purchased by the Marine Corps, on defense communications and on the unauthorized flight of a Cuban aircraft to New Orleans.

In July 1970, the House subcommittee issued Congress' first committee study on the massacre at My Lai, South Vietnam. Among the conclusions of the report were: that the My Lai incident was probably covered up at several different levels within the Army and that "a tragedy of major proportions involving unarmed Vietnamese" had occurred at My Lai 4.

Closed Sessions. The Armed Services Committees, like all other committees in Congress, has the option of meeting in executive session (no public or press) or in open session.

The Senate Armed Services Committee during the three years 1969-1971 met increasingly behind closed doors. In 1969 the committee met in executive session 56 percent of the time. In 1971, the closed session vote had increased to 79 percent. No other Senate committee met behind closed doors during 1971 more often than did the Armed Services Committee (118 closed sessions and 32 open).

The House Armed Services Committee showed an increasing tendency to open its doors. In 1969 the House committee met in executive session 64 percent of the time. By 1971 the percentage of closed sessions was down to 41.

Of the 23 committees measured by Congressional Quarterly, this 41 percent total of closed sessions placed the House Armed Services Committee in a tie as the fifth most secretive committee in the House. The tie was with the District of Columbia Committee.

"There are so many meetings that are closed that must be closed," Hebert said. "You can't have a full and open discussion of a lot of things in public. But eventually, what people overlook, eventually that testimony gets out to the public (in censored form)."

Rep. Harrington attached to the fiscal 1972 defense procurement bill committee report (H Rept 92-232) his views on committee secrecy: "Many members of the committee...often express their concern that today the defense establishment is passing through a very difficult period.... It is said that the public does not really understand defense issues and the problems of the military and that the people are tired of war and lash out irrationally at military spending.

"I am struck by the unwillingness or inability of members of the committee to understand the extent to which its (the committee's) functioning contributes to the strident conflict and deep disagreement that has arisen around defense issues," Harrington said.

"Almost all of our sessions (on procurement) are held in secret. There seems to be a conscious effort to minimize public knowledge and discussion of defense issues, particularly those that are controversial or might expose the military to criticism. There are also very large expenditures (in excess of $1-billion) that most of the members of the committee are not permitted to know anything about."

Symington described the closed sessions as "incredible secrecy, unwarranted secrecy" much of the time. "My experience in all of government is that if you're not supervised, you're bound to get careless."

DEFENSE SUBCOMMITTEES: PROFILES OF TWO KEY GROUPS

From 1947, when Congress consolidated the Army, Navy and Air Force into the Department of Defense, until 1966 the House Appropriations Committee consistently cut the Pentagon's budget requests.

For 20 years, the House committee set a trend of chopping more from the Defense Department's annual money requests than did its Senate counterpart.

But traditional patterns have given way to new roles for the committees, reflecting changing attitudes about national defense in Congress.

• Since 1967 the Senate Appropriations Committee has taken over the role as the leading defense budget cutter.

• The House committee has increasingly engaged in defense policy-making, a role normally left to the legislative committee responsible for defense matters—the Armed Services Committee.

Key to the changing trends were the Appropriations Defense Subcommittees of the House and Senate. These subcommittees have operated with a high degree of autonomy (more so in the House) and rarely have either the full committees of the House and Senate altered the subcommittees' recommendations on defense appropriations.

For example, George Mahon (D Texas), who has been chairman of the House Defense Subcommittee since it was created in 1947, has not lost a floor fight on a defense appropriations bill since 1958. In other words, the House adopted the position Mahon took on all amendments. (*Subcommittee record, p. 9*)

The record for Mahon's counterpart in the Senate (three men have held the position) was unblemished for 20 years until Allen J. Ellender (D La.) became subcommittee chairman early in 1971. Ellender, often an outspoken critic of high defense spending, lost three floor battles his first year. In each case he was opposing amendments which sought to add funds to the bill his subcommittee had reported.

The changing roles of the Appropriations Committees in reviewing defense budgets has reflected in part growing dissatisfaction in Congress with the rising cost of buying weapons and with long-range administration defense planning. An additional irritant has been discontent with the war in Indochina.

The impact of these issues has been felt more in the Senate than in the House, according to a Congressional Quarterly study which included interviews with members of Congress, committee staff aides and congressional scholars.

"The Senate as a body tends to be more closely in tune with the American electorate," said Donald W. Riegle (R Mich.), a member of the House Appropriations Committee.

"Senators are more visible and more closely reported," Riegle continued. "They tend to reflect more

fully the very dramatic shift in national priorities that has taken place with respect to the electorate."

It had been the House Appropriations Defense Subcommittee which first reviewed the Pentagon's massive budget requests, the House committee which went further in analyzing the budget request and the House committee that first reported a version of the defense appropriations bill to Congress.

Until 1967 the Senate committee would wait until the House committee had finished with the defense appropriations bill before they even began hearings. But under the leadership of Richard B. Russell (D Ga. 1933-1971), the Senate subcommittee began holding simultaneous hearings on the defense appropriations bill. One Senate staff member said the subcommittee also began independently digging into more of the specific programs covered by the bill. In years before 1967, the Senate subcommittee relied heavily upon the work of its House counterpart.

Gordon Allott (R Colo.), a member of the Senate Defense Subcommittee, said that "in a true sense, as a matter of practice on most appropriations bills, the Senate has become sort of an appeal committee."

Advocate Or Overseer. Most of those Congressional Quarterly interviewed said the Defense subcommittees were more overseers than advocates for the Defense Department.

One committee member, Rep. Riegle, said the question was academic. "What happens is the enormity of the federal bureaucracy is such—particularly in the Defense Department which is the biggest of the big ones—that decades ago we lost any real control over monitoring their activity.

"We go through the motions of saying we do it, but as a practical matter, it's just not physically possible for us to keep up the way we're staffed," he said.

Joseph P. Addabbo (D N.Y.), a member of the House committee, said: "As long as we're limited on staff (the Defense Subcommittee has five professional staff members) and we have to face this tremendous mass of the Pentagon machine," it is all the subcommittee can do just to keep up.

Structure and Powers

To coordinate efforts in Congress to cut spending, the House in 1865 and the Senate in 1867 reorganized their committee systems. The task of reviewing appropriation requests was centralized in two groups—the newly formed Committees on Appropriations.

Jealousy concerning the new committee's autonomy in making decisions was the primary motivating factor which led the House to emasculate systematically the committee's original role. Between 1877 and 1885, the House stripped the Appropriations Committee of its jurisdiction in eight of the 14 appropriations areas—this included loss of control over appropriations for the Army, Navy and consular and diplomatic affairs. *(CQ Guide to Congress, p. 39)*

Full authority to review appropriations requests and to recommend funding levels for all government agencies was returned to the House committee June 1, 1920. The House had anticipated an executive branch reorganization which centralized the federal government's budgetary process—the Budget and Accounting Act of 1921.

Both the House and Senate Appropriations Committees have over the years reorganized their subcommittee structures to conform to changes in the executive branch.

When in 1947 the Departments of the Army and Navy were put under the broad control of the Defense Department and the Air Force was made a co-equal of the other two services, the Appropriations Committee adjusted their subcommittee structure accordingly. The Defense Subcommittees were formed to handle the appropriations requests of the consolidated department.

The House Defense Subcommittee, however, maintained three separate panels within the subcommittee itself to review independently the funding requests of the Army, Navy and Air Force.

Clarence Cannon (D Mo. 1923-1964), who was chairman of the House committee for more than 20 years, abolished the three-panel Defense Subcommittee structure in 1956 because he found that inter-service rivalries for funds were rubbing off on the respective subcommittee panels.

Since 1956 both the House and Senate Defense Subcommittees have remained structurally constant. The units have been responsible each year for reviewing appropriations requests for the Defense Department and for recommending spending levels to the full committee and the House and Senate.

Authorizing and Appropriating. Prior to 1960 the Defense Subcommittees appropriated funds for weapon systems with little interference from other committees. The Armed Services Committees made lump-sum authorizations which did not specify amounts for particular programs. This left the Appropriations Committees free to divide these authorized subtotals in any way they saw fit within the limits of budget requests by the Defense Department.

But since the early 1960s the House and Senate Armed Services Committees have gained substantial powers. The two committees authorize appropriation levels in the elastic spending areas of weapons research, development and purchasing. The Armed Services Committees set limits for spending on individual weapons programs and the Appropriations Committees must fund the systems within those limits. *(Armed Services Committee, p. 3)*

Two-thirds of the Pentagon's annual budget request does not require authorization by the Armed Services Committees, however. Most of these funds which come before the Defense Subcommittee are fairly stable amounts which do not receive the kind of attention that has been commonly directed toward the weapons programs.

The areas which fall into the category of not requiring prior authorization every year by the Armed Services Committees are operation and maintenance funds ($20.3-billion in fiscal 1972), retirement funds ($3.7-billion in fiscal 1972) and salaries and benefits for

Subcommittee Record On Floor

Since fiscal 1967 the House Defense Subcommittee has without exception reported larger defense appropriations bills than has its Senate counterpart. For 19 of the 20 preceding years it was always the Senate subcommittee which reported the larger bill. The exceptional year was 1952.

Not since fiscal 1959 has the House adopted an amendment to the defense appropriations bill without the full support of the subcommittee chairman. The Senate had not overruled the Defense Subcommittee chairman for 20 years until consideration in 1971 of the fiscal 1972 defense appropriations bill. At that time the chairman's position was overruled on three occasions.

Floor Changes. Since fiscal 1952, the House subcommittee's recommended total for the defense appropriations bill was altered by floor amendments seven different years. Five of those seven years the House voted to add money to the subcommittee's recommended total.

Since fiscal 1952, the Senate subcommittee's recommended total for the defense appropriations bill was changed by floor amendments 11 different years. In six of the 11 years, the Senate added funds to the subcommittee's recommended total.

Seven times since fiscal 1950 Congress adopted larger defense bills than the administration had requested. This happened in fiscal 1951, 1957, 1959, 1961, 1962, 1963 and 1967.

military personnel ($21-billion in fiscal 1972). Salary levels are set by the Armed Services Committees (with the approval of the Senate and House), but annual appropriations requests for salaries go directly to the Defense Subcommittees.

Committees At Work

In both the House and Senate, membership of the Appropriations Committees tends to be more conservative than the norm for their respective chambers.

Rarely do members find themselves assigned to the prestigious Appropriations Committees during their first few years on Capitol Hill.

Even after his assignment to the committee, however, a member usually serves an apprenticeship period on the less important appropriations subcommittees before being assigned to the Defense Subcommittee.

Riegle, a member of the House committee and its Foreign Operations Subcommittee, said: "There's a long-term tendency to put the more progressive and liberal members on the authorizing committee where they can sort of vent their fury, but then to maintain an arm-lock on the final expenditure of money by putting the more conservative members on the Appropriations Committee."

Riegle said he got his assignment to the committee before the Republican leadership knew what his ideas were. Once on the committee, Riegle spoke out against the war in Indochina and against high levels of defense spending. He rated his chances of ever being assigned to the Defense Subcommittee as extremely poor.

In the House, the committee chairman and ranking minority member make the subcommittee assignments. On the Senate committee, members choose subcommittees on the basis of their seniority on the full committee.

The role of the full Appropriations Committee in passing judgment on the recommendations of the Defense Subcommittees has been minimal. All persons interviewed by Congressional Quarterly were quick to say that all the subcommittee's work had to pass the scrutiny of the full committee before a bill was reported to the floor, but no one in either committee could recall the last time that the full committee did anything to a defense appropriations bill once it left the subcommittee.

Riegle said: "There have been occasions when some members of the full committee would get up and offer amendments to the defense appropriations bill, but it is basically an exercise in futility."

House Subcommittee

The House Appropriations Committee functions as one of the most autonomous groups in the House. Most of the members have only the one committee assignment.

The Defense Subcommittee also has great freedom to operate without interference or much oversight by the full committee. Most members have just one other subcommittee assignment which leaves them free to devote much more time to subcommittee work than their Senate counterparts. *(Box this page)*

Sen. Allott said the autonomy of the House Appropriations Committee was "characteristic of all committees in the House. They are just much more of a solid unit (than Senate committees) and the House structure tends to give the chairmen an opportunity—and they do use it—to control their committees much more than is done in the Senate in any of the committees."

Riegle said that once the Defense Subcommittee had finished its work on a defense appropriations bill, getting support to amend that bill becomes difficult.

"There's this time crunch," Riegle said. "Once the bill is reported out there's this deluge of material that goes with it. For anybody to wade through that and come up with a credible recommendation to cut funding on a certain helicopter or tank is nearly impossible.

"The established momentum of the House," Riegle continued, "is almost certain to carry the day against amendments to reduce spending that don't have Mahon's support."

Unlike the Senate group, the House Defense Subcommittee has few dealings with the Armed Services Committee. Subcommittee members do not generally read the hearings or reports produced by the Armed Services Committee, admitted one representative. Staff members, he said, do read some of the other committee's material.

The top three Democrats on the Defense Subcommittee are the same men who sat on the subcommittee when it was established in 1947. They are Chairman Mahon, Robert L. F. Sikes (Fla.) and Jamie L. Whitten (Miss.).

"The House subcommittee is strikingly interested in policy-making contrary to traditional impressions of what their role is supposed to be," said Kerry Jones, Indiana State University professor of political science.

Subcommittee Workload

Several quantitative comparisons of the House and Senate Appropriations Defense Subcommittees can be made with regard to how much time they devoted to examining the budget requests and the type of outside and internal resources that were applied to the task.

Hearings. The House subcommittee held 56 days of hearings for the fiscal 1972 defense budget request and published 8,296 pages of declassified testimony in nine volumes.

The Senate subcommittee held 30 days of hearings while examining the same budget request and published 4,873 pages of declassified testimony in four volumes.

Special Reports. The House subcommittee deliberations were supplemented by 29 investigative reports performed by the committee's surveys and investigations staff and by 19 reports prepared by the General Accounting Office (GAO) at the request of the subcommittee.

The Senate subcommittee requested no GAO investigations and all studies pertaining to the defense budget were conducted by the subcommittee staff, according to a subcommittee spokesman.

Busy Committee Members. The House Appropriations Committee has 55 members and the Senate committee 24 members. From the full committee membership the subcommittees draw their manpower.

All but three of the 11 members on the House Defense Subcommittee have just one committee assignment—Appropriations. About half of the members on the Senate Defense Subcommittee have at least four full committee assignments. Twelve of the 16 Senate subcommittee members (including the three ex officio members) have at least three committee assignments.

On the Appropriations Committees themselves, the committee members often serve on several subcommittees. The average number of subcommittee assignments on the House Appropriations Defense Subcommittee was two (including the defense subcommittee). The average number for the Senate subcommittee members was five subcommittee assignments.

Jones said he found that the House subcommittee "is interested in shaping a strong national defense policy. They've developed a new role—guardians of the national security rather than guardians of the treasury."

The report (H Rept 92-666) which the subcommittee wrote to accompany the fiscal 1972 defense appropriations bill to the floor of the House stated: "The Committee on Appropriations continues in its strong belief that adequate military strength is the foundation of national survival and must be given the highest priority in the allocation of federal funds."

Rep. Addabbo, a member of the subcommittee, said: "In our case the only real place where the subcommittee has gone into it (policy-making role) in any real degree has been in the case of the Navy. There are many who believe that our Navy has become almost second rate and I'm one of them.

"The administration plays games in submitting their budget," Addabbo said. To keep a low budget total for defense, he said, the administration purposely undercuts an area which the subcommittee feels is essential—such as the Navy—"knowing there will be ample justification presented to almost force us to increase areas where they have not made requests."

Both chairmen of the Defense Subcommittees in the House and Senate also serve as chairmen of the full Appropriations Committees.

Unlike his counterpart in the Senate, Mahon has long experience as the top man on the Defense Subcommittee—more than 25 years—and has built a reputation as a tough budget trimmer in all appropriations matters. Mahon's critics contend he sometimes leans more heavily on social programs than on defense requests when pushing for budget cuts.

"Mahon has a good sense of what the House is feeling at any given time," Addabbo said. "He has mellowed to a certain extent since the days of Cannon (Mahon's predecessor as committee chairman). He still has his own ways of operating, but has liberalized things in certain ways. He tries to give junior members a little more chance to operate—to chair the subcommittee."

Riegle, often a critic of the war and military spending levels, said: "I've found that Mahon rules much more by persuasion and reason than he does by an arbitrary use of power.

"He's just a much more reasonable man in terms of his basic demeanor and approach to problems than certain other chairmen in Congress," Riegle continued. "He's not heavy-handed."

A lobbyist, who most often works for legislation aimed at reducing defense spending, said: "Mahon's operation of the committee is far more closed than the way it is handled in the Senate....Mahon isn't as accessible to suggestions from other people—either House members or the public."

Senate Subcommittee

The Senate Appropriations Defense Subcommittee, as its House counterpart, also tends to have a membership slightly more conservative than the norm.

The subcommittee operates quite differently from the House subcommittee. Because there are fewer senators than representatives, members of the Senate are required to sit on at least two full committees. Seventy-five percent of the Defense Subcommittee members, however, serve on at least three full committees and have as many as 20 subcommittee assignments.

According to staff sources on the subcommittee, the members have time only to delve into about 20 or 25 areas of major controversy or concern each year when they consider the defense appropriations bill. Ninety percent of the subcommittee's focus, staff sources said, was directed toward the weapons procurement and research and development portions of the budget.

The Senate Defense Subcommittee has extensive interplay with the Armed Services Committee. The chairman of the Armed Services Committee, John C. Stennis (D Miss.), and the ranking minority member,

Spending and Districts

The Department of Defense spent three times as much money as any other federal agency in fiscal 1971 and 1972. *(Chart p. 105)*

In 21 states (42 percent), Pentagon spending ranked above outlays from any other federal source in fiscal 1971. In 18 states the Department of Health, Education and Welfare ranked as the top federal agency in spending. In the other 11 states, top federal agency spenders were the Agricultural Department and the Atomic Energy Commission.

Sixty-nine percent (11 of 16) of the members serving on the Senate Armed Services Committee and 64 percent (25 of 39) of those serving on the House committee were from states or districts for which the number one source of federal outlays was the Defense Department.

Defense Subcommittees. Forty-four percent (7 of 16) of the members serving on the Senate Appropriations Defense Subcommittee (including the three ex officio members) represented states for which Pentagon spending was the top source of federal income during fiscal 1971. This percentage was only *slightly above* the average for the Senate.

Thirty-six percent (4 of 11) of the House Appropriations Defense Subcommittee membership represented districts for which Defense Department outlays ranked as the top source of federal expenditures in fiscal 1971. This percentage was *slightly below* the average for the House.

Sen. Allen J. Ellender (D), chairman of the Senate Appropriations Committee and its Defense Subcommittee, represented Louisiana. Despite the fact that Louisiana has been well represented on key defense committees—for example, Chairman F. Edward Hebert (D) of the House Armed Services Committee—the state showed no drastic jumps in its share of defense outlays or in prime defense contracts since Ellender and Hebert became chairmen in 1971.

Rep. George Mahon (D), chairman of the House Appropriations Committee and its Defense Subcommittee, represented a district in Texas. Although Texas has moved from the seventh to the third largest recipient of defense prime contracts in the last decade, the state population and general growth of industry paralleled the increase in defense dollars.

Margaret Chase Smith (R Maine), have both been members of this appropriations subcommittee for more than a decade.

In addition to Stennis and Smith, the Defense Subcommittee has three ex officio members from the Armed Services Committee. Each appropriations subcommittee has ex officio members from the pertinent authorizing committee.

The ex officio members have full voting rights in the subcommittee—no votes at the full committee level—and one ex officio member sits with the conference committee when the Senate and House are ironing out differences in their versions of appropriation bills.

The three ex officio members of the Defense Subcommittee are chosen by Stennis, chairman of the Armed Services Committee. Stennis also names the one ex officio member who sits with the conference committee.

Ex officio members of the subcommittee during 1972 were Stuart Symington (D Mo.), Henry M. Jackson (D Wash.) and Strom Thurmond (R S.C.).

According to staff sources, the ex officio members participate just as fully in subcommittee hearings and mark up sessions for appropriations bills as do the regular subcommittee members.

One senator on the subcommittee told Congressional Quarterly that these members participate too much. Sen. Allott said: "The subcommittee members who are ex officio do consume in my opinion an inordinate amount of time to the point of where they actually restrict the time that should be available to the (regular) committee members." Allott called ex officio membership a remnant of the past that no longer served a useful purpose.

In commenting on the Senate committee's organization, Rep. Addabbo said: "If you're going to start doing that (heavy interaction with Armed Services Committee), then you might just as well have one committee—one combined committee. In other words, there would be no reason to have a legislative committee and an appropriations committee."

A new rule, adopted as part of the Legislative Reorganization Act of 1970, stipulated that although each senator had to sit on at least two full committees, no member could hold seats simultaneously on more than one of the big four committees—Appropriations, Armed Services, Foreign Relations and Finance.

Members who were sitting on more than one of these four committees when the act was passed were not required to drop off in order to conform with the new rules. The rules applied only to future committee assignments.

Symington's committee assignments were a prime example of what the new rule sought to prevent. He was a member of the Armed Services and Foreign Relations Committee as well as ex officio member to the Defense Subcommittee of the Appropriations Committee. Symington had votes in three of the four most powerful committees in the Senate.

When Ellender, 81, became chairman of the full Appropriations Committee in 1971, he also took over the chairmanship of the Defense Subcommittee—a marked contrast to his prior 35 years in the Senate as a specialist in agriculture and forestry.

As the Defense Subcommittee chairman, Ellender replaced Richard B. Russell (D Ga. 1933-Jan. 21, 1971) who at one time was chairman of both the Defense Subcommittee and the Armed Services Committee. Russell gave up the Armed Services Committee position in 1969 when he took over as chairman of the Appropriations Committee. Russell's knowledge of military matters was extensive, according to both staff and fellow senators.

"It does make a difference not having that vast reserve of experience," said a subcommittee member who compared Russell's experience in military affairs to Ellender's. "The meetings tend to go a little bit slower now."

From another senator on the subcommittee: "It could be said in all fairness that he is not generally sympathetic to the military. He feels there is a great deal of wasted money. He does not feel that the Russians

Defense Appropriations 1950-72

(in thousands)

Fiscal Year	Budget Request	Appropriation
1972	$73,543,829	$70,518,463
1971	68,745,666	66,595,937
1970	75,278,200[1]	69,640,568
1969	77,074,000	71,869,828
1968	71,584,000	69,936,620
1967	57,664,353	58,067,472
1966	45,248,844	46,887,163
1965	47,471,000	46,752,051
1964	49,014,237	47,220,010
1963	47,907,000	48,136,247
1962	42,942,345	46,662,556
1961	39,335,000	39,996,608
1960	39,248,200	39,228,239
1959	38,196,947	39,602,827
1958	36,128,000	33,759,850
1957	34,147,850	34,656,727
1956	32,232,815	31,882,815
1955	29,887,055	28,800,125
1954	40,719,931	34,371,541
1953	51,390,709	46,610,938
1952	57,679,625	56,939,568
1951	13,078,675	13,294,299
1950	13,248,960	12,949,562

1 Original Johnson administration request was $2.5-billion higher.

NOTE: *Above amounts do not include any supplemental estimates or appropriations not considered or made in the regular annual Defense Appropriation Act.*

SOURCE: House Appropriations Committee

or the Chinese constitute any threat to us of any significance. Therefore, he is not as sympathetic to many of the long-range things that many of us feel are necessary."

One of the ex officio members to the subcommittee said that Ellender was the man to watch in the Senate when it came time to push for budget cuts in defense bills. "A lot of moderates and liberals for the first time have somebody in a key position to do something about this defense budget," he said.

A staff member characterized Ellender: "Anybody who is looking to cut $10-billion from the defense budget does not have a friend in Allen Ellender. On the other hand, anybody from the Pentagon who is trying to sell us some program that is heavy on sophistication but marginal in value will definitely have an enemy in Ellender."

A defense lobbyist told of how Ellender's chairmanship of the Defense Subcommittee had altered his social life.

"There's a story that goes around," the lobbyist said, "about Ellender and his home movies of the Soviet Union. He's made many trips over there and always invites people to see his home movies when he gets back.

"Nobody ever used to go see Ellender's movies," he continued. "Well, now that he's chairman of that subcommittee, everybody goes—from the Joint Chiefs of Staff on down."

FOREIGN POLICY COMMITTEES AND MILITARY ASSISTANCE

The Senate Foreign Relations and House Foreign Affairs committees, though not primarily concerned with military matters, control one of the Defense Department's major programs—foreign military aid.

The two committees bring another perspective to the congressional oversight of the Pentagon: the implications of U.S. military aid and training overseas to the nation's commitments to other countries.

From its inception as the World War II lend-lease program, U.S. foreign aid has been regarded as part of the nation's military posture. The rationale and the mix of economic and military assistance varied by time and geography, but one purpose lay behind most dollars dispatched abroad: the support of a friendly nation that the United States might need as an ally in war.

The post World War II military aid program began with the Truman Doctrine in 1947 when the United States gave' assistance to the Greek government in its civil war against communist insurgents. Except for military aid to Greece and Turkey and small amounts to Nationalist China, the emphasis remained on economic assistance until the 1949 Mutual Defense Assistance Act.

The Korean war accelerated a shift from economic to military aid to Asian as well as European allies. By 1953, military aid reached $4-billion a year.

At President Kennedy's request, Congress in 1961 passed the Foreign Assistance Act of 1961 separating the administration of economic and military aid. The act created the Agency for International Development (AID) to handle economic assistance and assigned military aid to the Defense Department.

Military aid stayed within the jurisdiction of the Foreign Affairs and Foreign Relations Committees. One form of economic aid—supporting assistance to nations fighting or preparing for wars—was closely related to military assistance although administered separately by AID until 1971 reorganizations.

The foreign military sales program, started in 1962 and reorganized in 1968, increasingly replaced grant assistance during the 1960s as the principle means of distributing military equipment and training to other nations. It also came under Foreign Affairs and Foreign Relations committee jurisdiction.

The Vietnam war raised new doubts about military aid as members examined the roots of U.S. involvement. By assigning arms aid a major role under the Nixon doctrine of restraint in direct foreign involvements, the Nixon administration sharpened misgivings among influential senators.

Fulbright and Morgan

Differences between the House and Senate committees over foreign military assistance reflect in part the different approaches of their chairmen to the congressional role in foreign policy.

Military Aid Programs

The Senate Foreign Relations and House Foreign Affairs committees have jurisdiction over legislation authorizing appropriations for three types of foreign military aid:

Grant military assistance—authorized under the Foreign Assistance Act of 1961, includes outright gifts to foreign governments of military equipment, training and services.

Security supporting assistance—authorized under the Foreign Assistance Act of 1961, provides economic assistance to help nations offset the economic strains imposed by fighting or preparing for war.

Military credit sales—authorized by the Foreign Military Credit Sales Act of 1968, under which the federal government arranges for sale of arms to other nations on credit with ten years for repayment.

The three programs constitute only a portion of total U.S. military assistance to other nations. The Foreign Relations Committee's fiscal 1973 recommendations for the the three programs made up only $1.65-billion of a total program of $4.7-billion, the committee stated in its report on the fiscal 1973 authorization bill.

A total of $2,055,000,000 in military aid planned for South Vietnam and Laos was not included in the authorization request submitted to the Foreign Relations and Foreign Affairs committees. Funds for grant aid to those nations were made a part of the Defense Department budget during the 1966-67 U.S. military buildup in South Vietnam. Authorization requests are considered as part of the Pentagon budget by the House and Senate Armed Services committees.

Other forms of arms assistance include loans of U.S. ships, gifts of surplus military equipment and commercial cash sales of arms by private companies to foreign governments.

Foreign Relations Chairman Fulbright, a persistent critic of the Vietnam war, believes Congress should take part in a whole range of foreign policy decisions, particularly in those that threaten to bring involvements such as in Vietnam.

Foreign Affairs Chairman Thomas E. Morgan (D Pa.), until 1972 a consistent supporter of U.S. policy in Vietnam, views the role of Congress in foreign affairs as more limited.

Led by Morgan, the House committee frequently cut foreign aid requests and sometimes questioned aid to certain nations, for instance Greece and Pakistan. But except for a few members, the committee has not ques-

Military Assistance Authorizations, Fiscal 1968-72 [1]

(thousands of dollars)

Fiscal Year	Budget Request	Foreign Affairs Committee	House	Foreign Relations Committee	Senate	Conference
1972	$1,983,000	$2,015,000	$2,015,000	$1,185,000	$1,503,000	$1,518,000
1971 [2]	1,214,600	1,050,000	1,050,000	1,050,000	1,044,200	1,050,000
1970	1,214,600	1,090,000	1,144,100	1,014,600	1,014,600	1,014,600
1969	1,311,000	1,161,000	1,106,000	1,061,000	1,056,000	1,081,000
1968	1,400,100	1,370,000	1,310,000	1,075,000	1,075,000	1,170,000

1 Includes grant military assistance, economic supporting assistance and military credit sales (after 1968).
2 Does not include President's supplemental fiscal 1971 request.

tioned the need for continuation of the military aid program.

Fulbright and senators close to his views question the justification for sending arms to other nations.

In June 1972, Fulbright declined to handle the fiscal 1973 military aid bill on the Senate floor, citing his reservations about the amounts authorized even by the committee's scaled-down version. As committee chairman, Fulbright normally would have managed the bill.

In 1971, Fulbright presented the previous year's economic and military aid authorization bill "with great reluctance" and termed the amounts recommended by the committee "much too generous for the circumstances and the times."

Fulbright voted against that bill (HR 9910), contributing to its defeat by the Senate, 27-41. Congress kept the aid program alive by clearing a substitute bill (S 2819) authorizing $1.5 billion, $205 million less than Fulbright's committee had recommended for arms aid in HR 9910.

Morgan, on the other hand, led House floor arguments for enactment of HR 9910 including higher authorizations for military assistance recommended by his committee.

"Foreign aid is built into our defense strategy," he said, and "is a major instrument in the conduct of our foreign policy."

The contrasting positions of the committees—and the contrasting views and personalities of their chairmen—have produced some ill feeling.

During 1972 hearings on military aid authorizations, William S. Broomfield (R Mich.), the House committee's third-ranking Republican, asked Secretary of State William P. Rogers for "your suggestions on how our committee could bypass the Foreign Relations Committee in considering this legislation.... Our work is usually undone by the Senate Foreign Relations Committee."

Foreign Affairs Committee

The Foreign Affairs Committee has consistently backed the Vietnam policies of both President Johnson and President Nixon and has been reluctant to challenge the President on other foreign policy issues, including military assistance requests.

"The history of the committee and the history of the House has been more in support of military assistance" than the Senate, Harry C. Cromer, staff consultant to the committee's Subcommittee for Review of Foreign Aid Programs, told Congressional Quarterly.

For fiscal 1972, the committee actually recommended that the administration's military aid requests be increased by $32-million. The recommended increase, all in security supporting assistance, was intended to make additional funds available to Israel.

In previous years, the committee reduced arms aid requests, but by lesser amounts than the Senate committee. For fiscal years 1968-71, for instance, House committee reductions averaged about $108-million a year whereas the Senate committee's cuts averaged more than $350-million a year. *(Box this page)*

Also in contrast to the Foreign Relations Committee's activities in 1971-72, the Foreign Affairs Committee has used policy amendments to foreign aid bills sparingly.

"In terms of using the foreign aid bill as a vehicle for all kinds of aches and pains," Cromer said, "the Foreign Affairs Committee never has done that."

The committee has used legislative amendments "when something needed to be said," he added, referring to amendments added to the fiscal 1972 authorization bill prohibiting continued aid to Greece and Pakistan.

In general, the committee majority shares Morgan's views on military aid, although some liberal members echo the Senate committee's doubts and some conservative members question the cost.

Of six members who voted against reporting the fiscal 1972 authorization bill, only Ronald V. Dellums (D Calif.), a freshman member, filed minority views questioning the purposes of military aid.

In separate minority views, Republicans H. R. Gross (Iowa), Edward J. Derwinski (Ill.) and Vernon W. Thomson (Wis.) opposed the bill, but mostly on the ground of cost to the U.S. economy. Derwinski also opposed the provision cutting off aid to the military government of Greece, which he defended as a faithful U.S. ally.

Morgan has kept foreign aid authorization bills under his own control, resisting suggestions by some committee members that the administration's requests be broken up for consideration by subcommittees dealing with particular regions of the world. Morgan contends that consideration by subcommittees would make the foreign aid mark-up process unwieldy.

Under existing committee practice, Morgan and the full committee staff draw up a bill for consideration by the full committee, leaving other members the opportunity to offer amendments during mark-up sessions.

Fiscal 1972 Foreign Military Aid Authorizations

(in thousands of dollars)

Program	Administration Request	Foreign Affairs Committee	House	Foreign Relations Committee	Senate	Conference
Grant Aid	$ 705,000	$ 705,000	$ 705,000	$ 350,000	$ 452,000	$ 500,000
Supporting Aid	768,000	800,000	800,000	435,000	651,000	618,000
Credit Sales	510,000	510,000	510,000	400,000	400,000	400,000
Totals	$1,983,000	$2,015,000	$2,015,000	$1,185,000	$1,503,000	$1,518,000

To date, the process has frustrated some members' efforts to revise the bill along the lines suggested by the Senate committee. In particular, four Democrats— Donald M. Fraser (Minn.), Benjamin S. Rosenthal (N.Y.), John C. Culver (Iowa) and Lee H. Hamilton (Ind.)—are leaders in such efforts.

The four, who in 1971 assumed positions of potential influence within the committee as subcommittee chairmen, "have growing and deep reservations about the whole military aid program," said Clifford P. Hackett, staff consultant to Rosenthal's Subcommittee on Europe.

Fraser, for instance, during mark-up introduced an amendment to the fiscal 1973 bill to lower the ceiling on aid to Cambodia to the same level as approved by the Senate committee. The four also ask searching questions of administration witnesses who appear on behalf of foreign aid.

The four remain relatively isolated among committee Democrats, however, with more conservative members both above and below them in seniority. Morgan and the next three ranking Democrats—Clement J. Zablocki (Wis.), Wayne L. Hays (Ohio) and L. H. Fountain (N.C.)— are in general agreement on military aid and indeed most foreign policy questions.

While the highest ranking committee Democrats sometimes question the amounts and usefulness of aid to particular nations, they normally are content to impose reductions in overall administration requests.

One result of the committee's way of handling authorization requests, some sources say, has been a dwindling of interest in foreign aid among committee members. In June 1972, for instance, the committee scheduled several mark-up sessions on the fiscal 1973 military aid bill but failed to muster a quorum for any meeting.

Foreign Relations Committee

The Foreign Relations Committee's skepticism about foreign military aid grew along with most of its members' opposition to the Vietnam war.

"The dilemma of aid is not fundamentally different from the dilemma of Vietnam," committee member Frank Church (D Idaho) said in arguing for defeat of the original fiscal 1972 foreign aid bill. "It is a problem of power—our own power, the uses to which we wish to put it, and the moral and intellectual limitations which have resulted in such wide discrepancies between our intentions and our accomplishments.... The military assistance program has become a preposterous scandal. It should be drastically curtailed, not enlarged."

Fund Cuts. For the five fiscal years, 1968-72, the Foreign Relations Committee recommended reductions averaging $354.6-million in the President's budget requests for military assistance, supporting assistance and credit sales. *(p. 14)*

The largest cut, $798-million, was recommended in the committee's report on the fiscal 1972 military aid authorization bill which replaced the aid bill defeated in the Senate. Although the Senate subsequently restored $318-million for grant aid and supporting assistance, the bill as passed by the Senate authorized $480-million less than the President's request.

The committee report had recommended reductions of $355-million in grant aid, $333-million in supporting assistance and $110-million for credit sales.

For fiscal 1973, the committee in June 1972 again recommended reductions in the administration's military aid requests: grant aid to $600-million from $780-million, supporting assistance to $650-million from $844-million and credit sales to $400-million from $527-million.

Policy Amendments. In another approach to curbing what it considered excesses in U.S. foreign aid, the Foreign Relations Committee attached a series of policy amendments to the fiscal 1972 and fiscal 1973 authorization measures.

"The last couple of years have been really quite distinct from Fulbright's earlier activities," a Senate source told Congressional Quarterly. Frustrated by executive disregard for the views expressed by himself and other members, Fulbright has been "moving from recommendations to putting something into a piece of legislation," the source added.

Both the fiscal 1972 and 1973 bills included committee-attached end-the-war amendments by Majority Leader Mike Mansfield (D Mont.). The committee's fiscal 1973 bill also includes an amendment cutting off funds to implement executive agreements with Portugal and Bahrain unless the agreements were submitted for Senate approval as treaties.

Other committee-initiated amendments added in 1971-72 more directly restricting aid programs included:

• A ceiling on total aid to Cambodia. (Fiscal 1972-73 bills)

• Restrictions on U.S. financing of third country forces operating in Laos, Thailand or North Vietnam. (Fiscal 1972-73 bills)

• Prohibition of all military aid to South Asia, including India and Pakistan. (Fiscal 1973 bill)

• Limits on the executive branch authority to transfer foreign aid funds from program to program. (Fiscal 1972-73 bills)

• A requirement that certain nations receiving military aid or excess defense equipment make a partial payment in their own currencies. (Fiscal 1972-73 bills)

• Reduced ceilings on credit sales and excess equipment donations. (Fiscal 1973 bill)

Ceilings Considered. The committee's report on the fiscal 1973 military aid bill noted "some sentiment for imposing specific all-inclusive ceilings on arms aid either on a country-by-country or a regional basis, as the committee has done in the case of Cambodia."

In promising further consideration of the ceilings proposal for fiscal 1974, the committee hinted that it might attempt to put more constraints on the amounts of assistance, both military and economic, that could go to a particular country.

Under existing practice, Congress merely authorizes and appropriates funds for various categories of aid, leaving the administration considerable discretion as to how much each recipient nation actually receives.

Committee Sentiments. Fulbright and Church generally are regarded as the Senate's most vocal critics of military aid. The committee, however, includes members who represent other points of view.

Gale W. McGee (D Wyo.), a firm supporter of U.S. Vietnam policy under both the Johnson and Nixon administrations, is regarded as the strongest committee supporter of continued military assistance.

Among other committee Democrats, Mansfield and Stuart Symington (D Mo.), who also serves on the Armed Services Committee, are regarded as closest to Fulbright and Church and their views on military aid. Among Republicans, Clifford P. Case (R N.J.) is close to the Fulbright-Church position.

Although the committee majority remains opposed to many administration policies, a series of votes on the fiscal 1973 State Department-U.S. Information Agency authorization bill, approval of the fiscal 1973 funding for Radio Free Europe and Radio Liberty and votes on policy amendments added to the fiscal 1973 foreign aid bill were interpreted by some observers as a weakening of committee support for Fulbright.

"In the last 12 months," McGee told *Congressional Quarterly*, "there's been quite a shifting around in the committee. I'm not as lonely as I once was.

"There's a mood that maybe the committee has overreached itself," McGee added. "The committee seems to be moderating its stance to a more refined and sophisticated attitude" toward military aid requests.

Administration Concern

The Nixon administration, in messages to Congress and testimony before both the House and Senate committees, has made plain its view that approval of its military aid requests is essential for U.S. security.

In a June 9, 1972, letter to Mansfield and Minority Leader Hugh Scott (R Pa.)—both Foreign Relations Committee members—President Nixon urged the Senate to reject fund reductions and policy amendments added by the committee to the fiscal 1973 military aid bill.

Nixon said "the foreign assistance appropriations for fiscal year 1972 were below the minimum level required to attain our foreign policy and national security goals. Such reductions and restrictions, if imposed by Congress again in 1973, will call into serious question the firmness of our commitments abroad."

In his March 1972 foreign aid testimony before the House committee, Rogers said the administration was "in close agreement with your committee" on the need for security assistance.

In the Senate, in contrast, the administration in 1972 has had to rely on floor amendments in efforts to overcome opposition to its program by the Foreign Relations Committee. Sympathetic committee members have offered some administration-backed amendments designed to reverse committee actions.

During debate on the fiscal 1973 bill in June 1972, for instance, McGee and Republican leader Scott sponsored amendments to raise the committee-imposed ceiling on aid to Cambodia and to increase authorizations for grant military assistance.

Perhaps because of the Senate committee's opposition, Secretary of Defense Melvin R. Laird has proposed transfer of military assistance and credit sales funds to the Defense Department budget. The transfer, first suggested by former Secretary of Defense Robert McNamara, would place authorizing legislation for the programs within the jurisdiction of the House and Senate Armed Services Committees, generally more favorable to administration policies.

In testimony before the House committee in 1972, Laird said grant aid and credit sales "could be better handled as part of the Defense Department's budget so we could take into consideration the military assistance as part of our total force planning...."

The administration has not pushed the proposal, however, and Senate Armed Services Committee Chairman John C. Stennis (D Miss.) and House Armed Services Committee Chairman F. Edward Hebert (D La.) have not sought control over military aid.

Stennis has said he would not object to returning grant aid and credit sales to South Vietnam and Laos to the regular military assistance program after the Indochina war ends. During the 1966-67 U.S. buildup in South Vietnam, assistance funds to those nations and to Thailand were transferred to the defense budget because the programs were closely related to the U.S. war effort.

In 1971, arms assistance to Thailand was returned to the military aid budget—and thus to the Foreign Relations and Foreign Affairs jurisdiction—by a Foreign Relations Committee amendment to the fiscal 1972 aid bill.

Largely because of Stennis' opposition, however, provisions that would have returned South Vietnamese and Laotian aid to Foreign Relations and Foreign Affairs were dropped from the fiscal 1972 and 1973 bills.

Morgan and Fulbright—and indeed most members of their committees—agree that military aid should stay within their purview. Responding to Laird's proposal, Morgan said "if the military assistance program were buried in the Defense budget, there would be no effective controls and it would grow like Topsy....Because the authorization for military assistance funds requires action by the Committee on Foreign Affairs and Committee on Foreign Relations...we are able to keep a brake on the amount spent for such assistance."

CIA: CONGRESS IN DARK ABOUT ACTIVITIES, SPENDING

Since the Central Intelligence Agency was given authority in 1949 to operate without normal legislative oversight, an uneasy tension has existed between an uninformed Congress and an uninformative CIA.

In the last two decades nearly 200 bills aimed at making the CIA more accountable to the legislative branch have been introduced. Two such bills have been reported from committee. None has been adopted.

Some members of Congress insist they should know more about the CIA and about what the CIA knows. Clandestine military operations in Laos which were run by the CIA provided Congress with an opportunity to ask questions about the intelligence operation during 1971. *(Congress and Laos, p. 68)*

Sen. Stuart Symington (D Mo.), a member of the Armed Services Intelligence Operations Subcommittee and chairman of the Foreign Relations subcommittee dealing with U.S. commitments abroad, briefed the Senate June 7, 1971, behind closed doors on CIA involvement in Laos. He based his briefing on a staff report.

He told the Senate in that closed session: "In all my committees there is no real knowledge of what is going on in Laos. We do not know the cost of the bombing. We do not know about the people we maintain there. It is a secret war."

As a member of two key subcommittees dealing with the activities of the CIA, Symington should be privy to more classified information about the agency than most other members of Congress. But Symington told the Senate he had to dispatch two committee staff members to Laos in order to find out what the CIA was doing.

If Symington did not know what the CIA was doing, then what kind of oversight function could Congress exercise over the super-secret organization?

A Congressional Quarterly examination of the oversight system exercised by the legislative branch, a study of sanitized secret documents relating to the CIA and interviews with key staff members and members of Congress indicated that the real power to gain knowledge about CIA activities and expenditures rests in the hands of four powerful committee chairmen and several key members of their committees—Senate and House Armed Services and Appropriations Committees.

The extent to which these men exercise their power in ferreting out the details of what the CIA does with its secret appropriation determines the quality of legislative oversight on this executive agency that Congress voted into existence 25 years ago.

The CIA Answers to...

As established by the National Security Act of 1947 (PL 80-253), the Central Intelligence Agency was accountable to the President and the National Security Council. In the original Act there was no language which excluded the agency from scrutiny by Congress, but also no provision which required such examination.

To clear up any confusion as to the legislative intent of the 1947 law, Congress passed the 1949 Central Intelligence Act (PL 81-110) which exempted the CIA from all federal laws requiring disclosure of the "functions, names, official titles, salaries or numbers of personnel" employed by the agency. The law gave the CIA director power to spend money "without regard to the provisions of law and regulations relating to the expenditure of government funds." Since the CIA became a functioning organization in 1949, its budgeted funds have been submerged into the general accounts of other government agencies, hidden from the scrutiny of the public and all but a select group of ranking members of Congress.

THE SENATE

In the Senate, the system by which committees check on CIA activities and budget requests is straightforward. Nine men—on two committees—hold positions of seniority which allow them to participate in the regular annual legislative oversight function. Other committees are briefed by the CIA, but only on topical matters and not on a regular basis.

Appropriations. William W. Woodruff, counsel for the Senate Appropriations Committee and the only staff man for the oversight subcommittee, explained that when the CIA comes before the five-man subcommittee, more is discussed than just the CIA's budget.

"We look to the CIA for the best intelligence on the Defense Department budget that you can get," Woodruff said. He said that CIA Director Richard Helms provided the subcommittee with his estimate of budget needs for all government intelligence operations.

Woodruff explained that although the oversight subcommittee was responsible for reviewing the CIA budget, any substantive legislation dealing with the agency would originate in the Armed Services Committee, not Appropriations.

No transcripts are kept when the CIA representative (usually Helms) testifies before the subcommittee. Woodruff said the material covered in the hearings was so highly classified that any transcripts would have to be kept under armed guard 24 hours a day. Woodruff does take detailed notes on the sessions, however, which are held for him by the CIA. "All I have to do is call," he said, "and they're on my desk in an hour."

Armed Services. "The CIA budget itself does not legally require any review by Congress," said T. Edward Braswell, chief counsel for the Senate Armed Services Committee and the only staff man used by the Intelligence Operations Subcommittee.

The role of the Armed Services Committee is not to examine the CIA's budget, Braswell said, but rather to review the programs for which the appropriated funds pay.

Symington told Congressional Quarterly in early 1972 that the Armed Services oversight subcommittee had not met for 18 months, but that Chairman John C. Stennis (D Miss.) had been taking care of the subcommittee's business by himself primarily.

"The people who run the CIA budget are the five senior members of the Appropriations Committee," Symington said. That included both Stennis and Margaret Chase Smith (R Maine), ranking minority member of the Armed Services Committee. *(Box p. 19)*

"I can find out anything from Mr. Helms (CIA director) that I want to find out because we're friends, but that's not the proper way to do it," Symington continued.

"As a member of the Foreign Relations Committee and the ranking member of the Armed Services Committee I am denied the details of the money being spent by the Central Intelligence Agency." Symington would not deny that he knew details of the CIA budget, only that he was denied the information when he went through proper committee channels.

"The budget is gone into more thoroughly than people (on the committee) would admit," Braswell explained. "It's just reviewed in a different way than, say, the State Department's budget is." The committee's chief counsel said the budget review was conducted by a "very select group...more select than the five-man subcommittee."

Foreign Relations. Since the CIA never has been recognized officially as an agency involved in making foreign policy, the operations of the agency have not regularly been scrutinized by the Foreign Relations Committee. The Armed Services Committee reviews the agency's program annually because threats to the United States, against which the CIA guards, traditionally have been military in nature. The Appropriations Committee checks on the CIA's budget because the committee examines all money requests of government agencies; the CIA provides valuable intelligence on Pentagon programs about which the committee has an interest. In 1967 the Foreign Relations Committee became a newcomer into the circle of CIA-knowledgeable committees.

In the spring of 1967, secret CIA aid for student activities became the cover story for *Ramparts* magazine. The national press picked up the story and soon it became widely known that the CIA had been contributing money to the National Student Association (NSA) and other tax-exempt foundations and was playing more than a casual role in jockeying CIA personnel into leadership positions in the various organizations.

The response in Congress to the NSA story was the introduction of seven bills in one month—all aimed at allowing Congress a closer look at the CIA. One proposal, sponsored by Sen. Eugene J. McCarthy (D Minn. 1959-71), would have involved an investigation of the CIA by a select committee armed with subpoena power. A proposal to set up a similar oversight and investigating committee had been killed in 1966 on a procedural ruling regarding committee jurisdiction. With the new series of embarrassing CIA revelations, the McCarthy proposal posed a threat to the long-standing oversight system.

'I Have Not Inquired'

The following exchange was excerpted from the Nov. 23, 1971, Senate debate over a floor amendment to place a $4-billion annual ceiling on U.S. intelligence activities.

Allen J. Ellender (D La.), chairman of the Appropriations Committee and head of its five-man Intelligence Operations Subcommittee, discussed his knowledge of CIA-run operations in Laos with J. W. Fulbright (D Ark.) and Alan Cranston (D Calif.).

Fulbright: "Would the Senator (Ellender) say that before the creation of the army in Laos they (the CIA) came before the committee and the committee knew of it and approved it?"

Ellender: "Probably so."

Fulbright: "Did the Senator approve it?"

Ellender: "It was not—I did not know anything about it."

Fulbright: "So the whole idea of Congress declaring war is really circumvented by such a procedure, is it not?"

Ellender: "Well, Mr. President, I wish to say that—"

Fulbright: "Is it not?"

Ellender: "No, I do not think so."

Fulbright: "Well, if you can create an army and support it through the CIA, without anyone knowing about it, I do not know why it is not..."

Ellender: "I wish to say that I do not know. I never asked, to begin with, whether or not there were any funds to carry on the war in this sum the CIA asked for. It never dawned on me to ask about it. I did see it publicized in the newspaper some time ago."

Cranston: "...the chairman stated that he never would have thought of even asking about CIA funds being used to conduct the war in Laos....I would like to ask the Senator if, since then, he has inquired and now knows whether that is being done?"

Ellender: "I have not inquired."

Cranston: "You do not know, in fact?"

Ellender: "No."

Cranston: "As you are one of the five men privy to this information, in fact you are the number-one man of the five men who would know, then who would know what happened to this money? The fact is, not even the five men know the facts in the situation."

Ellender: "Probably not."

Don Henderson, a Foreign Relations Committee staff member, said that in an effort to undermine support for the McCarthy bill, the Foreign Relations Committee was invited to send three members to all CIA joint briefings held by the Armed Services and Appropriations Committees. The original members were J. W. Fulbright (D Ark.), Mike Mansfield (D Mont.) and Bourke B. Hickenlooper (R Iowa), who was replaced by George Aiken (R Vt.) when Hickenlooper retired in 1968.

Woodruff, counsel for the Appropriations Committee, said that the committee had not met jointly on CIA business with the Appropriations Committee for at least one year. "Maybe it's been two years," he said, "I'm not sure."

CIA Director Helms, however, appeared before the Foreign Relations Committee for special briefings in 1971 and 1972.

"I have known," Fulbright told the Senate during the June 7 closed session, "and several (other) Senators have known about this secret army (in Laos). Mr. Helms testified about it. He gave the impression of being more candid than most of the people we have had before the committee in this whole operation. I did not know enough to ask him everything I should have...."

THE HOUSE

Two committees in the House acknowledge that they participate in oversight of the CIA—Armed Services and Appropriations. The Armed Services Committee has a five-man subcommittee reviewing the programs of all intelligence organizations. The Appropriations Committee refused to say who on the committee reviews the CIA budget.

Armed Services. A subcommittee formed in July 1971 filled a hole on the committee that was left since F. Edward Hebert (D La.) reorganized the Armed Services Committee and abolished the CIA Oversight Subcommittee that had been run by the late L. Mendel Rivers, chairman of the committee until his death Dec. 28, 1970.

Hebert's plan was to democratize the committee by allowing all to hear what the CIA was doing instead of just a select group of senior members. Freshman committee member Michael Harrington (D Mass.) said that Hebert was making an honest attempt to spread the authority, but the full committee CIA briefings were still superficial. "To say that the committee was performing any real oversight function was a fiction," Harrington said.

When Helms came before the full committee, Harrington asked what the CIA budget was. Helms said that George Mahon (D Texas), chairman of the Appropriations Committee, had instructed him not to reveal any budget figures unless Armed Services Chairman Hebert requested the information. Hebert said "no" according to Harrington and the budget figures were not disclosed.

As in the Senate, the House Armed Services Committee is responsible more for what the CIA does than how much it spends, according to the committee's chief counsel, John R. Blandford. The Armed Services Committee does not meet jointly for CIA briefings with the Appropriations Committee or with the Foreign Affairs Committee, Blandford said.

The new subcommittee, responsible for reviewing all aspects of intelligence operations, was put under the leadership of Lucien N. Nedzi (D Mich.)—a leading House opponent of the Indochina war and critic of Pentagon spending. Hebert said he chose Nedzi "because he's a good man, even though we're opposed philosophically." Hebert's predecessor as committee chairman, Mendel Rivers, regarded the oversight subcommittee as so important he named himself as subcommittee chairman. Nedzi said that Hebert had placed no restrictions on how the subcommittee should be run or what it should cover.

Appropriations. In interviews with two staff members of the House Appropriations Committee, Congressional Quarterly learned that the membership of the intelligence oversight subcommittee was confidential. When

---

CIA Oversight Subcommittees

Four subcommittees have the official function of monitoring Central Intelligence Agency programs and passing judgment on the agency's budget before the figures are submerged in the general budget.

Senate. Armed Services Committee, Central Intelligence Subcommittee (reviews CIA programs, not the budget)—*John C. Stennis (D Miss.), Stuart Symington (D Mo.), Henry M. Jackson (D Wash.), Peter H. Dominick (R Colo.) and Barry Goldwater (R Ariz.);

Appropriations Committee, Intelligence Operations Subcommittee comprised of the five ranking members on the Defense Subcommittee—*Allen J. Ellender (D La.), John L. McClellan (D Ark.), Stennis, Milton R. Young (R N.D.), Margaret Chase Smith (R Maine);

Foreign Relations Committee in 1967 was invited by Stennis and Ellender to send three members to any joint briefings of the Appropriations and Armed Services oversight subcommittees. The three members were J.W. Fulbright (D Ark.), George D. Aiken (R Vt.) and Mike Mansfield (D Mont.). There have been no joint meetings in at least the last year. However, CIA Director Richard Helms did appear once in March before a Foreign Relations subcommittee.

House. Armed Services Committee, Intelligence Operations Subcommittee (created in July)—*Lucien N. Nedzi (D Mich.), William G. Bray (R Ind.), Alvin E. O'Konski (R Wis.), O. C. Fisher (D Texas), Melvin Price (D Ill.), with *ex officio* members F. Edward Hebert (D La.) and Leslie C. Arends (R Ill.).

Appropriations Committee, Intelligence Operations Subcommittee—membership undisclosed. Believed to be the five ranking members of the Defense Subcommittee headed by committee chairman George Mahon (D Texas). Also would include Robert L. F. Sikes (D Fla.), Jamie L. Whitten (D Miss.), William E. Minshall (R Ohio), John J. Rhodes (R Ariz.).   * *Indicates subcommittee chairman.*

---

asked why the membership was a secret, Paul Wilson, staff director, said: "Because that's the way it's always been." Ralph Preston, a staff man for the Defense Subcommittee, said the information was a secret, but admitted that more members than just Chairman Mahon were responsible for reviewing the agency's budget.

Rep. Harrington said he has requested the composition of the subcommittee and has been refused the information. "I'm just sure the CIA committee consists of the five ranking members of Mahon's subcommittee on defense," Harrington said. *(Box this page)*

Quality of Congress' Oversight

Because most members of Congress have not been aware of what the CIA was planning until long after the agency had already acted, more than one Senator or House member has made embarrassing statements out of line with fact.

Former Sen. Wayne Morse (D Ore. 1945-69), a member of the Foreign Relations Committee, took the Senate floor April 20, 1961—five days after the Cuban Bay of Pigs invasion—and said: "There is not a scintilla of evidence that the U.S. government has intervened in the sporadic rebellion which has occurred inside Cuba. That rebellion has been aided from outside by Cuban rebel refugees who have sought to overthrow the Castro regime."

Four days later Morse admitted: "We now know that there has been a covert program under way to be of assistance to the Cuban exiles in an invasion of Cuba and that assistance was given by the United States government. We did not know at the legislative level, through the responsible committees of the Senate, what the program and the policies of the CIA really were."

The Morse speech, delivered nine days after the Bay of Pigs invasion, was the first mention in either the House or Senate of U.S. involvement in the invasion attempt.

While explaining the details of the Central Intelligence Act of 1949, former Sen. Millard E. Tydings (D Md. 1927-51) said in a May 27, 1949, floor speech: "The bill relates entirely to matters external to the United States; it has nothing to do with internal America. It relates to the gathering of facts and information beyond the borders of the United States. It has no application to the domestic scene in any manner, shape or form."

Committee investigations into tax-exempt foundations in 1964 produced an informal report issued by Rep. Wright Patman (D Texas) labeling the Kaplan Fund as a conduit for CIA money. The fund described its purposes in its charter as to "strengthen democracy at home." Patman later agreed to drop the committee investigation saying, "No matter of interest to the subcommittee relating to the CIA existed."

In the spring of 1967, another example of domestic CIA programming emerged as it became known that the National Student Association was receiving money from the CIA and that the agency had been involved in manipulating the leadership of the student organization.

Laos. Another illustration of congressional ignorance of CIA activities was in the series of revelations which came from the June 7, 1971, closed Senate session briefing on Laos requested by Symington.

Three times during the two-hour session, Symington, a member of the Armed Services subcommittee on CIA oversight, said that although he knew the CIA was conducting operations in Laos, he did not know how extensive the program was.

"Nobody knows," Symington said, "the amounts the CIA is spending while under orders from the executive branch to continue to supervise and direct this long and ravaging war (in Laos)."

Minutes after Symington said that in all of his subcommittees—which included the Armed Services Intelligence Subcommittee under the chairmanship of John C. Stennis (D Miss.)—there was "no real knowledge about what is going on in Laos." Stennis took the floor and said: "The CIA has justified its budget to our subcommittee and as always they have come with expenditures right in line with what they were authorized expressly to do....They (CIA) have told us from time to time about their activities in Laos."

Intelligence Reorganization

In a move to trim costs and improve the output of the U.S. global intelligence system, President Nixon Nov. 5, 1971, disclosed details of a reorganization plan for the nation's intelligence program. The plan contained the following changes:

• It gave authority to Richard Helms, Director of Central Intelligence, to review the budgets of the CIA, the FBI, units within the Defense and State Departments and the Atomic Energy Commission. It was believed $1-billion could be cut from the $5-billion to $6-billion the U.S. spends yearly to ascertain Soviet and Chinese Communist military developments.

• It created a new intelligence subcommittee under the National Security Council to tailor the results of the nation's vast overseas intelligence network closer to the needs of the President and his top staff.

• It created a "net assessment group" inside the National Security Council to compare over-all U.S.S.R. forces and capabilities with those of the U.S.

• It created an Intelligence Resources Advisory Committee headed by Helms to advise on the preparation of a consolidated program budget. This would permit Helms to see the Department of Defense intelligence budget—estimated to be 80 percent of everything the U.S. spends for intelligence—and advise on it before its submission.

"It has been said that we all know about what the CIA is doing," Fulbright retorted. "I have been on the CIA oversight committee and I have never seen any detailed figures (on Laos) whatever."

Stennis said that the secret report on CIA activity in Laos, compiled by Foreign Relations Committee staff members, contained some information he was not familiar with, information he had not been told in his capacity as chairman of the Armed Services Intelligence Operations Subcommittee.

"I think we all know," Stennis said, "that if we are going to have a CIA, and we have to have a CIA, we cannot run it as a quilting society or something like that. But their money is in the clear and their forthrightness, I think, is in the clear."

Sen. Miller criticized Symington for saying the Congress was appropriating money blindly: "We should not leave the impression that the Senate somehow or other has been helpless in this matter. We are all mature individuals and we know what we are doing....

"But let us not say the Senate has been hoodwinked or leave the impression we have been misled and have not known what is going on. I think we may have lacked information on the specifics, and the Senator (Symington) is pulling out information on specifics, but the Senators who voted on these appropriations for the CIA voted for them with our eyes wide open, knowing what we were doing. Maybe we should change it. It is something for future debate."

"I would be the last to say he (Miller) had been hoodwinked," Symington commented, "or that any other member of the Senate had been hoodwinked. But I have been hoodwinked, and I want the Senate to know this afternoon that that is the case."

PROBLEMS IN THE RANKS

Vietnam Disenchantment, Drug Addiction,

Racism Contribute to Declining Morale

The nation's armed forces have been struggling with increasing turmoil in the ranks since the late 1960s—about the time U.S. military involvement in Indochina began increasingly to trouble the American public.

With no victory at hand in war-torn South Vietnam, the military found itself fighting a frustrating campaign on three fronts—against an elusive enemy in the field, against a growing hatred for the war at home and against a massive depression of morale among the rank and file soldiers.

Heroin addiction among GIs began to climb as did charges of racism and bigotry in the command by minority racial groups in the armed services. The number of persons refusing inductions into the Army and those evading the draft by other means increased along with the thousands of GIs who were fed up with military life and deserted as a result. Reported incidents of fragging—where a soldier throws a fragmentary grenade under the bunk of a sleeping platoon leader or fellow enlisted man—were also on the rise in the late 1960s and early 1970s.

Images of slaughtered Vietnamese peasants at My Lai haunted the nation as did the drawn-out trial of Lt. William Calley who many thought was being used as the Army's scapegoat for the massacre. Headlines of graft and corruption among U.S. generals and enlisted men in charge of the military post exchange system in Vietnam added fuel to the rising anti-military sentiment.

Despite the many passionate debates over military morale problems, Congress failed to do much to ease the situation during the 1960s—perhaps because Congress was not sure what had to be done.

In hopes that higher pay for military people would ease some of the discontent in the ranks, Congress doubled the recruits' pay in 1971 and substantially increased salaries for all military personnel. The move was heralded as the first step toward an all-volunteer military, a program which would eliminate the unpopular draft and the unwilling recruit. President Nixon's target date for phasing out the draft, however, was not until mid-1973.

While Congress was not particularly active in legislating solutions to the military's difficult problems, forces from within the uniformed services mounted active campaigns to improve the military's image as it was seen by the public and by its own members. Some of the top personnel in the Pentagon said they equated good morale with an effective fighting force and as a result they pushed hard for needed reforms in the regulations and for innovative programs and recruiting methods.

Presidential initiatives in 1971 set the pace and direction for the fight against drug abuse in the armed forces. Congress issued half a dozen reports over a three-year period documenting the extent of the problem and its potential for harm to the military and the individuals involved, but not until 1972 did the Armed Services Committee report a bill aimed directly at the situation.

On the question of racial strife within the ranks, Congress did nothing officially. The Armed Services Committees, with two decades of chairmen representing states below the Mason-Dixon line, ignored the racial problem. Only the Congressional Black Caucus, holding ad hoc hearings on the situation late in 1971, made an attempt to investigate charges of racism and discrimination.

The racial tension and drug abuse among GIs were to a degree only symptoms of greater underlying morale problems which were perhaps not amenable to solution by government action. Capt. Dean M. Steffy, a Ph. D in anthropology who spent a year organizing one of the military's drug rehabilitation centers, said: "We're suffering from the fact right now that we have a bunch of young people in the military who...haven't been prepared for what's going on here in the military. They hate the Army. They just hate it. It blows their minds."

MILITARY DISCIPLINE: DESERTIONS, FRAGGINGS ON THE RISE

Almost 100,000 men walked away from their military duties in fiscal 1971 and became part of the United States' army of deserters. Once every six minutes a soldier called it quits.

A field commander in the Army could have expected 73 of every 1,000 men to desert during fiscal 1971. The rate for the Marine Corps was 56 of every 1,000 men. Since the Pentagon began keeping service-wide desertion statistics during World War II, the problem has never been greater.

Despite the shrinking size of the U.S. garrison in South Vietnam, the Pentagon reported a rising number of incidents in 1971 involving enlisted men who tried to murder either their officers or their peers with fragmentation grenades—a practice known as fragging.

While the estimate of attempted fraggings increased for 1971, the success attributed to the fraggers declined. Only 12 men were fragged to death in the first 11 months of 1971, compared with 34 deaths in all of 1970.

The Pentagon made no estimates for the number of men cut down by rifle fire from their own lines, but Defense Department sources said the number of GIs killed this way in combat was probably far greater than those murdered by fragmentation grenades.

The rising desertion rate and the increased number of attempted fraggings during 1971 were but two of the indicators which told of the military's ebbing morale.

"The Army must adjust to new realities, engage in introspection and undergo a revitalizing and rebuilding process," said Gen. William Westmoreland, Army chief of staff, in 1971. "Problems must be identified, causes isolated and solutions aggressively sought. This effort is well underway. I doubt if any institutions have engaged in more intensive, searching introspection."

In response to the military's vow to look inward for solutions to the morale problem, the House Armed Services Committee announced that it would be doing some looking of its own during 1972. Committee Chairman F. Edward Hebert (D La.) and the ranking minority committee member, Leslie C. Arends (R Ill.), told reporters Sept. 17, 1971, that new subcommittees were being established in "an all-out effort to get at the roots of the multi-faceted problems" facing the military.

"These problems include not only drugs," Hebert said, "but also the incidents of fragging, desertions, absence without leave, serious disciplinary infractions and even more important, the ability of the armed forces to conduct combat operations in the event of an emergency."

By May 1972, no hearings had been held, and the committee staff men assigned to the new subcommittee told Congressional Quarterly that there were no plans for hearings into the specific problems of fragging, desertion or absence without leave (AWOL). One of the subcommittees, however, has studied the drug abuse problem in the military for more than two years.

Nine special subcommittees had been formed by Hebert by February. The subcommittees were to deal with the following subjects: civil defense, defense communications, drug abuse, intelligence, North Atlantic Treaty Organization commitments, nonappropriated fund activities, recruiting and retention of personnel, transportation and survivors' benefits.

Defining Terms. Congressional Quarterly interviewed three members of the House Armed Services Committee, who have expressed differing points of view, on the military's morale problem. Congressional Quarterly also examined General Accounting Office reports and committee findings and interviewed career military officers.

The various sources agreed that the morale situation involved a circle of interlocking problems. They disagreed, however, on which problems could be defined as cause and which as effect.

Among the factors cited as contributing to the morale problem were anti-military sentiment in the United States, the war in Indochina, bad press coverage, lack of direction in the military, boring jobs for the enlisted men, the draft and lack of discipline.

Seen as the results, or symptoms, of these problems were the rising rate of desertions, the emergence of fragging as a means to defy command and undermine both discipline and authority, incidents of soldiers refusing to risk their lives in Vietnam when they questioned the value of their mission to the over-all campaign, an increase in racial tension within the ranks and a drug problem among the enlisted men and draftees which was described by the Pentagon's highest-ranking doctor as being of epidemic proportions at one point.

Roots of Problem

On April 20, 1972, after the United States had been taking casualties in Vietnam for more than 11 years, the U.S. command announced that those killed in Vietnam since 1961—North and South Vietnamese, Americans and other allies—totaled more than one million persons.

The number of U.S. soldiers killed in Vietnam by that time totaled more than 55,000 persons—45,600 dead from combat and another 10,100 from causes other than hostile action.

From the beginning of 1966 to the middle of 1968 when the United States reached its peak involvement in the Indochina war, the Army expanded by more than 50 percent with its greatest influx of manpower coming from the draft. More than 12 percent of the men who were inducted into the armed forces and ranked as privates were college graduates.

It was this 12 percent minority that after 1968 became involved in scattered incidents of soldiers refusing to go on patrol in Vietnam when they regarded their assignment as involving a high risk factor with little re-

Desertion and AWOL

DESERTION*

(Rate per 1,000 men)

Fiscal Year	1967	1968	1969	1970	1971
Army	21.4	29.1	42.4	52.3	73.5
Marine Corps	6.8	30.7	40.2	59.6	56.1
Navy	9.7	8.5	7.3	9.9	11.1
Air Force	.4	.4	.6	.8	1.5
All Services	13.2	15.7	21.1	25.8	32.7

ABSENT WITHOUT LEAVE (AWOL)**

(Rate per 1,000 men)

Army	78.0	89.7	112.3	132.5	176.9
Marine Corps	Not available			174.3	177.8
Navy	22.4	14.4	13.5	17.5	19.0
Air Force	3.6	3.6	4.4	5.9	9.4
All Services	46.8	38.5	46.9	66.3	80.8

*Absent without permission for more than 30 days.
**Absent without permission for 30 days or less.

SOURCE: Office of Defense Secretary

turn for that risk. Increasingly, military commanders were faced with the problem of getting their men to fight when those men were draftees.

During the era of Vietnam, the Army lowered its acceptance requirements for inductees and enlisted men, bringing into the ranks a group which had twice the disciplinary problems of the higher achiever group, according to Westmoreland in an interview with the *Armed Forces Journal.*

Also during the years in which the United States was involved in Vietnam, the Indochina war became so unpopular that the issue was credited with forcing Lyndon B. Johnson to retire instead to seeking a second full term after 1968 as President.

"There is definitely an anti-military trend running in this country right now, particularly among the young," said 33-year-old Les Aspin (D Wis.), freshman member of the House Armed Services Committee and former economic adviser to Defense Secretary Robert S. McNamara. "There is a revulsion against things that are military."

Samuel S. Stratton (D N.Y.), 55, sixth-ranking Democrat on the 40-man House Armed Services Committee and six years younger than any man with higher seniority, told Congressional Quarterly: "I can only assume that it (the decline in morale) is because of the basic anti-military attitude that has developed in this country in the last few years as a result of the frustrations of Vietnam."

"This has obviously affected the young people," Stratton said, "who get from the newspapers and many of the people they associate with this attitude that military service is to be avoided at any cost."

Otis G. Pike (D N.Y.), seventh-ranking Democrat on the House Armed Services Committee, from a Long Island area with major aerospace and defense contractors, characterized the withdrawal period from Vietnam as "a time of wound-licking and an attempt at recovery of prestige, status and respect in the nation."

Pike said: "A national view of our military and particularly our professional career military is about as low as I've ever seen it.... I frankly think it is lower than it ought to be. Our career military people are not the ogres or dumbheads that they are frequently characterized as in the press."

Boring Jobs. One of the recurring causes cited throughout congressional and Pentagon studies of drug abuse, racial tension and discipline problems has been the boredom of the jobs to which many men have been assigned.

In a survey of 200 men at Ft. Dix, New Jersey, who were scheduled for honorable discharges, Pike found that 32 percent of the men regarded their jobs as both physically and mentally "too easy" and 50 percent said their military service had been a waste of taxpayers' money.

A General Accounting Office (GAO) report in May 1971 noted that 10 percent of the enlisted men surveyed "were assigned to duties for which they had not been trained." The GAO survey was taken at four military installations in the United States. A similar GAO study in 1964 found the corresponding figure was 4 percent.

"With regard to Army personnel assigned outside the continental United States," the GAO report said, "we found that in a review recently completed in Korea, the misutilization rate of personnel in the 8th Army was about 21 percent." Similar problems appeared in European installations maintained by the U.S. military, the report said.

A sergeant who had 19 weeks of special training in communications and supposedly was assigned to a position for that task was tending bar at an officers' club, the GAO report stated. A specialist fourth-class who had been trained as a helicopter repairman was working as a legal clerk one day every week and spending the rest of his time as a janitor.

Stratton, who had just returned from an inspection tour of European military facilities, said: "There was a rather woeful lack of matching up an individual with his specialty (the job he was trained for).... Nothing can drive a man wilder than having a particular specialty and then be sitting around and not using it."

"We were told at headquarters," Stratton said, "that many of these problems were being worked out and had been worked out. After we got this pitch from headquarters, we went and had lunch with some of the men." Stratton said that progress toward solving the problems was not as far along as headquarters had led him to believe.

Vietnam. During the more than three years that the United States was making withdrawals from Vietnam, morale among GIs stationed in that country dropped steadily.

"They have very little to do," Stratton said. "They don't feel that they have any particular mission there. As a result, morale sinks. And I think this is largely the reason for the high incidence of drug abuse and the other problems that really weren't known two or three years ago."

When asked about the living quarters improvements that have been made, Aspin said: "I don't see how the hell painting the barracks is going to make a guy feel good if he thinks he's fighting in an immoral war."

Pike said that much of the military's morale problem could be blamed on the Indochina conflict, but that the sheer bureaucracy of the military was also a causal factor. "One of the ways you deal with the problem is to get rid of some of the layers of bloat and fat and brass which weighs so heavily on our force structure," Pike said.

"Discipline in the military has become too lax," Pike added. "Commanders have turned their backs on too many incidents which should have resulted in punishment of some kind. I think this is a cancerous disease and spreads terribly rapidly."

The Symptoms

Among the indicators the Pentagon uses to gauge morale in the armed forces are the desertion rate and the reported incidents of fragging.

Other indicators are racial disturbances and the number of men using drugs or alcohol. *(Racial tensions p. 34; drug abuse problems p. 28)*

Desertion. "Desertion from the military service has through history been recognized as one of the most heinous of offenses," a Senate Armed Services subcommittee reported in 1969 after studying the situation. "The problem of desertion should constantly be of deep concern to military and civilian officials. They must recognize their legal and moral obligation to work unceasingly to reduce its frequency and to deal with it firmly when it occurs."

"The subcommittee noted a discernible tendency on the part of some officials associated with the administration of military justice to place overemphasis on leniency when prescribing the sentence for desertion," the report continued.

Two years after the subcommittee studied the phenomenon, the desertion rate had increased by 50 percent. The number of persons absent without leave (AWOL) for less than 30 days had nearly doubled. *(Box preceding page)*

"Desertion has nothing to do with the physical life soldiers lead," Pike told Congressional Quarterly. "It has to do with the fact that there is no respect for the war which is being fought. There is no respect for the people who are commanding in that war. And, accordingly, there is no motivation to stick in there and do the job."

Fragging. It was after an April 20, 1971, floor speech by Senate Majority Leader Mike Mansfield (D Mont.) that the word "fragging" became commonly used by the news media for the act of a GI attempting to murder one of his fellow-servicemen with a fragmentation grenade.

"One week ago yesterday," Mansfield said with a shaking voice, "an Army first lieutenant was to have ended his tour of duty in Vietnam. He was a West Point graduate, an honor student in high school.... He graduated from the military academy near the top of his class, served on the honor committee and following graduation, completed a course in Ranger training. In every

---

Fragging Incidents

In 1969 the Pentagon began keeping special records on the number of incidents of fragging—murder or attempted murder of a fellow-serviceman with a fragmentation grenade.

Year	Confined incidents	Number of Deaths
1969	96	39
1970	209	34
1971 (first 11 months only)	215	12

---

respect, this young Montanan had every right and every reason to live.

"Like many other young men today," Mansfield said, "he volunteered for service in Southeast Asia to carry on a war, not of his making or choice, but prosecuted pursuant to policies formed and implemented here in Washington."

Mansfield continued: "On March 15, just four weeks before his tour was to end, this young Montanan was killed. He was not a victim of combat. He was not a casualty of a helicopter crash or a jeep accident.

"In the early morning hours of March 15, the first lieutenant from Montana was 'fragged' to death as he lay sleeping in his billet at Bien Hoa. He was murdered by a fellow serviceman, an American GI.... It is a grim statistic of this war that I shall not lose sight of."

Sen. Charles McC. Mathias Jr. (R Md.) said: "In all the lexicon of war there is not a more tragic word than 'fragging' with all that it implies of total failure of discipline and the depression of morale, the complete sense of frustration and confusion and the loss of goals and hope itself."

The Pentagon reported 215 confirmed incidents of fragging during the first 11 months of 1971 and 12 resulting fatalities. A Pentagon spokesman also reported an additional 98 suspected fragging incidents. *(Box above)*

What Can Be Done

As military morale indicators hit new lows, suggestions on how to improve the situation were plentiful.

Two of the most widely touted cure-alls for the military's ills were to end U.S. involvement in Indochina and to end the draft.

Congress debated both of these proposed solutions for months during 1971. The military draft extension bill (HR 6531—PL 92-129), which was passed by the House April 1, 1971, cleared Congress six months later after becoming bogged down in debate over the Indochina war and the all-volunteer military program. *(Draft bill p. 46)*

Contained in the draft extension bill were provisions aimed at creating an all-volunteer military—such as higher pay and more attractive barracks. The legislation extended the draft for only two years instead of the customary four years and President Nixon announced he was planning to achieve a "zero-draft" by the June 30, 1973, expiration date of draft authority.

Also part of the draft extension bill was a provision directed at U.S. involvement in Indochina—Mansfield's

(Continued on p. 26)

My Lai Massacre Damaged Military's Image

One event during the Vietnam war which severely tarnished the image of U.S. fighting men and affected morale in the ranks was the disclosure in November 1969 of the 1968 massacre of Vietnamese civilians at My Lai village, and the ensuing trial of platoon leader Lt. William Calley.

The nation's first reaction in the massacre of more than 100 Vietnamese peasants by U.S. soldiers was one of shocked disbelief, disgust and anger. But when it became apparent, nearly two years later, that the only GI who was going to pay for the massacre was Lt. Calley, the mood of the nation split. Some said the Army was using Calley as a scapegoat and urged that he not be punished unless everyone involved was also punished. Others said Calley should pay for what he did regardless of all other circumstances.

Disclosure. Seymour M. Hersh, who won a Pulitzer Prize for his reporting of the massacre, gave the My Lai story to the press Nov. 13, 1969.

Eight days after the Hersh account of My Lai appeared in the national press, the Army announced it was investigating 26 men, 15 of them civilian, in connection with the massacre. Lt. Calley was court martialed Nov. 24 on charges of premeditated murder of at least 109 Vietnamese civilians "of various ages and sexes."

Two days after Calley was court martialed, the House and Senate Armed Services Committees began hearings on the incident.

Sixteen months after the initial charges were brought against Calley, he was convicted of premeditated murder of at least 22 Vietnamese civilians and on March 31, 1971, Calley was sentenced to life imprisonment.

Congressional Reaction. Immediately after Calley's conviction there was an outpouring of protest from Congress. Sen. Abraham Ribicoff (D Conn.) said: "The tragic events at My Lai are reflective of the tragedy of the entire Vietnam war. All sides have committed horrible atrocities. Lt. Calley should not be made to bear sole responsibility for all wrong-doing."

Sen. Herman Talmadge (D Ga.) said: "Most Americans believe that he (Calley) is assuming the burden for the entire war, including the errors of his superiors....I am saddened to think that one could fight for his flag and then be court martialed and convicted for apparently carrying out his orders."

In the House, Rep. Joe D. Waggonner Jr. (D La.) said: "Lt. William Calley was convicted...for criminal responsibility in the death of 22 of the Viet Cong enemy...Lt. Calley has been made a scapegoat and there is no honor in that course. The Army does not know what it is doing. I protest the verdict and urge others to join me."

President Nixon intervened twice on behalf of Calley in the days after the conviction. On April 1, 1971, Nixon ordered that Calley be removed from the stockade and placed instead under house arrest in his apartment. On April 3 the President announced through one of his aides that he would personally re-view the Calley case when all avenues of appeal were exhausted.

Sen. Hugh Scott (R Pa.), minority leader, said that Nixon intervened "in response to enormous public reaction to this case."

But another Republican, Jacob Javits (N.Y.), told the Senate: "If the nation really is encouraged to believe that he (Calley) did nothing wrong—indeed he is a hero—then we have changed as a people during the course of this tragic war even more disastrously than I had imagined."

Draft Debate. The conviction of Lt. Calley was announced during the middle of House debate on the military draft extension bill. *(1971 draft bill, p. 46)*

Minutes before the final roll-call vote on the bill Edward J. Derwinski (R Ill.) told the House: "I do not believe that good judgment was shown by the majority leadership in bringing this bill to the floor this week. It is difficult to maintain composure and objectivity with the debate over the Calley case reaching a peak as a result of the decision and sentencing..."

Rep. M. G. Snyder (R Ky.) told the House: "There is no question but that we must maintain an adequate military force to defend our country and I can and will support legislative efforts to do this. But I cannot in good conscience vote to send American boys to fight a 'no win' war for a government that then allows the American boys to be tried for discharging that obligation."

Post-mortem. By mid-1972 the Calley case was in its second appeal and the defendant had spent more than one year living in his Fort Benning, Ga., apartment under house arrest. The original life sentence had been commuted Aug. 20, 1971, to 20 years during the first appeal.

Rep. Samuel S. Stratton (D N.Y.), a member of the Armed Services Committee and its My Lai investigating subcommittee, told the House Feb. 8, 1972: "I am profoundly dissatisfied with the way the Army has allowed this complex, tragic and highly damaging case to simply peter out. If the Army leaves this case unresolved, unexplained, unexamined and uncommented upon...then its failure can only have the most damaging impact on the Army and the American defense establishment."

"Twenty-five officers and men were originally charged in connection with the killings at My Lai and their subsequent coverup within the Army," Stratton continued. "Charges against 19 of the 25 were dropped without trial. Five were acquitted. Only one, Lt. Calley, was convicted."

Rep. Les Aspin (D Wis.) told the House April 4, 1972: "The most distressing aspect of this entire tragic chapter in the history of the Vietnam war is that the Pentagon is covering up its own investigation which first unearthed the initial conspiracy guide of the truth about My Lai. The military is guilty of a double cover-up—first with the massacre and now with the investigation."

Army Desertion Rate
(PER 1,000 MEN)

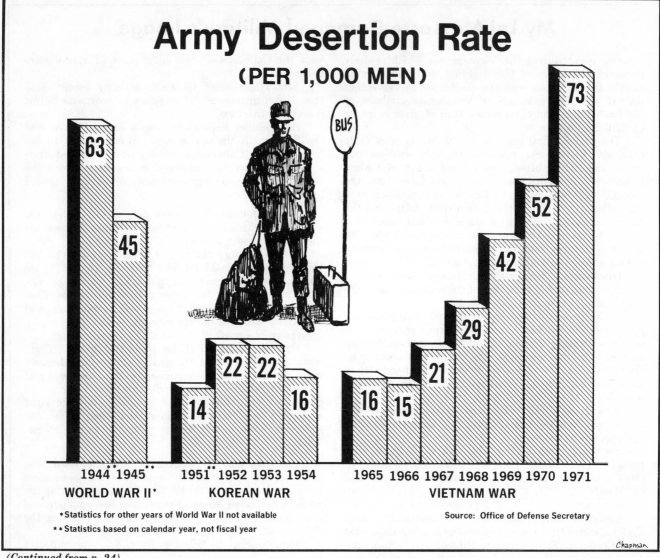

1944 ** **1945** **   **1951** ** **1952** **1953** **1954**   **1965** **1966** **1967** **1968** **1969** **1970** **1971**
WORLD WAR II   **KOREAN WAR**   **VIETNAM WAR**

*Statistics for other years of World War II not available

**Statistics based on calendar year, not fiscal year

Source: Office of Defense Secretary

Chapman

(Continued from p. 24)

amendment, which in its final version contained no deadline for the withdrawal of U.S. troops but urged that the President set a deadline. The Mansfield amendment was signed into law as part of the draft bill and thus became Congress' first legislation calling for setting a withdrawal date for U.S. troops in Indochina. *(Vietnam debate p. 70, 76)*

The Senate in 1971 twice again adopted amendments aimed at forcing a withdrawal of U.S. troops from Indochina.

One of the Senate amendments was watered-down by the House, the other deleted by the House.

All-Volunteer Military. Congress acted during 1971 to give the military additional funds preparing for the day when the draft would not be needed to meet manpower requirements. The Pentagon, however, already had been experimenting with new approaches to training, to recruiting and to promoting the military's strong points with the general public. *(Box p. 27)*

"Obviously, if only those who wanted to go into the military were the ones who were in the military," Stratton said, "the morale problems might be a little different. Even then, however, I think you'd find that morale problems would not be missing."

Aspin said: "Gen. Westmoreland thinks the volunteer army is going to solve all his problems. He talks about his problems—the black militants, underground newspapers, drugs. The poor guy thinks that as soon as we get an all-volunteer army all of a sudden a whole stream of crew-cut guys are going to come floating in. And anybody who's going to be bored with a military job won't volunteer."

The Army has been "forced through a real re-thinking of its role," Aspin said. The military's accepted routine has been challenged. "How much of this spit and polish, up early in the morning, clean barracks, drill formations is really necessary? What really does this have to do with a fighting man? ...Is it a time filler or is it valuable?"

Vietnam. Some of the suggested solutions for the military's morale problem involved mixtures of ending the draft and pulling out of Indochina.

"Sending draftees to a war which we are getting out of, in this stage of our history, is going to do nothing but create these problems of desertion, fragging, drug abuse, lack of discipline and refusal to obey orders," said Pike.

Training Experiments to Improve Morale in the Ranks

On March 1, 1971, the Army began making life easier for its recruits in a much-publicized experiment at Ft. Ord, California. The experiment was linked to the all-volunteer military program which was being heralded by President Nixon and legislated by Congress. While the Senate and House were debating bills that eventually more than doubled a recruit's pay, the Army, for its part, showed a willingness to experiment. Beer vending machines in the mess halls, no more reveille-blasting bugles at dawn, private cubicles in the barracks replete with curtains were all part of the fringe benefits tossed into the experimental program for recruits. *(Volunteer army in a draft debate p. 46)*

Eight months after the experiment began, it ended. The Army announced Jan. 20, 1972, that recruits would bunk together in one big room in barracks of olive drab and that beer could be obtained at a base canteen but no longer from vending machines in the mess halls. The experimental program was never expanded beyond Ft. Ord.

The Army's reasons for tightening recruit training were two-fold: The men were not learning enough to provide them with maximum training for combat; the men themselves were complaining that their training was not sufficiently rigorous.

The second phase of the Army's experimental training program came as the logical revision of the first eight months. Physical exercise was increased, classroom lectures were replaced where possible by field training exercises that allowed the men to practice what they were learning and discipline was tightened. Training was decentralized, allowing local commanders the freedom to try different training methods with end results as the criteria for success or failure.

From the first eight months of the experiment, the Army learned that reveille at dawn was an unnecessary harassment. If a recruit could not drag himself out of bed in the morning, then he would not get off base on weekends.

For the soldier who had finished basic training, the Army provided certain accoutrements to make daily living more pleasurable. The enlisted men's club at various bases boasted a night club atmosphere with go-go girls and live music. As Congress legislated the funds, the Army began pouring money into barracks improvement programs. Enlisted men would be provided with semi-private living quarters, an Army spokesman said, as soon as the semi-private quarters could be built.

KP for Civilians. One of the most aggravating duties to which a private might be assigned was kitchen police, popularly known as KP. Starting in mid-1971, the Army began turning over some of its kitchens on an experimental basis to food contractors who come onto a base, cook the meals, serve the food and wash the dishes. The Army's European command announced Jan. 12 that 1,000 civilians were being hired to take over positions which included janitors and truck drivers.

At Ft. Jackson, South Carolina, the Army announced Feb. 1 that it would allow a potential enlistee to view military life on a trial basis—for three days—before deciding if he wanted to spend two years or more at the job. The "try it—you'll like it" approach to military recruiting may be expanded beyond Ft. Jackson, a military spokesman said in February, if the experiment proved successful.

"We're not engaged in exercises in permissiveness," said Gen. William Westmoreland, Army chief of staff. "Quite the contrary. We are tightening up. We are being more discriminating in accepting men for enlistment and have turned down many applicants in recent months."

"I think the problems will diminish as the number of draftees diminish."

Aspin said public revulsion about Vietnam could have been "a tremendous good force for restructuring some of the spending in this country." The anti-military sentiment, however, was channeled against the men in uniform instead of the policies that guide them, he said.

Stratton said the problems of sinking morale were not unique to Vietnam. "We've got these problems in Germany as well as in Vietnam.... I don't know if they've gotten around to fragging yet, but there's a lot of discontent."

Defining the Role. "If you really want to do something about the morale of the armed forces, you've got to make sure what the armed forces stand for and what we do with them is channeled in better directions," Aspin said.

Stratton said that members of Congress were not going to their constituents enough to explain the world situation. "A congressman has not only a responsibility to reflect and represent the views of his constituency, he

also has an obligation to explain to them what's going on in Washington and what some of the obligations and requirements of our country are. One of those in the modern world and today's predatory world is the maintenance of an adequate military force to defend yourself."

Limits of Congress. "There are certain things that Congress has done and will continue to do," Pike said. "For example, you've got to make life livable for a soldier. One of the things we've agreed to do is pay them a lot more and put a lot of the money into housing."

There were also things which Congress, apparently, could not do. "How can Congress legislate a change in morale? I don't know," Pike continued. He said that trying to investigate the problems of desertion or of fragging would not prove very much. Change would have to start at home with the public's attitude about the military changing toward the positive.

"Congress can't run the day to day operations of the military," Pike said. "How you change the motivation of 2.5 million men—or even 10 percent of that number—I simply don't know."

NARCOTICS, AMPHETAMINES, ALCOHOL IN THE MILITARY

"It's ironic indeed that in the last two years of the war our biggest casualty figures will come from heroin addiction, not from combat." Unnamed soldier in Vietnam.

"They walk as the living dead, not buried in the grave somewhere but returned to the streets of America, driven to steal because they must feed an addictive habit they no longer can control." Sen. Harold E. Hughes (D Iowa).

One of every 10 men in the armed forces during 1971 depended on either drugs or alcohol to get through the day, according to reports issued by Congress, the Pentagon and the General Accounting Office.

Heavy users of narcotics, amphetamines and barbiturates have been estimated at from 2 percent to 7 percent of the military population with most reports tending toward the higher figure. Servicemen in this category have served less than two years in the military, generally, and do not plan to make the armed forces their career.

Approximately one in every 20 members of the armed services has an alcohol problem. Most in this category have served 10 years or longer in the military. *(Box p. 30)*

During 1971, Congress issued four reports on the military's drug problem. Although Assistant Defense Secretary Richard S. Wilbur claimed that "we've turned the problem around," the pictures painted by reports from Congress got progressively darker the later the study was conducted.

Despite the severity of the problem outlined in the thousands of pages of testimony submitted to committees, Congress did little aimed directly at easing the military's problem during 1971.

During 1972, however, Congress moved to officially give the armed forces the authority to combat drug problems—authority for programs the Pentagon had already initiated a year before.

President Nixon on June 17, 1971, launched the first high-visibility executive drive to expand drug control and rehabilitation programs in both the civilian and military sectors of society.

The Defense Department has known of the increasing drug problem within the ranks since the beginning of U.S. escalation in Vietnam. Not until mid-1971, however, did the Pentagon order all services to establish amnesty rehabilitation programs for drug-dependent persons. At the same time, the services began their first extensive program aimed at detecting hard narcotics users.

In testimony taken by several committees late in 1970, it became apparent to members of Congress that the military services faced a major drug problem. Instead of alcohol, the younger members of the armed services were turning first to marijuana as a diversion in their off-duty hours.

Heroin-Opium Facts

The Bureau of Narcotics and Dangerous Drugs estimated that in 1970 330,000 persons in the United States were narcotics addicts. The National Institute of Mental Health put the figure at 250,000 persons.

According to Rep. Seymour Halpern's (R N.Y.) report on drug abuse:

• The United States has the largest heroin addict population in the world.

• At least five Americans die every day as a result of narcotics abuse.

• Up to 50 percent of all metropolitan area property crimes stem from the addict's need to support his habit.

The United States consumes about five to six tons of heroin illegally each year. That amount of heroin is distilled from 50 to 60 tons of opium.

World Opium. World production of opium is estimated at 3,000 tons annually—1,200 tons for legal medical uses and 1,800 tons for illicit purposes.

Primary suppliers of opium for legal uses throughout the world have been Turkey, India, the Soviet Union and the People's Republic of China. Primary suppliers of opium for illicit uses have been Turkey, Burma, Thailand and Laos.

Of the illegal opium by-products being consumed in the United States, 80 percent is estimated to come from the poppy fields of Turkey, 15 percent from Mexico with the remainder coming from the "golden triangle" of Burma, Thailand and Laos.

Of the illegal opium by-products being consumed by American soldiers in South Vietnam, most—if not all—of the drug comes from Laos, Thailand and Burma (the largest illicit drug-producing nation in the world).

Source: *Bureau of Narcotics and Dangerous Drugs, Department of Defense and reports from the House Foreign Affairs Committee and House and Senate Armed Services Committees.*

In Vietnam, military authorities began a massive crackdown on marijuana in 1970. Simultaneously, the Army noted an increase in personnel using opium and the opium derivative, heroin.

Unlike the stereotype of a heroin user in the United States, the serviceman in Vietnam did not generally inject the drug with a syringe. So pure was Southeast Asian heroin that by smoking or sniffing the drug a person could get an acceptable high without the needle. Addiction, however, was just as likely whether the drug was injected, smoked or snorted.

Heroin-using servicemen who returned to the United States from Vietnam found that their $2 to $6 a day

(Continued on p. 30)

Chronology of Action Involving Drug Abuse in the Military

1969

July 14—President Nixon's message to Congress on drug abuse prevention. No mention of military.

October—Army establishes the military's first amnesty program for drug abusers providing rehabilitation and limited protection from prosecution.

1970

March, August and November—Hearings related to the drug problem in the military conducted by Special Subcommittee of the House Armed Services Committee, the Senate Labor and Public Welfare Special Subcommittee on Alcoholism and Narcotics and the Senate Judiciary Subcommittee on Drug Abuse.

October—Defense Department recommends that amnesty program for drug abusers be adopted by all branches of the military.

October—Congress clears the Comprehensive Drug Abuse Prevention and Control Act (PL 91-513) which contained no mention of the Defense Department or the Veterans Administration.

1971

March 8—Air Force starts amnesty program.

April 20—Senate Armed Services Special Subcommittee on Alcoholism and Drug Abuse, chaired by Harold E. Hughes (D Iowa), issued staff report on drug abuse in military jointly with Labor and Public Welfare Committee.

April 23—The House Armed Services Special Subcommittee to Investigate Alleged Drug Abuse in the Armed Services issued a report concluding that "there is a serious drug problem in the military," estimating that as many as 10 percent of the men stationed in Vietnam were heroin users.

May 27—The House Foreign Affairs special study mission on the world heroin problem issued a report estimating that from 10 to 15 percent of U.S. troops stationed in Vietnam were using heroin; "in some units heroin addiction might be as high as 25 percent."

May 30—Navy starts amnesty program.

June 1—During President Nixon's news conference he gives first indication that the drug problem in the military is a major one; announces that his program will include holding addicts in military for treatment although their term of service may have expired.

June 4—Defense Secretary Melvin R. Laird announces that he is not completely satisfied that the government of South Vietnam is doing all it can to stem the flow of heroin into the country.

June 9—Senate adopts an amendment authorizing drug control and rehabilitation programs in military.

June 15—Sen. Alan Cranston (D Calif.) announces that the Veterans Administration is treating a total of 219 drug patients at just five centers.

June 17—President Nixon announces the establishment of a special action office within the Executive Office to "develop over-all federal strategy for drug abuse programs"; requests $14-million increase in the Veterans Administration budget for rehabilitation efforts of veterans and appoints Dr. Jerome H. Jaffe as consultant to the President on narcotics.

June 22—Veterans Administration announces it will open 27 new drug treatment centers by Oct. 1 bringing to 32 the number of specialized treatment centers.

June 30—Pentagon submits to Congress a supplemental budget request for fiscal 1972 of $34,225,000 for drug abuse prevention and rehabilitation programs.

July 7—Pentagon announces that any serviceman who volunteers for drug treatment cannot be disciplined under the Uniform Code of Military Justice and cannot be discharged administratively under dishonorable conditions.

July 13—Army extends urinalysis tests to European theater.

Sept. 21—Brig. Gen. John K. Singlaub is named to fill the new position of Deputy Assistant Defense Secretary for drug and alcohol abuse.

Sept. 28—President Nixon signs the military draft extension bill (HR 6531—PL 92-129) which included authorization for the Defense Secretary to "utilize all practical available methods" to identify, treat and rehabilitate military personnel who are drug or alcohol dependents.

Oct. 24—Rep. Seymour Halpern (R N.Y.) issues a report on his special study mission of the heroin problem and estimated that from 20 percent to 30 percent of the servicemen in Vietnam were using heroin.

Dec. 16—The Army sent 132 enlisted men and officers to Yale University, New Haven, Conn., for the Army's first two-week intensive training program at the University's Drug Dependence Institute; the Army allotted $342,000 for the training program and the men from each of the two-week sessions were to be sent all over the world.

Dec. 26—Rep. G. V. (Sonny) Montgomery (D Miss.) tells newsmen after his tour of Vietnam that the military's drug program "hasn't reduced the problem percentage-wise that much but it's under control and it doesn't affect the over-all efficiency."

1972

Jan. 7—Dr. Richard S. Wilbur, Assistant Defense Secretary, announces that the military had "reversed a heroin epidemic in Vietnam" and that the percentage of drug abusers in Vietnam had been reduced to 4.5 percent of the men checked in unannounced tests.

April 17—The House Armed Services Committee reported a bill (HR 12846) aimed at dealing with the military's drug problem. "The Defense Department is making encouraging advances in attacking the drug problem," the committee report stated. "However, this advance is modest and much remains to be done." *(Provisions of bill, box p. 33)* habit in Vietnam cost $50 to $200 a day in the United States. They also found U.S. black market heroin to be so diluted (5 percent pure) that intravenous injections became necessary to obtain the same kick from the drug they got from smoking the 95-percent pure heroin of Vietnam.

Dimensions of Problem. In trying to establish the extent of drug abuse in the military, the House Armed Services Committee commented: "We have about as many statistical definitions to deal with as we do the various drugs of abuse."

The committee noted in its investigation of the Army's 25th Infantry Division stationed in Vietnam that "roughly 10 percent of the men tested presently use hard drugs (heroin, opium, morphine)." Other reports from congressional fact-finding missions put the number of users in Vietnam at totals ranging from 10 percent to 30 percent.

Representatives of the executive branch from the White House and the Defense Department pegged narcotic drug abuse among U.S. troops stationed in Vietnam at from 5 percent to 6 percent and the use of hard drugs among the entire military population at about 3 percent.

The reports issued by Congress that studied drug abuse in Europe and the United States estimated that although heroin and opium use was lower in those areas among U.S. troops, the use of other drugs—LSD, amphetamines and barbiturates—was greater than in Vietnam.

Action by Congress

Prior to 1970, Congress demonstrated little inclination toward investigating the drug problem in the military or seeking a legislative solution. As shown by which committees studied the phenomenon and who the witnesses were during hearings, drug abuse was defined by members of Congress before 1970 as a civilian problem to be dealt with by the Departments of Justice and Health, Education and Welfare.

The rising number of hard drug users among servicemen stationed in Southeast Asia during 1970 brought the issue home to Washington, however. Through the news media, through increasing command-level problems in dealing with drug abuse and finally through field investigations by members of Congress and committee staff personnel, news reached Congress that the military was plagued with a problem as pervasive as that found in civilian society.

Results of congressionally initiated studies were issued in four reports during 1971—two from the House Foreign Affairs Committee, one from the Senate Armed Services Committee in conjunction with the Labor and Public Welfare Committee and one from the House Armed Services Committee.

Hughes Staff Report. Sen. Harold E. Hughes (D Iowa), chairman of the Alcoholism and Narcotics Subcommittee of the Committee on Labor and Public Welfare and chairman of the special armed services subcommittee on the same topic area, issued a staff report April 20, 1971, based on a nearly year-long investigation of the drug problem in the armed forces.

The subcommittee staff report, based on hearings and on-site inspections of military installations, empha-

---

Alcoholism in Military

The General Accounting Office (GAO) issued a report Nov. 2, 1971, estimating that about 5 percent of the members of the armed forces were alcoholics.

"Alcoholism was most prevalent among senior noncommissioned officers and commissioned officers," the report stated, "primarily effecting personnel who had 10 or more years of military service."

The low cost of alcoholic beverages for servicemen combined with long separations from families were two of the reasons for the persistent problem in the military, according to the GAO report.

If half the alcoholics in the military were either cured or removed from the armed forces, the government would save an estimated $120-million annually, the report stated.

"Little has been done by the military establishment to deal with the problem of alcoholism unless an individual has become at least partially ineffective in his duties or absent without leave, drunk and disorderly, or involved in some traffic mishap while intoxicated.... Most of the bases that we visited had no regulations on how to handle an alcoholic or a problem drinker," the GAO report stated.

Pentagon Study. The Defense Department's Advanced Research Projects Agency surveyed 36,510 enlisted men in all branches of the service and concluded May 30, 1972, that drinking and alcoholism constituted a "far more pervasive" personnel program than illegal use of drugs.

Of the enlisted men surveyed, 57 percent said their officers opposed drug use while only 9 percent had an objection to drinking.

"The use of alcohol in the services thus appears to be condoned, if not promoted," the report said. "The situation for narcotics is quite the reverse."

Less than 2 percent said they needed help with their drug problem while more than 5 percent admitted they needed counseling for their drinking habits.

The report said that drinking and alcoholism "appear to be serious problems that deserve study on a level commensurate with the attention being expended in the study of the use of drugs in the services."

---

sized the use of marijuana among U.S. troops in Vietnam. The report said that the marijuana-sniffing dogs used by the military to locate marijuana stashed in the barracks or among a soldier's equipment were "probably justified by the deterrent effect their reputation has" although the staff investigators "suspect their actual detection value."

Citing a 1969 in-service study on drug abuse, the Hughes subcommittee staff report stated that in 1969 only 2.2 percent of the servicemen leaving Vietnam had sampled heroin while 17.4 percent had tried opium (generally smoked). Fifty percent of those leaving Vietnam in 1969 had used marijuana while in Vietnam. The in-service study found that 6.3 percent of the servicemen arriving in Vietnam had used opium and that 17.4 percent of those leaving Vietnam had tried it.

The staff investigation found "very little indication of heroin or cocaine use" among servicemen in Germany.

"Hashish is by far the drug of choice and is in widespread use," the report said. Also a problem in Germany was the over-the-counter sale of amphetamines, Librium, Valium and Darvon. "LSD is also used in significant amounts by troops in Germany," the report noted.

Although the report pegged primary causal factors for drug use to low education, broken-home background and a history of emotional problems, also cited as important contributing causes were "lack of sense of value which many soldiers feel about their job," peer group pressure and, in Vietnam, the stress of combat.

"We did not find that the use of drugs has a significant direct impact upon the military mission of the armed services," the report stated. "We saw no evidence that any mission or operation had been jeopardized by drug use.... However, it is clear that drug abuse does impose an indirect but significant burden upon the entire military community and organization."

Hagan Subcommittee. The House Armed Services Special Subcommittee to Investigate Alleged Drug Abuse in the Armed Services held hearings during 1970 and conducted an inspection tour of Southeast Asian military facilities in January 1971. The subcommittee's 70-page report was issued April 23, 1971. Hearings by the subcommittee continued after issuance of the report until Congress adjourned at the end of the 1st Session of the 92nd Congress in December 1971.

The House Armed Services Committee April 17, 1972, after two years of investigating the military's drug problem, reported a bill (HR 12846) to the House. The proposal essentially gave the armed forces legal authority for programs that had been underway for more than a year. *(Box p. 33)*

The subcommittee, headed by G. Elliott Hagan (D Ga.), found "there is a serious drug abuse problem in the military largely because there is a serious drug abuse problem in our civilian society."

The subcommittee concluded that "40-50 percent of the men entering military service have at least experimented with marijuana; 50-60 percent of the men in service have at least experimented with drugs, principally marijuana; some 20 percent of our military personnel may be marijuana users; upwards to 10 percent of our personnel in Vietnam could be using hard narcotics."

Although the Hughes subcommittee report found the use of marijuana-sniffing dogs of questionable value, the Hagan subcommittee report stated: "The use of dogs in marijuana detection is a highly effective device."

The report noted a "rapid rise in heroin use by our men in Vietnam, commencing in the spring of 1970," and concluded that the increased supply and use was not part of any enemy strategy but rather the result of enterprising Chinese entrepreneurs in Laos, Thailand and Burma.

"Drug abuse in the military is confined principally to those in the 17-23 age group who are in the first five grades (E-1 through E-5) on their first enlistment and their drug is usually marijuana," the report stated. Peer pressure was cited as a most significant cause for experimenting with drugs in the military.

"This subcommittee does not for one moment favor the coddling of the drug abuser.... We favor affording the drug experimenter an opportunity for rehabilitation, but if he does not respect that opportunity, he should be dealt with firmly.... There is no excuse for breaking the law. Any challenge of its provisions, regardless of the anthropological tendencies in some quarters to condone the extramedical use of drugs, finds not one scintilla of support in this subcommittee," the report stated.

Murphy-Steele Report. Representatives Morgan F. Murphy (D Ill.) and Robert H. Steele (R Conn.), both members of the House Foreign Affairs Committee, conducted a special study mission on the world heroin problem April 3 through April 23, 1971.

"Best estimates available are that 10 to 15 percent of all U.S. troops currently in South Vietnam are addicted to heroin in one form or another," their final report, issued May 27, 1971, stated. "It is estimated that in some units heroin addiction might be as high as 25 percent.... Contributing to this epidemic use of heroin is its ready availability, the frustrations and boredom growing out of the war and the fact that the drug culture in the armed forces reflects American society as a whole....

"However, most of the addicts in South Vietnam become addicted in that country—usually within the first 30 days.... Of the heroin users among the U.S. military in South Vietnam, it is estimated that 40 to 45 percent sniff, 50 percent smoke and between 5 and 10 percent inject.

"Those who have become addicted to the high quality heroin available in South Vietnam will have no choice but to inject the much more diluted heroin that is available in the United States."

The heroin used by U.S. troops in Vietnam is produced from poppies grown in the "remote mountain areas of Burma, Laos, Thailand and parts of the Yunan Province in Communist China," the report said. "Unfortunately, no government exercises effective administrative or political control over these areas.

"Prospects for stopping poppy cultivation and the production of heroin in Southeast Asia in the near future are dim. Efforts must be directed toward stopping the illegal flow of heroin into South Vietnam. If these efforts fail, the only solution is to withdraw American servicemen from Southeast Asia.

"Heroin addiction is essentially an American problem and most countries view it as such. As a result there is a great deal of talk about cooperation with the United States but there is very little action."

Halpern Report. After a fact-finding mission which took him to 12 countries in Europe, the Middle East and Southeast Asia, Rep. Seymour Halpern (R N.Y.) compiled a 171-page report entitled "The International Narcotics Trade and Its Relation to the United States." The report was released Oct. 24, 1971, for the use of Halpern's committee, House Foreign Affairs, and the public.

"My findings while in Vietnam," Halpern wrote, "led me to believe that at least 20 to 30 percent of our forces in Southeast Asia were at the time of this mission using heroin. This would translate into more than 60,000 men. Even this shocking figure, I feel, is conservative."

Halpern said that "marijuana is not as prevalent as heroin in most units in the armed forces in Vietnam." Why? Because it becomes "too easily detectable by its odor when smoked or by trained dogs who have been able to sniff it out from its hiding places."

"Until about a year ago," Halpern continued, "heroin use was more the exception among our troops in Vietnam. Now it's the rule."

According to Halpern's report, the heroin available to servicemen in Vietnam "is so pure that the user can get a full high by merely inhaling it through sniffing or smoking. What he doesn't realize is that it's just as addictive this way as it is through taking it by needle into the veins....

"And what is so terrifying about this is that the $2 to $6 a day habit in Vietnam could well become a $50 to $200 a day habit here in the States. The heroin that he will obtain here (in the United States) is so diluted that the effect the GI now realizes by snorting or smoking heroin will be nil when he returns home.... To feed his dependency which he had thought of in Vietnam as a transient phenomenon, the ex-GI must now turn to repeated daily intravenous injections," Halpern stated.

Halpern was critical of the urinalysis testing programs being administered to servicemen in an effort to detect heroin use. Because he had little faith in the accuracy of these tests, he questioned the official estimates for drug addiction among the troops.

Dr. Jerome Jaffe, special assistant to the President in charge of coordinating drug programs, announced July 17, 1971, that 4.5 percent of U.S. servicemen in Vietnam were using heroin. On July 30, Jaffe revised his estimate to 5.5 percent of the men in Vietnam.

"There have been reports of some GIs buying urine samples from their non-using buddies to use during the heroin tests," Halpern said. "Also, it has been reported that apple juice and other substances are being substituted."

"In the view of this study, these estimates (Jaffe's) are understatements and are unrealistic," Halpern said. He said Jaffe did not include in his percentage estimates those servicemen who had been arrested for dealing or using drugs or those who had been granted amnesty. During the first half of 1971, about 3,300 drug-related arrests were made in Vietnam and nearly 9,000 servicemen turned themselves in for treatment under the amnesty program.

Legislative Action. Congress in 1970 adopted a massive drug control bill that ignored the growing drug problem in the military. The Comprehensive Drug Abuse Prevention and Control Act of 1970 (PL 91-513) allocated $189-million to the Department of Health, Education and Welfare for rehabilitation and education programs; $220-million to the Justice Department to improve enforcement of the drug laws, and $6-million to the Bureau of Narcotics and Dangerous Drugs, also to improve enforcement of the drug laws.

In another measure, Congress gave the Department of Health, Education and Welfare an additional $58-million for drug abuse education programs.

Not until 1971 did Congress aim its first legislative proposal directly at the military problem. As an amendment to the military draft extension bill (HR 6531—PL 92-129), the Senate adopted a drug and alcohol rehabilitation and treatment program. In the House-Senate conference on the bill, House conferees insisted that all specific proposals in the amendment be deleted and replaced by general authorizing language which gave the Defense Secretary broad authority to develop programs.

"The conferees desire that the language of the conference report as adopted be considered an interim step," the conference report said. "The conferees of both houses believe that additional effective legislation will probably be necessary to combat the serious drug abuse problem in

the armed forces and that consideration of such legislation should commence at the earliest practical date."

The Defense Secretary was authorized to use all available methods and facilities to "identify, treat and rehabilitate members of the armed forces who are drug or alcohol dependent persons." No specific funding was provided by the bill.

Pentagon Programs

"It wasn't until the summer of 1970 that the defense establishment realized the full impact of the acute drug abuse situation that existed in all of the services," stated the Hagan subcommittee report of the House Armed Services Committee.

The office of the Defense Secretary, however, "saw the beginnings of a serious problem in 1967 after looking at monthly service reports based on drug abuse investigations over a period of about three years," according to the subcommittee report. In the wake of the 1967 findings, the office of the Defense Secretary issued its first major program directives concerning drug abuse. The programs were aimed at education and control, not rehabilitation.

The Pentagon's first Task Force on Drug Abuse was appointed in 1967 and reported its findings in February 1968. The Task Force recommended increasing further the department's drug education and suppression efforts and called for the establishment of a service-wide committee to deal with the problem—later called the Defense Drug Abuse Control Committee. Each service, under the oversight of the control committee, was allowed to proceed with its own drug programs at its own pace.

As a result, the Army began to experiment with an amnesty program in early 1968 and expanded the amnesty concept to all commands of the Army in October 1969. It would be more than a year before the Air Force and the Navy followed the Army's lead with the amnesty program. *(Chronology, p. 29)*

A second Pentagon task force was appointed May 1970 to study and revise the Defense Department's drug abuse policies. As a result of the second task force study, the Pentagon issued an Oct. 23, 1970, directive which laid the groundwork for the department's drug abuse program in the coming years. Rehabilitation became an important consideration and all services were urged, but not ordered, to establish an amnesty program.

Paralleling the Pentagon's increased interest in establishing drug abuse programs was a statistical picture which showed growing numbers of drug-related deaths in the service, triple the number of drug abuse investigations by the armed forces and a new civilian problem caused by drug-addicted veterans who had been dishonorably discharged from the armed forces and were barred from Veterans Administration drug rehabilitation facilities.

Amnesty, Drug Tests. The Defense Department entered into a new and more aggressive phase of its campaign against drug abuse after the President announced June 17, 1971, his "over-all federal strategy" for dealing with the problem.

Immediately after the President's announcement, the Army began using a urinalysis testing method to determine recent drug use among soldiers returning from duty in Vietnam. The Army July 13, 1971, extended the tests to European-based servicemen. In late August, the Pentagon ordered spot checks of all military personnel in Southeast Asia and the tests were to be unannounced.

Three weeks after the President's June 17 announcement, the Pentagon issued a directive clarifying how the various amnesty programs, established by all services but the Marines at that time, were to work.

Any servicemen who volunteered for drug treatment, the July 7 directive stated, could not be disciplined under provisions of the Uniform Code of Military Justice and could not be discharged administratively under dishonorable conditions. Amnesty would not be granted to the drug-using soldier if he already was under investigation or indictment by the military for a drug-related offense.

In an early September 1971 tour of drug rehabilitation facilities in Vietnam, Dr. Jaffe and Dr. Richard S. Wilbur, Assistant Secretary of Defense (health and environment), noted deficiencies in the military's education program and its rehabilitation approach. Using various civilian programs as models, Wilbur brought trained ex-addicts to Vietnam to help structure the education and rehabilitation programs. Treatment of drug abusers in Vietnam was modified into a two-phased program—detoxification followed by group therapy.

Wilbur told a Jan. 7, 1972, news conference at the Pentagon that the "Army had succeeded in a social area where civilian programs never have...by reversing a heroin epidemic in Vietnam."

The education program for servicemen in Southeast Asia was a success, Wilbur said. As an indicator of the program's effectiveness, he noted that in June 95 percent of the courts-martial against drug abusers and pushers were initiated by the military's law enforcement investigating teams. By November, Wilbur continued, 50 percent of the cases were initiated by tips provided by men within the ranks.

Wilbur said that use of marijuana went "down drastically as heroin came in." He credited the drop in marijuana use partly to the military's enforcement efforts and partly to the new interest in using heroin.

White House Moves

The White House did not openly begin pushing for anti-drug abuse measures in the military until a June 1, 1971, news conference where the President said: "I think it is well for us first to put the problem of drug addiction in Vietnam in perspective. It is not simply a problem of Vietnam veterans. It is a national problem."

The President went on to say that servicemen in Vietnam with a drug problem would be held in that country for a detoxification program. Mr. Nixon stressed that a stepped-up effort in prosecuting pushers was needed as well as more effective education programs for all military personnel.

From June 1 to June 17 the President met several times with his Pentagon and civilian advisers concerning the drug abuse problem. In a prepared statement he read June 17, Mr. Nixon threw his full support behind a multipronged drug abuse offensive.

He created a new position within the Executive Office to coordinate all programs of drug abuse rehabilitation and control at the White House level. Dr. Jaffe was named special consultant to the President for narcotics and dangerous drugs.

The President asked Congress to give the Pentagon authority to hold a drug abuser in the military, against his will if necessary, for 30 days after his tour of duty

Drug Treatment Bill

The bill (HR 12846) which was designed to implement the President's June 17, 1971, program was reported from the House Armed Services Committee April 17, 1972. The bill's provisions:

• Authorized defense secretary to require all members of armed forces to submit to drug detection tests.

• Directed the defense secretary to "prescribe policies encouraging members who are drug-dependent to identify themselves as such and seek treatment... voluntarily."

• Authorized the defense secretary to require treatment of a drug-dependent person without the individual's consent and to extend the individual's stay in the military 30 days beyond his scheduled release date for treatment if necessary.

• Provided that a member of the armed services could not be prosecuted under terms of the Uniform Code of Military Justice "solely on the basis that he has been examined and determined to be drug dependent."

• Provided that time spent undergoing treatment for drug problems would be counted toward a patient's total obligation to the armed forces and a patient would continue to receive regular pay.

• Provided that persons who had been held for the 30-day period for treatment after their obligation to the military had expired would not be included in the armed forces' total strength count.

ended. The extension was to provide the person with a detoxification and rehabilitation program before turning him loose as a civilian. The President's request was sent to Congress in the fall of 1971 as HR 9503.

Among the measures proposed by the President June 17 was a $14-million increase for drug programs run by the Veterans Administration (VA). This brought the VA fiscal 1972 request for drug programs to $17-million.

As a result of the President's increased budget request, the VA began a massive expansion program of its treatment facilities. To the VA's five experimental drug treatment centers—the first of which was opened in October 1970—were added 27 new centers in four months. By November 1971, the VA was operating 32 treatment centers. A spokesman for the Veterans Administration told Congressional Quarterly that 12 additional treatment centers were planned for 1972.

In 1969, the Veterans Administration handled 289 patients with a narcotics dependence problem. In 1970, more than four times (1,374 men) as many veterans were handled with the same problem. Figures nearly doubled in 1971 with 1,188 drug addicts being handled in the first half of the year.

The President appointed Jaffe to a White House level position to allow him the freedom to work with all agencies of the executive branch and not to be a part of any one in particular. Hence, under the Nixon plan, the Defense Department acquired the active cooperation in drug programs of the Veterans Administration and the Department of Health, Education and Welfare as well as the enforcement efforts of the Department of Justice and Bureau of Narcotics and Dangerous Drugs.

BLACKS IN MILITARY: PROGRESS SLOW, DISCONTENT HIGH

At the beginning of 1948, the Navy had a total of four Negro officers, the Marine Corps had one, the Air Force 310 and the Army 1,306. They all commanded black units.

Midway through 1948, President Harry S Truman took an historic step toward eliminating discrimination in the military services. Four administrations later, the armed forces still were struggling to become an equal opportunity employer—although by 1948 standards, the changes have been revolutionary.

By more current standards, however, the revolutionary changes have been those that threaten to erupt from discontent within the ranks. Racial dissent has been smoldering—sometimes bursting into flames—in the armed forces since the peak years of the Vietnam war.

Team after team of Pentagon civil rights experts has ventured into the field to study the race relations problem. Stacks of reports have been filed warning of unresolved frustrations within minority groups. And, scores of policy directives have been issued.

Congress, with exception of the House Black Caucus, has done little either to investigate charges of racial discrimination in the military or to legislate measures designed to deal with the problem. *(p. 38)*

In 1948 the Navy had just four black officers; by early 1972 it could boast a minority representation of about 520 Negro officers or seven of every 1,000 officers. The Marine Corps reported a slightly higher ratio of 13 black officers in every 1,000 for a total of 218 Negroes with the rank of second lieutenant or above. Nationwide, 111 persons of every 1,000 were black (11.15 percent of the population), according to the 1970 census. *(Box p. 36)*

President Truman told newsmen in 1950 that as a result of the changes he had forced upon the military, equality within the ranks would be achieved "within the reasonably near future." But equality had not been achieved by the early 1970s and as a result:

• After a three-week tour of European bases, a report issued by the Pentagon's civil rights division in November 1970 said: "We did not anticipate finding such acute frustration and such volatile anger as we found among the blacks...."

• The NAACP warned in April 1971 after a tour of European military installations that "an uncomfortable number of young Negro servicemen are disenchanted, alienated and have lost faith in the capacity and the will of the armed forces to deal honestly with their problems."

• A second Pentagon civil rights study group toured U.S. installations in Southeast Asia and reported in June 1971: "We found that blacks and whites were moving farther and farther away from each other, resegregating through accelerated racial polarization."

• An Air Force human rights team toured 15 domestic bases and reported in July 1971 that "there is discrimination and racism in the command and it is ugly." The

Blacks In Armed Forces

The following figures represent the number of Negro enlisted men and officers (and their percentage of the total strength) in the active armed services as of March 31, 1971:

	Officers	Enlisted	Total
Army	5,480 (3.5%)	140,625 (13.7%)	146,105 (12.3%)
Navy	518 (.7%)	29,660 (5.3%)	30,178 (4.8%)
Marine Corps	287 (1.3%)	22,296 (11.2%)	22,583 (10.2%)
Air Force	2,216 (1.7%)	74,745 (11.9%)	76,961 (10.2%)
TOTAL	8,501 (2.2%)	267,326 (11.1%)	275,827 (9.9%)

According to the Pentagon, blacks comprise 11.2 percent of those stationed in Vietnam (12.3 percent of the enlisted men; 2.7 percent of the officers). Of those killed in action from 1961 through the first quarter of 1971, 12.4 percent or 5,570 were black (13.6 percent of the enlisted men killed; 2 percent of the officers killed).

The 1970 census showed that 11.15 percent of the population in the United States was black.

report urged base commanders to stop "gambling with festering frustrations" and to enforce civil rights measures.

• Past director of the Pentagon's program to promote racial harmony Frank Render charged in November 1971 that "basically the equal opportunity complaint system (in the military) is bankrupt."

Old Habits

President Truman, after trying for a year to push through equal opportunity legislation, issued an executive order July 26, 1948, which shook the Defense Department to its foundations. The order provided for "equality of treatment and opportunity for all persons in the armed forces without regard to race, religion or national origin" and that promotions were to be based "solely on merit and fitness." Segregation within the armed services, however, was not officially done away with until 1950.

Prior to the Truman directive, the Army had rigidly segregated units and a strictly enforced 10-percent quota for Negroes in the entire Army. The Navy, which had abolished segregation officially during World War II, had just four black officers in 1948 and 95 percent of the mess attendants were Negroes until the mid-1950s.

Before Mr. Truman made his announcement, Richard B. Russell (D Ga.; 1933-1971), later chairman of the Senate Armed Services Committee, delivered a bitter floor speech aimed at blocking the President's move. "The mandatory intermingling of the races throughout the services will be a terrific blow to the efficiency and fighting power of the armed services," Russell argued. "It is sure to increase the numbers of men who will be disabled through communicable diseases. It will increase the rate of crime committed by servicemen."

Defense Secretary Louis A. Johnson May 11, 1949, appointed James C. Evans, a Negro civilian, as his consultant on race relations—the Pentagon's first. Evans noted the progress that had been made in the Army with respect to the blacks. In 1939, there were five Negro officers in the Army and a decade later the Army led all services with 1,173 Negro officers and 71,189 enlisted men (all in segregated units).

After the appointment of Evans, the four branches of the military began a slow process of desegregating. The Army was the last service to officially submit, on Jan. 16, 1950, a plan for desegregating its ranks.

Civil Rights in Pentagon. After Congress had passed two major pieces of civil rights legislation (the Civil Rights Acts of 1957 and 1960) and with President Kennedy exerting pressure for a third and more sweeping legislative program, the Pentagon was pushed to take action of its own in 1963.

Exactly 15 years (to the day) after Mr. Truman made his historic announcement about equal opportunities for all races in the military, President Kennedy went a step further by issuing an executive order aimed at protecting the civil rights of military personnel both on base and off. The Kennedy directive held base commanders responsible for enforcing the policy. The Pentagon is still working on the problem.

Mr. Kennedy established a division in the Pentagon responsible for civil rights and equal opportunities. L. Howard Bennett, a black municipal court judge from Minneapolis, was named the division's first administrator. He held the position until Nov. 30, 1971, when he was replaced by Curtis R. Smothers, a 28-year-old lawyer.

Mr. Kennedy issued his civil rights directives July 26, 1963. Two months later, the Civil Rights Commission issued its third biennial report.

Although the commission statement commended the military for "considerable progress" since 1948, the report condemned the wide disparities which still existed between black and white military personnel. "The Navy," the report stated, "has shown little or no improvement since 1948."

Persistent Problems

An outgrowth of the civil rights movement was a new awareness and pride in being black. During the late 1960s, manifestations of black awareness were appearing in the military. The Afro hair style, black unity salutes and handshakes became targets for white segregationists.

"We cannot shrug off the black power movement in the military as simply some integration situation," said Rep. John R. Rarick (D La.) on Sept. 23, 1969. "For by their handshakes, their salutes and flag, these dupes openly identify themselves as members of an international movement whose allegiance is ultimately to Moscow."

The Pentagon was aware of the problems and polarization caused by self-emphasis of a minority group within the ranks. In the fall of 1969, Bennett, the Penta-

gon's chief civil rights man, took a one-week tour of military installations in Southeast Asia. Bennett said he noticed a "dramatic new dimension in young black troops expressing a far greater concern for their black brothers and sisters on the outside than had their predecessors."

Bennett cited two major problems that he observed on his trip. First, blacks were not being promoted according to their performance or training. Second, blacks were being denied the symbolism of black unity salutes and the Afro styled hair.

A year after Bennett's tour to Southeast Asia, race-related violence among servicemen was increasing, not diminishing. Another Pentagon tour was planned. A White House spokesman said the President was "deeply concerned about the increasing number of incidents between black and white servicemen."

President Nixon appointed Frank W. Render II, a 34-year-old educator, as Deputy Assistant Secretary of Defense in charge of the equal opportunity division (civil rights). Render became Bennett's superior and headed the investigating team.

The Nov. 2, 1970, report by Render to Defense Secretary Melvin R. Laird outlined the failure of command leadership to exercise authority and responsibility in race-related problem areas, the failure by white leaders in the military to understand the difference between black awareness and black militancy, the unequal administration of military justice with the scales weighted against the black serviceman.

Recommendations in the Render report included establishment of a race-relation education program in all branches of the armed forces, removal of officers who demonstrated a bigoted or insensitive attitude toward racial problems, establishment of human relations councils whereby an informal structure would be provided for the airing of grievances and assignment of an equal opportunity (EO) officer at all major military installations. The EO officer would have a direct line to the base commander, thus eliminating the chain of command communications system on human relations issues.

All of Render's program recommendations were adopted to some degree. The military launched an across-the-board race relations education program and at the same time established a race relations institute at Patrick Air Force Base, Fla., which was responsible for training instructors to teach the service-wide course. The institute's first 100-man class was scheduled to begin its six-week training program Oct. 1. The starting date was delayed, however, and the class size reduced.

The first class of 79 students graduated from the race relations institute March 17, 1972, after a seven-week course of instruction. A Pentagon spokesman said the military hoped to graduate at least 1,000 persons from the school each year.

Render told reporters July 27, 1971, that 10 or 12 officers, from company commanders up to generals, had been relieved of command, transferred or reprimanded because of their racial attitudes. Gen. James H. Polk, who was in charge of Army forces in Europe, received a premature retirement in March after his lack of initiative on racial problems in the European theater had been chronicled and criticized by an NAACP investigating team and by Render's own study group.

Percentage of Blacks in Military

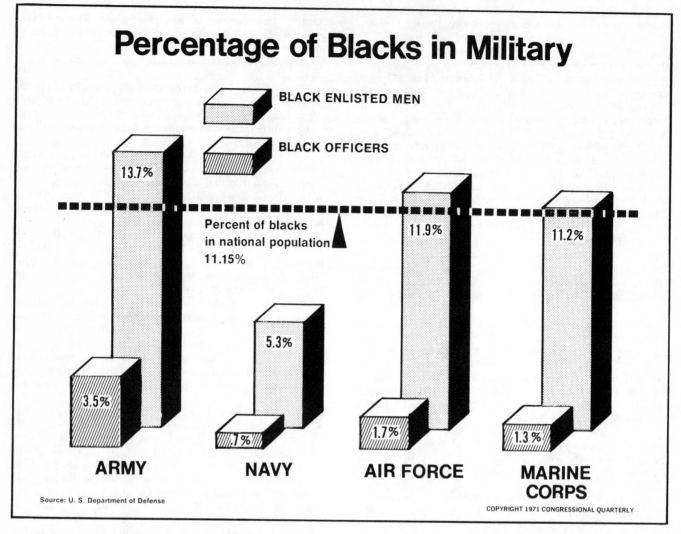

■ BLACK ENLISTED MEN

▨ BLACK OFFICERS

13.7%

Percent of blacks
in national population
11.15%

11.9%

11.2%

5.3%

3.5%

.7%

1.7%

1.3%

ARMY　　**NAVY**　　**AIR FORCE**　　**MARINE CORPS**

Source: U. S. Department of Defense

COPYRIGHT 1971 CONGRESSIONAL QUARTERLY

Rep. William Clay (D Mo.), a black House member, said: "It is common knowledge among black GIs that Gen. Polk is a bigot...." Clay's statement was included in the March 25, 1971, *Congressional Record.* According to him, Polk was forced to resign "because he adamantly refused to carry out the established regulations and policies of the military."

Polk was replaced by Gen. Michael S. Davison, who said since he had taken charge of the European based troops a number of officers had been relieved of their command because of racial considerations. Davison refused to say how many or who the officers were. The Army's record on race relations will, in the final analysis, depend on the quality of its leadership, Davison said. He also noted that race relations among U.S. troops stationed in Europe were worse than those in Vietnam where the men were forced to find a greater degree of harmony in the face of a shooting enemy.

Second Render Report. Despite the scope and variety of the plans proposed by Render after his first tour of military installations and the fanfare which the Pentagon gave Render's finds and recommendations, the racial situation continued to deteriorate.

A second tour of military installations, this time in Southeast Asia, was conducted by a 15-man team headed

by Render during the spring of 1971. The report June 15 told of "blacks and whites moving farther and farther away from each other" and of minority group frustration that was "so great and their pent up fury so high that many of them have exceeding difficulty expressing themselves and articulating their complaints....The conditions that affected them were so overwhelming that it was producing a verbal paralysis."

The men interviewed by Render's team did not describe an easing of racial tension, but rather "situations pregnant with the potential for serious disorders." Despite the ominous picture drawn by the report, Render expressed hope because of "a command awareness, resourcefulness and leadership in this area that did not exist two or three years ago."

The report described military justice as one of the major points of racial irritation. "The severest scrutiny must be given to the use of the administrative discharge to preclude its utilization as a means to unfairly remove blacks from the services," the report stated. "Every effort must be made and action taken to preserve the integrity of the administration of military justice and the proceedings of non-judicial punishment....Blacks especially must have their confidence restored...and assured of the inherent impartiality...of these proceedings."

Render's second report again stressed massive race relations education programs, human relations councils and improved communications between command leadership and the enlisted man.

Render was asked to resign from his position as head of the Pentagon's civil rights division by Defense Secretary Laird and did so Aug. 26, 1971. Although both Render and the Pentagon were cautious in their statements to the public, the Pentagon said that during Render's one year with the Defense Department, the racial tension had not been significantly eased, and the number of complaints from minority servicemen had not significantly declined.

Render later told the congressional Black Caucus that his superiors in the Defense Department regarded his program to promote racial harmony in the military "as a necessary evil."

"Laird's objectives for racial harmony are the same as ours," Render said, "but he is surrounded by people who cannot give him the proper advice. He is isolated and insulated. We must convince him that the problem is more serious than he realizes, that it is more than an assault at a base or lack of chitlins in a post snack bar."

Laird named Render's replacement Nov. 19, 1971. Donald L. Miller, 39, a black shipbuilding executive, became deputy assistant secretary of defense for equal opportunity Dec. 1, 1971.

"We've got to get people to understand and make a commitment to the human goals program," Miller said Feb. 13, 1972. "They've got to understand that this is not a game and that we don't look at it as a game."

Miller noted that while 23 percent of people involved in food service in the military were from minority groups in 1971, only two percent of the officer corps was drawn from minority groups. This trend must not continue, he said.

Air Force Report. A human relations team dispatched by the Air Force issued a scathing report on race relations July 26, 1971. The Air Force did not release the report, however, until it was leaked to *The New York Times* in late August.

After touring 15 domestic Air Force installations in the spring of 1971, the 15-man team reported:

• "The gut feel that we have is that supervisors, and we mean the vast majority of supervisors of all ranks, are simply not doing their job....All up and down the chain of command there is a tragic indifference to human needs."

• "Whites misunderstand the meaning of the symbols of black culture or signs of solidarity....Blacks and whites don't communicate freely to dissolve these misunderstandings."

• "Unequal treatment is manifested in unequal punishment, offensive and inflammatory language, prejudice in the assignment of details, lack of products for blacks in the PX, harassment by security police under orders to break up five or more blacks in a group, double standards in enforcement of regulations. The cause of this is blatant supervisory prejudice in many cases, but for the most part it was the result of supervisory indifference."

Contained in the Air Force report, which had not been meant for public perusal, was a stinging indictment of the latest innovations for easing racial tensions in the military—the Render program. Although all of Ren-

---

Black General Officers

On active duty in the Army, Navy, Air Force and Marine Corps, there are 1,328 officers with general rank (brigadier general or above; rear admiral or above). In the history of the United States, 15 blacks have held a general officer's position in all the military services (including the reserves). Twelve of the 15 were promoted after Jan. 1, 1971.

ARMY—Maj. Gen. Frederick Ellis Davison, the third Negro to attain general's rank, promoted 1968; Brig. Gen. Rosco L. Cartwright, promoted 1971; Brig. Gen. James F. Hamlet, promoted 1971; Brig. Gen. Oliver W. Dillard, promoted 1971, and Brig. Gens. George Schuffer Jr., Harry Brooks Jr., Edward Greer, Julius Becton Jr. and Arthur J. Gregg who were all promoted in 1972.

NAVY—Rear Adm. Samuel Lee Gravely Jr., promoted 1971.

AIR FORCE—Maj. Gen. Daniel James, promoted 1972.

MARINE CORPS—None.

The National Guard and the Army Reserves each has one Negro general—Brig. Gen. Cunningham C. Bryant, National Guard, promoted 1971; Brig. Gen. Benjamin L. Hunton, Army Reserve, promoted 1971.

The first Negro to be promoted to general was Brig. Gen. Benjamin O. Davis Sr., who was promoted to the rank temporarily in 1940 and retired nine months later. Davis was recalled to active duty as a brigadier general after the outbreak of World War II and served until July 13, 1948, when he retired. Davis died at the age of 93 Nov. 26, 1970. His 50 years with the military were spent in segregated units.

Lt. Gen. Benjamin O. Davis Jr., the son of Brig. Gen. Davis, was the second Negro to attain general's rank in the military, the first in the Air Force. He was promoted to the rank of brigadier general in 1954, major general in 1959 and lieutenant general in 1965. Davis retired in 1970.

---

der's recommendations had not yet been put into effect, those that had were criticized by the human relations team for not producing the intended results.

The report was made at the request of Lt. Gen. George B. Simler, the man in charge of the Air Force training command. In an interview with *The New York Times* Sept. 2, Simler said he had already begun a quiet program aimed at correcting the problems outlined in the report.

When asked how he would combat the incidents of racial slurs, the General said: "I've got an aggressive chief of chaplains, and I've told him to get out of church and onto the flight line. The men tend to cut out that language when the chaplain is around."

Housing Discrimination. One of the most persistent irritants to race relations in the military has been the inability of black servicemen to live or socialize in some of the communities which surround military installations.

When the government looks for land upon which to build military installations, the regions that have the greatest supply of land at the lowest prices are rural, far from major metropolitan centers. The towns that are near such a base are therefore often rural and generally lacking the breadth of racial mixtures that a major city provides.

President Kennedy's 1963 directive to the Pentagon held base commanders responsible for stopping discrimination against servicemen in surrounding communities. Kennedy's plan did not work. As a result, base commanders were ordered in 1970 to use economic clout on local residents by declaring an establishment or an entire town "off limits" if there was not compliance with the anti-discrimination laws. That directive had limited success.

A March 19, 1971, directive from Army Secretary Stanley R. Resor said, "Increased emphasis is being placed on eradicating the serious problem of discrimination in off-post housing which continues to plague the minority group soldier and his family."

Navy Secretary John Chafee, who is responsible for both the Navy and the Marine Corps, issued a memorandum Aug. 12 which stated that "in-depth investigation confirms that discrimination is widespread despite the equal opportunity gains made in the past few years." Chafee ordered base commanders to "advise local governmental officials, community leaders and private groups that future base closure decisions will take into account local area practices with respect to open housing."

The most blatant instances of housing discrimination have occurred overseas, specifically in West Germany and Japan. The latest and highest level move taken to alleviate the problem was a joint communique issued by the Departments of State and Defense Sept. 7 to all U.S. diplomats and military commanders overseas. The message said President Nixon regarded the unequal treatment of black Americans in uniform "a matter of serious concern" and therefore a "top priority matter." The communique marked the first time that diplomatic missions had been involved in trying to exert a broad-based pressure on foreign governments to enforce a nondiscriminatory policy toward minority group American servicemen.

Congress Stands Back

The impetus for change of policy in the military regarding racial problems has traditionally come from either the President or from the Pentagon's own personnel offices, not from Congress. An equal opportunity regulation aimed specifically at racial discrimination was put on the books by President Truman nine years before Congress passed the first of several civil rights laws in 1957.

Although Congress at first refused to approve an equal opportunity policy for the military, the three civil rights acts of the 1960s went beyond anything the armed forces already had accomplished. Prior to the passage of the open housing law in 1968 (PL 90-284), the military was not obligated to pressure communities surrounding military bases for equal treatment of all soldiers.

There has been little action and no proposed legislation coming from either the House or Senate Armed

---

Black Ship Brown

The Navy March 18, 1972, launched the USS *Jesse L. Brown*—the first ship to be named after a Negro officer.

The 438-foot escort ship was named after the Navy's first black aviator. During the Korean War Ensign Brown was killed when his plane was shot down.

Services Committees concerning equal rights in the military. Since the early 1950s, five men have been in charge of the two committees. They have all represented states from the deep South and not a single one voted for the Civil Rights Acts of 1957, 1960, 1964 and 1968.

Black Caucus. For three days—Nov. 16-18, 1971—the congressional Black Caucus, composed of 12 voting members of the House and one non-voting delegate from Washington, D.C., held ad hoc hearings on the racial situation in the military.

"It's tragic that in 1971," said caucus member Ronald V. Dellums (D Calif.), "the Black Caucus has to find independent resources to hold these ad hoc hearings when there are millions of dollars and resources available to the House Armed Services Committee which did not see fit to address itself to this very serious problem."

Shirley Chisholm (D N.Y.), also a member of the caucus, said: "If something doesn't happen legislatively as the result of our hearings then all we can say is that time has run out."

During the hearings the caucus released three letters that had previously been classified. The Defense Department would not deny the authenticity of the letters which carried dates ranging from 1961 to 1970.

The letters substantiated charges by the caucus that the military knowingly entered into an oral agreement with Iceland to limit the number of black GIs stationed at U.S. installations on the island. "The Icelandic government will have no objections to three or four colored servicemen in the defense force but hope that they will be carefully chosen in light of the special conditions existing in Iceland," stated a 1961 letter allegedly written by William C. Burdett, former acting deputy assistant defense secretary.

Defense Secretary Laird acknowledged that there had been racial quotas for blacks assigned to Iceland duty, but they had been rescinded early in his term.

"If any instructions issued by previous administrations or by subordinate components of the Department of Defense deny or limit equal opportunity," Laird said, "such instructions or limitations were rescinded by the human goals program (established by Laird in 1969)."

The Black Caucus investigation which preceded the hearings unearthed a "subtle racism that has literally crippled and impaired the effectiveness of American troops in NATO countries," the investigation report stated. The racism manifests itself through discrimination in military justice, promotions and off-base military housing, the report said.

"I don't want to become an alarmist," said Ralph H. Metcalfe (D Ill.), a caucus member, "but the situation is becoming explosive."

CASE STUDIES

Congress Tempers Long-Standing Support

for Defense Policy with Debate, Investigations

Pentagon policy requires congressional approval. Without Congress to provide the money, the Defense Department cannot carry out its policies nor can it exercise its massive purchasing power.

Despite the many heated debates on defense that occur on Capitol Hill, the Pentagon and a majority of the members of Congress—particularly those on the key committees—are generally in full harmony with each other. The Pentagon asks and Congress gives (after hearings, debates and many votes).

In recent years, however, certain areas of the old relationship have been called into question—particularly in foreign policy matters. Military operations have been discovered in Laos about which Congress had no knowledge. In weapons-buying programs cost overruns have become common to the procurement process—the C-5A and F-14 aircraft. A growing minority in the Senate and House has resisted the temptation to push through complicated military bills without at least a cursory examination on the floor of the implications.

Bitter debates over the Indochina war have stalled Senate consideration of bills for months. But Congress, especially the House, voted to leave with the President the responsibility for extricating U.S. forces from the unpopular war. The Senate, in early 1972, moved to prevent future Vietnams by clarifying the procedures by which the United States could again send troops to foreign soil, but again the House showed little interest.

The committee investigation has become the most common vehicle for congressional dissent, but it does not carry the force of legislation. While it takes a majority of the House or Senate to pass a bill, it requires only a few subcommittee members to launch a probe that can be world-wide in scope. In addition, any member of Congress has the authority to set the investigating muscle of the General Accounting Office (GAO) in motion—the

GAO is an arm of the legislative branch—and many members use the GAO to probe the workings of the Pentagon.

Key to any attempt in Congress aimed at altering executive branch policy is support of the committees that deal with defense matters—Armed Services, Appropriations and Foreign Relations (Foreign Affairs in House). Without the support of these committees, there is virtually no chance of arresting the momentum already established for a Pentagon program.

The Defense Department annually submits voluminous justifications—often highly technical—for advancing its programs. A majority of Congress for the last two decades has been satisfied to buy most Pentagon programs, laying the most difficult burden of proof on those who would stop a program rather than with those who support it. Ready-made Pentagon arguments and statistics are used by members to justify their support.

It took three-quarters of a year for President Nixon to get a two-year military draft extension through Congress. But despite the debates over Vietnam and the temporary expiration of the draft for the first time since 1948, he did get the bill through. Annually the administration mounts a pervasive lobby campaign against amendments seeking to force withdrawal of U.S. troops from Indochina; as a result, no binding proposal has yet passed Congress. The Pentagon refused to let Congress look at the financial records of its largest defense contractor (Lockheed Aircraft Corp.), but Congress passed a $250-million loan guarantee for the company anyway.

The following case studies document some typical examples of how Congress has used its constitutional prerogatives to pressure the administration into action and also how Congress has declined to exercise its full powers when confronted by intensive lobbying from the White House and the Pentagon.

1972 SENATE BILL WOULD REASSERT CONGRESS' POWER

Is the power of declaring war necessary? No man will answer this question in the negative. It would be superfluous, therefore, to enter into a proof of the affirmative.

—James Madison, *The Federalist*

We live in a time when man probably will never again dare to declare war, even though he may be forced ...to wage one sort of conflict or another. This is where the Constitution has left us wanting.

—Sen. Gale W. McGee (D Wyo.)
March 29, 1972

War is "the most oppressive of all kingly oppressions," Abraham Lincoln wrote his law partner in 1848. For that reason, the framers of the Constitution "resolved...that no one man should hold the power of bringing this oppression upon us," Lincoln added.

By 1972, one man—the President—nevertheless held that power, and the authority of Congress set forth in the Constitution to check his use of it was in doubt.

"We live in an age of undeclared war, which has meant presidential war," Sen. Jacob K. Javits (R N.Y.) declared during hearings by the Senate Foreign Relations Committee in 1971 on the President's war powers. "Presidential war has created a most dangerous imbalance in our constitutional system of checks and balances"—

Senate Bill. The Senate April 13, 1972, passed a bill designed to place restrictions on the President's use of armed forces without prior congressional approval. The bill provided procedures whereby Congress could overrule the President's decision to commit troops to combat in undeclared wars. *(Provisions of S 2956 p. 41; Senate debate p. 43)*

The bill was intended as a supplement to the Constitution, which sponsors of the bill said only offered a vague definition of Congress' role in foreign policy making. The Constitution gives Congress the power to provide for the common defense, to declare war and to ratify treaties. Sponsors maintained that a more precise description and limitation of the situations in which a President could commit men to battle without congressional approval was required. Jacob K. Javits (R N.Y.) said situations arose "which require combat actions but which are not serious —or in which contemporary conditions make it undesirable—to enact a declaration of war."

As passed by the Senate the bill defined the emergency circumstances in which the President could act on his own and gave Congress the responsibility of exercising independent judgment short of a declaration of war.

The Nixon administration strongly opposed the bill and lobbied hard to kill it before passage. White House lobbyists were confident, however, of their chances of defeating the measure in the House if it ever reached the floor.

House Resolution. The House Aug. 2, 1971, by voice vote passed a resolution (H J Res 1) reaffirming the constitutional war-making powers of Congress and the President. H J Res 1 required the President to submit a written explanation to Congress if he acted without prior congressional consent in committing U.S. troops to combat, sending combat-equipped forces to foreign countries or significantly enlarging military forces already stationed abroad. The resolution also urged—but did not require—the President to consult Congress before sending Americans into armed conflict. It recognized the President's authority to defend the nation and its citizens without specific legislative approval in extraordinary and emergency circumstances.

The resolution, considered weaker than the Senate bill, was acceptable to the Nixon administration.

The Senate Foreign Relations Committee April 20, 1972, adversely reported H J Res 1, acting seven days after the Senate had passed the stronger war powers measure, S 2956.

By sending H J Res 1 to the Senate floor with a recommendation that it not be passed, the committee prepared the way for a possible attempt to substitute the provisions of S 2956 for the House-passed resolution. If this were done, there could be a House-Senate conference on the differing version of H J Res 1 and the stronger Senate war powers provisions would not have to go to the House Foreign Affairs Committee. The House committee had rejected proposals similar to S 2956 before reporting H J Res 1 in 1971.

Constitutional Powers

Art. I, Sec. 8: "The Congress shall have the power to...provide for the common defence...to declare war...to raise and support armies, but no appropriation of money to that use shall be for a longer term than two years; to provide and maintain a Navy; to make rules for the government and regulation of the land and naval forces...to make all laws which shall be necessary and proper for carrying into execution the foregoing powers, and all other powers vested by this Constitution in the government of the United States, or in any department or officer thereof."

Art. II, Sec. 2: "The President shall be Commander in Chief of the Army and Navy of the United States...he shall have power, by and with the advice and consent of the Senate, to make treaties, provided two thirds of the senators present concur; and he shall nominate, and by and with the advice and consent of the Senate, shall appoint ambassadors, other public ministers and consuls...."

As Congress moved toward recess in June 1972 for the political conventions, the prospect that either S 2956 or H J Res 1 would clear Congress appeared slim.

Background

In an age of nuclear stalemate and brush-fire wars, a declaration of war—an act with far-ranging implications for national mobilization and defense commitments—has been regarded by many as an archaic and inflexible power.

"Throughout the 19th and early 20th centuries," Javits told the Senate in 1971, "a body of precedents" for undeclared war "developed on an ad hoc basis, evolving essentially out of the case-by-case exercise of the discretionary executive authority of the President as commander in chief.

"Such cases arise in circumstances which require combat actions," he said, "but which are not sufficiently serious—or in which contemporary conditions make it undesirable—to enact a declaration of war."

Yale University law professor Alexander M. Bickel in 1971 told the Foreign Relations Committee that there was "utterly no reason to think that Congress has only the mega-power to declare war in the exact terms of the constitutional grant and no intermediate power to commit the country to something less than a declared war."

Former Under Secretary of State George W. Ball warned the committee that war powers legislation "represents an attempt to do what the Founding Fathers felt they were not wise enough to do: to give precision and automatic operation to the kind of legislative-executive collaboration which they deemed essential to prevent the unrestricted use of American forces by the executive... while...assuring him sufficient flexibility to defend the country."

In its Feb. 9, 1972, report on S 2956, the Foreign Relations Committee said the power of Congress to enact such legislation was based not only on the specific constitutional grants of authority to delcare war and raise and support armies. A strict interpretation of the constitutional clause giving Congress the right to "make all laws necessary and proper for carrying into execution" the federal government's powers permits Congress "to define and codify the powers of the government as a whole, including those of the President...," the committee said.

In the view of the committee's majority, S 2956 would fulfill "the intent of the framers of the...Constitution in order to assure that the collective judgment of both the Congress and the President will be brought to bear in decisions" involving the United States in hostilities—including future Vietnams.

But the Nixon administration saw such legislation threatening the President's constitutional powers to defend the nation—a dangerous development in a nuclear age.

Foreign Relations Committee Chairman J. W. Fulbright (D Ark.) cautioned that the bill's provisions might "have the unintended effect of giving away more power than they withhold."

Although S 2956 as passed by the Senate specifically exempted the ongoing Indochina war from its provisions, the manner in which the United States became involved in and its strategy for disengaging from that war provided the framework for the war powers debate.

Power of Past

Constitutional Theory. The American colonists who declared their independence from Britain in 1776 were deeply suspicious of standing armies and of the king who had sent British troops to the colonies. The distrust carried over after independence, contributing to a determination to subject military affairs to civilian control.

The Second Continental Congress had general oversight of the conduct of the Revolutionary War. It com-

---

Senate War Powers Bill

Provisions. As passed April 13, 1972, by the Senate S 2956:

• Provided that, in the absence of a declaration of war by Congress, armed forces could be committed to hostilities or to "situations where imminent involvement in hostilities is clearly indicated by the circumstances" only:

1. To repel an armed attack on the United States or to forestall the "direct and imminent threat of such an attack."

2. To repel an armed attack against U.S. armed forces outside the United States or to forestall the threat of such attack.

3. To protect and evacuate U.S. citizens and nationals in another country if their lives were threatened.

4. Pursuant to specific statutory authorization by Congress (not to be inferred from any existing or future law or treaty unless specific authorization was provided. Specific statutory authority also was required for assignment of U.S. military personnel to assist a foreign nation's forces in hostilities or situations where hostilities were imminent).

• Allowed the President to take armed action to protect U.S. citizens and nationals on the high seas.

• Assured continued participation by U.S. officers in joint military commands with other nations, such as NATO.

• Allowed the President to use the armed forces if necessary to protect U.S. forces as they withdrew from hostilities if Congress refused to authorize their continued use after 30 days or if an attack on the United States prevented Congress from meeting before the 30-day deadline expired on presidential action not authorized by Congress.

• Required the President to promptly report to Congress the commitment of forces for such purposes.

• Limited to 30 days the length of involvement of U.S. forces unless Congress by specific legislation authorized their continued use.

• Provided that Congress by act or joint resolution could terminate the use of U.S. forces by the President before the end of the 30-day period.

• Set procedures to require prompt consideration in both houses of any bill or joint resolution authorizing or terminating use of U.S. forces committed by the President.

• Made the bill's provisions effective on the date of enactment but exempted hostilities in which U.S. forces were involved on the effective date.

missioned George Washington to be commander in chief but instructed him "punctually to observe and follow such orders and directions...from this or a future Congress."

The Articles of Confederation, under which the new nation was governed from 1781 to 1789, did not establish an independent executive and left to Congress "the sole and exclusive right and power of determining peace and war...."

Recognizing the need for a strong chief executive who could respond to attacks, the Constitutional Convention of 1787 divided the war-making power between Congress and the President. The Constitution gave Congress the power to declare war and made the President commander in chief of the armed forces.

As first proposed, the Constitution would have given Congress the power to make war, but the convention, by a vote of eight states to one, later agreed to restrict Congress' role to that of declaring war in order to leave the President authority to repel sudden attacks.

A delegate from South Carolina, Pierce Butler, advocated "vesting the power (to declare war) in the President, who will have all the requisite qualities and will not make war but when the nation will support it."

George Mason of Virginia, on the other hand, opposed giving the President sole power to declare war because the executive "was not safely to be trusted with it."

Presenting the newly written Constitution to the nation, the authors of *The Federalist*—John Jay, James Madison and Alexander Hamilton—construed the President's war powers narrowly.

Richard B. Morris, professor of history at Columbia University, told the Foreign Relations Committee during war powers hearings in 1971 that it was "a fair inference from the debates on ratification and from...*The Federalist* papers that the war-making power of the President was little more than the power to defend against imminent invasion when Congress was not in session."

Historical Practice. Historically, the President has exercised much more than a defensive war-making power.

"The Constitution delegates to Congress the authority to *declare* war (with the consent of the President), but the commander in chief in practice *precipitates* war," James MacGregor Burns and Jack Walter Peltason wrote in their 1960 textbook, *Government by the People.*

Between 1789 and 1971 U.S. forces participated in military action overseas on more than 150 occasions, by some counts, but Congress declared war only five times: the War of 1812, the Mexican War, the Spanish-American War, World War I and World War II.

Although Congress has approved some actions by measures other than the constitutionally prescribed declaration of war, others were initiated by the President without specific congressional authorization.

"It has been recognized from the earliest days of the Republic, by the President, by Congress and by the Supreme Court, that the United States may lawfully engage in armed hostilities with a foreign power without a congressional declaration of war," Assistant Attorney General William H. Rehnquist wrote in 1970. "Our history is replete with instances of 'undeclared wars,' from the war with France in 1798-1800 to the Vietnamese war."

Rehnquist, now an associate justice of the Supreme Court, expressed this view in a defense of President

Nixon's authority ordering the 1970 incursion in Cambodia.

Secretary of State William P. Rogers, testifying on war powers legislation before the Foreign Relations Committee in 1971, said the 19th and early 20th centuries brought "an increasing exercise by the President of his constitutional powers to use American armed forces abroad, without the prior authorization of the Congress. And yet there was remarkably little complaint from the Congress."

Although the courts usually had refused to take jurisdiction on cases involving the war powers of the President and Congress, Rogers said, decisions on a few cases "indicate that the courts recognize and accept the President's authority to employ the armed forces in hostilities without express congressional authorization."

In a paper presented to the Center for the Study of Democratic Institutions in 1971, Louis Fisher of the Congressional Research Service of the Library of Congress traced recent presidential claims to expanded powers to a 1936 Supreme Court decision. *United States v. Curtiss-Wright Export Corp.,* 299 U.S. 304 (1936).

Speaking for the court in a case upholding the right of Congress to delegate embargo powers to the President, Justice George Sutherland said legislation in international matters must allow the President "a degree of discretion and freedom from statutory restrictions which would not be admissible were domestic affairs alone involved."

Going beyond the case at issue, Sutherland elaborated on the President's powers in "this vast external realm." Sutherland's "sweeping assertions have since been used to justify an expansion of presidential war powers based not on new powers delegated by Congress but rather on inherent executive powers," Fisher said.

The growth of presidential prerogatives in foreign policy accelerated during World War II and its aftermath as the United States attained—and exercised—worldwide power.

In 1971 testimony on war powers before the Foreign Relations Committee, Professor Alfred H. Kelly of Wayne State University listed "two decisive 'breaks' in the continuity of peace-war relationships between the executive and the Congress:"

● President Roosevelt's actions between May 1940 and U.S. entry into World War II in December 1941. Included in this period were the U.S. destroyer deal with Great Britain and the protection of British convoys in the North Atlantic.

● President Truman's military intervention in South Korea in 1950 and the stationing of seven U.S. divisions in Germany in 1951.

Congress in 1951 challenged Truman's actions but to little avail. Opening a three-month "great debate," Sen. Robert A. Taft (R Ohio) said Truman had "no authority whatever to commit American troops to Korea...without congressional approval" and "no power to agree to send American troops to fight in Europe in a war between the members of the Atlantic Pact and Soviet Russia."

The "great debate" proved inconclusive, however, since the House took no action on a Senate-passed resolution approving the dispatch of four divisions to Europe but declaring the sense of the Senate that congressional approval was required for further additions of ground troops.

(Continued on p. 44)

Senate Debate: Conflicting Views on War Powers

The Senate held 10 days of debate on the war powers bill (S 2956) from March 29 to April 13, when it passed the bill by a 68-16 roll-call vote. During debate the Senate adopted three amendments offered April 5 by the bill's sponsors to clarify provisions questioned by opponents of the legislation. All others were rejected by wide margins, as was a motion to refer the bill to the Senate Judiciary Committee for further study. *(Provisions of S 2956, p. 41)*

Highlights of the 10-day debate:

Jacob K. Javits (R N.Y.): S 2956 would not "deprive the President of authority essential to the security of our country." It would permit him to follow his own judgment in responding to emergencies, but would subject unauthorized action to a time limit of 30 days. "The important thing is that at some stage...(a presidential decision) ceases to be repelling or retaliating against an attack and becomes a basic commitment to war.... That requires the concurrence of Congress."

Gale W. McGee (D Wyo.): "We live in a time when man probably never again will dare declare war, even though he may be forced...to wage one sort of conflict or another.... This is where the Constitution has left us wanting."

John C. Stennis (D Miss.): It would be a "great tragedy if we don't get together some way and put some language on the books.... What the people want to know is what's going to be the rule. If they're called, they're going to be ready if they think" that the nation had been committed to war by proper constitutional procedures.

Barry Goldwater (R Ariz.): S 2956 was "jerrybuilt on false assumptions—false beliefs about the power of Congress to enact this kind of legislation, false claims of what the bill actually provides and false understanding of what the role of Congress has really been in shaping of important decisions bearing on war." The war powers issue should be addressed by constitutional amendment "so that Americans across this land could decide over an unhurried period of time whether it would be wiser to have 500 members of Congress decide about war in moments of grave threat or to have one man, with his staff, make the decisions...."

Peter H. Dominick (R Colo.): S 2956 "would virtually abrogate our 42 defense treaties around the world, severely limit our role in NATO...possibly deprive the President of the authority...to carry on a forward defense...preclude U.S. forces from protecting U.S. nationals on the high seas and...severely limit our credibility with our allies."

John Sherman Cooper (R Ky.): There is "nothing in this bill which denies the deployment of forces to protect the country, to protect our forces, to protect our ships. I know nothing that denies a proper show of force."

Herman E. Talmadge (D Ga.): "The single most important decision...a nation can make is the decision to go to war.... In the recent past, the President, acting alone, has determined whether we followed a course of war or peace. The decision is too great for one man to make...."

Lawton Chiles (D Fla.): "What we are attempting to do...is to provide that before the military is called upon to...run a war, we are going to see that a little more deliberation goes into whether it would be wise for this country to involve itself...and that always would be the decision of the civilians."

Roman L. Hruska (R Neb.): "In attempting to make specific what the Constitution has left general, and in trying to define in advance the outer limits of the President's authority to act in the interest of national security, S 2956 charts a precarious constitutional course."

Mike Mansfield (D Mont.): "What we want to do is try and correct by legislation some of the mistakes which have occurred in the past so that they will not occur again.... We have a responsibility; we have an institution we should fight to uphold. We should fight to uphold the integrity of the Senate...and we should not bow down to whoever happens to be President of the United States."

John G. Tower (R Texas): "The very philosophy at the root of the war powers bill is contradictory to the American constitutional tradition. The bill seeks a rigid definition of the powers.... The Constitution... (is) nowhere near so explicit and constrictive."

Mike Gravel (D Alaska), in support of his amendment to relate the provisions of S 2956 to the Indochina war (expressly excepted by the language of the bill): "We have been waging war in Southeast Asia but... have never bothered to declare war. Yet senators stand on this floor to insist and appeal that we should do more bombing.... We at least ought to have the gumption, the honesty and the straightforwardness to look them in the face and say, 'We declare war against you.' ...If we voted not to declare war, it would make our actions in Indochina look somewhat ridiculous to the world."

J. W. Fulbright (D Ark.), in support of his amendment recognizing a general presidential authority to respond to armed attacks and eliminating from S 2956 the specific circumstances under which the President could take emergency action: The list of emergencies in S 2956 was "broad enough to let the President do anything he wants, but it is narrow enough to give his action the appearance of congressional sanction in advance. My amendment will leave him with the same, but no greater, leeway, while depriving him of any appearance in advance of congressional sanction."

Javits, supporting a provision of S 2956 which restricted the scope of the President's response to attacks on U.S. troops overseas: "We want to make it clear that the order of response was not unlimited. We do not want to give a general hunting license. After all, we have troops all over the world....Let me remind my colleagues that in a limited juridical sense...we are still 'retaliating' against North Vietnam, seven years later, for the Aug. 2-4, 1964, attacks on the *Maddox* and the *Turner Joy* in the Gulf of Tonkin.

Consultation with Congress. Presidents beginning with Truman had made frequent use of their war powers, often with the cooperation of Congress, but in many significant instances without consultation.

"During 16 of the last 23 years," author Eugene G. Windchy wrote in the Jan. 29, 1972, issue of *The New Republic*, "American presidents have been waging undeclared wars."

"Five times in the past 10 years," historian Henry Steele Commager told the Foreign Relations Committee in 1971, "Presidents have mounted major military interventions in foreign nations without prior consultation with the Congress: the Bay of Pigs, the invasion of the Dominican Republic, the attacks on North Vietnam, Cambodia and Laos."

Congress, for its part, has usually been willing to delegate to the President decisions involving military actions abroad.

With little opposition Congress approved measures authorizing the President to commit U.S. forces to the defense of South Vietnam and Taiwan and to take whatever action was necessary to exclude Soviet nuclear missiles from Cuba.

In the view of successive presidents since Truman and, to date, of a majority of members of Congress, the free exercise of the President's constitutional powers to conduct foreign policy and defend the nation was required by modern diplomatic and military conditions.

The U.S. postwar role has brought "fundamental changes in the factual setting in which the war powers must be exercised," Rogers told the Foreign Relations Committee in 1971. And these changes increased the importance of "the institutional capacities of the presidency" for gathering information, maintaining secrecy and reaching quick decisions during crises, he maintained.

"Unlike the presidency," Rogers added, "the institutional characteristics of Congress have not lent themselves as well to the requirements of speed and secrecy in times of recurrent crises and rapid change."

Ten years ago, most members of Congress were willing to concede the need for executive supremacy.

In 1961, for example, Fulbright said in a Cornell University lecture: "The enhancement of presidential power is...a disagreeable and dangerous prospect. It is seen to be a compelling necessity, however, when set against the alternative of immobility which can only lead to consequences immeasurably more disagreeable and dangerous."

Soon after the advent of the large-scale commitment of U.S. armed forces in the Vietnam conflict in 1965-66, Fulbright began to oppose presidential monopoly in foreign policy decisions.

During the 1971 war powers hearings, Fulbright asserted that "it is very much in our interest to revive the participation of the Congress, not only to keep the country united but...to furnish some degree of deliberation and wisdom on the part of the decisions of the executive."

Impact of Vietnam

President Johnson's 1965 policy committing U.S. forces "to full-scale war in Vietnam...mark the farthest...extension of presidential power," Bickel told the Foreign Relations Committee.

"The decisions of 1965 amounted to an all but explicit transfer of the power to declare war from Congress...to the President...."

Sen. John C. Stennis (D Miss.), chairman of the Armed Services Committee, testifying before the committee, cited "...confusion over the legal justification for the war in Vietnam" as one reason legislation was needed to clarify the war powers of the Congress and of the President.

The Johnson administration maintained that the President had ample authority to undertake the U.S. armed intervention in Vietnam. In 1966, Leonard C. Meeker, the State Department's legal adviser, wrote that there was "no question in present circumstances of the President's authority to commit U.S. forces to the defense of South Vietnam. The grant of authority to the President in Article II of the Constitution extends to the actions of the United States currently undertaken in Vietnam."

The Johnson administration also claimed congressional authorization from the Gulf of Tonkin Resolution (H J Res 1145—PL 88-408), approved by Congress on Aug. 7, 1964, for its intervention.

The joint resolution, which had the force of law, was passed after the United States reported that two American destroyers had been attacked by North Vietnamese PT boats. H J Res 1145 declared congressional support for the President's "determination...to take all necessary measures" to repel attacks on U.S. forces and to prevent further aggression. It said the United States was prepared "as the President determines" to use force if necessary to assist any member of the Southeast Asian Collective Defense Treaty Organization.

In testimony before the Foreign Relations Committee on Aug. 17, 1967, Under Secretary of State Nicholas deB. Katzenbach said the Gulf of Tonkin Resolution was "'as broad an authorization for the use of armed forces...as any declaration of war so-called could be in terms of our internal constitutional process."

President Johnson, however, said at a press conference the next day that the administration "...did not think the resolution was necessary to do what we did and what we're doing."

"The exact trouble with the Tonkin Gulf Resolution was that it was misperceived, both by the Congress and by the executive branch...," McGeorge Bundy, special assistant for national security affairs in the Kennedy and Johnson administrations, told the Foreign Relations Committee in 1971.

The United States must "never again go to war without the moral sanction of the American people," Stennis said. "Vietnam has shown us that by trying to fight a war without the clear-cut prior support of the American people we not only risk military ineffectiveness but we also strain, and can shatter, the very structure of the Republic. ...it is not only our right, but our constitutional duty to insist that the President obtain the sanction of the Congress, the people's representatives, before he actually involves the nation in war."

Congressional Response. As opposition to the Vietnam war grew both among the public and in Congress, members sought to reassert the role of Congress in making decisions leading to war.

Several measures considered in recent years—such as the amendment proposed in 1970 by Senators John

Sherman Cooper (R Ky.) and Frank Church (D Idaho) barring use of funds for U.S. ground troops in Cambodia and the amendment proposed by Mike Mansfield (D Mont.) in 1971 declaring a policy of withdrawal from Indochina—were offered to prevent a widening of the war or to force an end to U.S. involvement.

Others, including S 2956, were addressed to the larger goal of reasserting the power of Congress to make decisions on future involvements in war.

The Senate in 1969 adopted a resolution (S Res 85) declaring the sense of the Senate that a national commitment could be made only "from affirmative action taken by the legislative and executive branches...by means of a treaty, statute, or concurrent resolution of both houses...specifically providing for such commitment."

S Res 85 did not have the force of law, however, and only admonished the President to consult with Congress in making commitments of U.S. forces or aid.

Congress in 1970 repealed the Tonkin Gulf Resolution through an amendment to the foreign military sales bill (HR 15628—PL 91-672), which was signed by the President on Jan. 12, 1971.

The Foreign Relations Committee Jan. 19 reported a bill (S 596—S Rept 92-591) requiring that Congress receive promptly the text of any international agreement made by the executive branch.

The Foreign Relations Committee Feb. 9 ordered reported S Res 214 expressing the sense of the Senate that any agreements with Portugal or Bahrain for military bases or foreign aid be submitted to the Senate as a treaty requiring ratification.

Nixon Administration Position

While President Nixon reduced U.S. troop strength in Vietnam after assuming office in 1969, his administration has insisted that the President as commander in chief had sole authority to conduct the war as he saw fit.

The President sought no authority from Congress when he sent U.S. troops into Cambodia in 1970 and provided support for the South Vietnamese invasion of Laos in 1971.

The administration did not oppose repeal of the Gulf of Tonkin Resolution, maintaining that it had not relied on it for authority to conduct the war.

In May 14, 1971, testimony before the Foreign Relations Committee, Secretary of State William P. Rogers opposed war powers bills similar to S 2956 because such legislation would "narrow the power given the President by the Constitution" and freeze the division of power between the President and Congress.

Asked his opinion of war powers legislation during an April 29, 1971, news conference, Nixon said that "limiting the President's war powers, whoever is President of the United States, would be a very great mistake.... We live in times when situations can change so fast internationally that to wait until the Senate acts before a President can act might be that we acted too late."

The administration conducted a major lobby effort against S 2956 when it reached the Senate floor.

Tom C. Korologos, a special assistant to the President, March 2 told Congressional Quarterly that the White House would lobby "hammer and tongs" against S 2956.

Cooper-Church Amendment

A precedent-setting attempt to put Congress' control of funding to use was made in 1970. On June 30 the Senate, by a 58-37 vote, adopted an amendment to the pending Military Sales bill (HR 15628) aimed to shut off the employment of American forces in Cambodia. Sponsored by Senators Frank Church (D Idaho) and John Sherman Cooper (R Ky.), the amendment would have forbidden government expenditures after July 1, 1970, to support U.S. combat operations in Cambodia or furnish military instruction to Cambodian forces. Conferees dropped the amendment from HR 15628, but the amendment in slightly different form was enacted as part of a supplemental foreign aid authorization bill (HR 19911). Its practical effect was limited, since the ground troops ordered into Cambodia by President Nixon on April 20 were withdrawn by July 1.

Following is the final text of the 1970 Cooper-Church Amendment:

"In concert with the declared objectives of the President of the United States to avoid the involvement of the United States in Cambodia after July 1, 1970, and to expedite the withdrawal of American forces from Cambodia, it is hereby provided that unless specifically authorized by law hereafter enacted, no funds authorized or appropriated pursuant to this act or any other law may be expended after July 1, 1970, for the purpose of—

"(1) retaining United States forces in Cambodia;

"(2) paying the compensation or allowances of, or otherwise supporting, directly or indirectly, any United States personnel in Cambodia who furnish military instruction to Cambodian forces or engage in any combat activity in support of Cambodian forces;

"(3) entering into or carrying out any contract or agreement to provide military instruction in Cambodia or to provide persons to engage in any combat activity in support of Cambodian forces; or

"(4) conducting any combat activity in the air above Cambodia in direct support of Cambodian forces.

"Nothing contained in this section shall be deemed to impugn the constitutional power of the President as Commander-in-Chief, including the exercise of that constitutional power which may be necessary to protect the lives of U.S. armed forces wherever deployed.

"Nothing contained in this section shall be deemed to impugn the constitutional powers of the Congress including the power to declare war and to make rules for the government and regulation of the armed forces of the United States."

Fulbright's proposed amendment granting a general presidential authority was a matter of "just trying to fog up the issue," Korologos added.

Harrison M. Symmes, deputy assistant secretary of state for congressional relations, said March 2 that State Department opposition expressed by Secretary of State Rogers in his 1971 testimony was unchanged.

DRAFT 1971: EIGHT-MONTH DEBATE, TWO-YEAR EXTENSION

It was the end of January 1971 when President Nixon sent Congress a military draft bill. He wanted a two-year extension of conscription and a $1.5-billion pay increase for men in uniform. The President got what he asked for, and more.

The draft bill (HR 6531—PL 92-129), which was cleared for the President's signature Sept. 21, 1971, on a 55-30 Senate roll-call vote, extended the draft two years—through June 30, 1973—and increased military pay and other benefits by $2.4-billion annually.

In both the House and Senate, the greatest threat to extending the draft in the manner requested by the White House came on votes aimed at renewing induction authority for just one year. In the House a one-year extension amendment was rejected by two votes, 200-198 recorded teller. There was a six-vote margin in the Senate, 49-43 roll-call.

Congress chose the draft bill as a vehicle to call for an end to the war in Indochina—the first time such a provision has gained majority support. The bill was used as a forum of debate on the United States' commitment to the North Atlantic Treaty Organization (NATO), on drug addiction in the military and dozens of issues peripheral to the draft.

Portions of the draft bill debate which dealt with amendments to withdraw troops from Vietnam and to reduce the number of troops stationed in North Atlantic Treaty Organization countries are not included in this chapter; Vietnam debate p. 70, 76; NATO debate p. 63; drug addiction p. 28.

Campaign Promise. In the 1968 presidential campaign, Richard M. Nixon promised to end the draft as soon as possible and to establish an all-volunteer military. In the four-bill package sent to Congress in January 1971, the President proposed measures that he said would reduce draft calls to zero by mid-1973.

Simultaneously, Mr. Nixon requested a two-year extension of the draft law.

By combining proposals that sought to extend conscription while offering to launch an experimental program aimed at ending the draft, the administration package had sections that appealed to many members of Congress. It was a compromise designed to undercut pending draft repeal bills with the promise that a volunteer army was in the works while assuring opponents of the all-volunteer concept that no rash moves were contemplated.

Final Action. HR 6531 cleared Congress Sept. 21 when the Senate broke the back of an emerging filibuster by draft opponents on a 61-30 cloture vote and passed the bill 55-30.

The House had accepted the conference report on the bill Aug. 4 but the Senate delayed action until after a Congressional summer recess despite heavy administration and Pentagon lobbying for earlier action.

The delay in Senate approval of the final bill resulted in almost a three-month interruption in the process of inducting young men into the armed forces, the first time the draft had not been in effect since 1948. *(Draft expiration p. 60)*

The President signed the bill into law (PL 92-129) Sept. 28, ending a legislative process which began seven months earlier.

During the debate, Congress considered 83 amendments to the bill, 60 in the Senate and 23 in the House. Twice the Senate reversed itself—first, adopting greater pay increases than the President had requested after rejecting a similar pay hike six days before; second, adopting for the first time a proposal calling for the withdrawal of U.S. troops from Indochina after rejecting a somewhat stronger measure two weeks before.

Congress rejected attempts to end or shorten the extension of the draft but expanded the rights of young men facing induction and broadened representation on local draft boards.

1971 Draft Bill Highlights

In its final form, the draft extension bill (HR 6531—PL 92-129) provided for *(complete provisions, appendix)*:

- A two-year extension of the draft to June 30, 1973.
- A sense of Congress resolution urging the President to negotiate for a Vietnam cease-fire and for the President to withdraw U.S. troops from Indochina at the earliest practicable date pending the release of all U.S. prisoners of war.
- An increase in pay and other types of compensation for servicemen estimated to cost a total of $2.4-billion the first year.
- A nationalized lottery call eliminating the local board quota system.
- The return to the President of authority to draft college students who entered school after the spring of 1971.
- Expanded the procedural rights of the draft registrant.
- Interim steps for setting up programs to treat, identify and rehabilitate drug addicts and alcoholics in the military.
- A 2.5-million-man ceiling on the armed forces' active duty strength and a 130,000-man ceiling on the number of men who could be drafted during fiscal 1972.
- An extension of the statute of limitations making a person who failed to register for the draft eligible for prosecution until age 31.

In most instances, Congress supported the views of the administration which, although committed to eventually ending the draft, insisted on extension of the draft, belatedly approved pay raises and vehemently opposed the European and Vietnam withdrawal amendments.

The lengthy debate was staged in the midst of related outside events which had mixed influence on the discussion in Congress. The disclosure of the secret Pentagon papers on the history of the Vietnam war was credited by some as influencing Senate approval of a strong amendment by Sen. Mike Mansfield (D Mont.) on Vietnam by a sizable 61-38 vote after it had rejected the earlier proposal by Senators George McGovern (D S.D.) and Mark O. Hatfield (R Ore.). Soviet moves toward negotiations on European troop reductions were seen as scuttling the Mansfield measure on that subject. Also taking place during the debate were the trial and conviction of Army Lt. William Calley for the murder of Vietnamese civilians in My Lai, the North Vietnamese offer to negotiate on mutual troop withdrawals and the repatriation of prisoners and the announcement of a visit by President Nixon to Communist China.

During congressional deliberation on the bill the administration and Pentagon officials and coalitions supporting an end the draft or a termination of U.S. involvement in Vietnam brought heavy lobby pressure to bear on Congress.

Changes in the Law. The end product of Congress' eight-month work on the bill was a substantial change in who would serve in the military services, how he would be chosen, who would sit on his draft board and what his rights were in dealing with that board.

The age group vulnerable to induction was unchanged (18-26). But within the framework of existing law fewer young men were able to escape draft eligibility. Student deferments were abolished for 1971 college freshmen, although the sophomores, juniors and seniors maintained their deferments.

A new set of procedural rights for the draft registrant was part of the draft law, including the right to present witnesses to the draft board, the right to appear in person, a requirement that the board have a quorum present when the registrant appears in person and the stipulation that if the registrant so requests, the board must provide him a written statement if it rules against his claim for a particular draft status.

Despite several attempts to revise the definition of a conscientious objector on the floor of the Senate and House, there was no change in existing law. The House-passed version of the bill extended an objector's term of alternate service to three years from two years. The extra year of service was removed from the bill in the House-Senate conference. The final version of the bill stipulated that a CO was subject to recall to his alternate service in case of a declared national emergency. *(Box, p. 53)*

Background: The Volunteer Army

The idea of replacing the draft with an all-volunteer system first was placed in the Republican platform during the 1964 presidential campaign. In 1968, stronger language was used. "When military manpower needs can be appreciably reduced, we will place the Selective Service System on standby and substitute a voluntary force obtained through adequate pay and career incentives," the platform stated.

The presidential platform of the Democratic party first included a phrase about the all-volunteer concept in 1968.

Two months after Mr. Nixon moved into the White House, he appointed a 15-man presidential commission to work out plans for conversion of the armed forces into an all-volunteer service. The commission, headed by former Defense Secretary Thomas S. Gates, reported its recommendations to the President Feb. 21, 1970.

The commission recommended implementation of an all-volunteer force by July 1, 1971. To obtain an all-volunteer force of 2.5 million men, the commission estimated additional costs of $2.7-billion for wages and total new costs of $3.2-billion. About 75,000 additional volunteers would have to be found.

Early Legislative Attempts. As a freshman senator in 1967 Hatfield in his first floor speech proposed an amendment to the draft extension bill of 1967 calling for initial steps toward "the prompt termination of involuntary inductions and a transition to an effective voluntary system." Hatfield's amendment was rejected May 11, 1967, by a 9-69 roll-call vote.

After the Gates Commission recommended that an all-volunteer military should be instituted by mid-1971, Hatfield cosponsored with Sen. Barry Goldwater (R Ariz.) an amendment to the fiscal 1971 military procurement authorization bill calling for implementation of the Gates commission's recommendations.

Although the second Hatfield proposal picked up 26 more votes than his 1967 attempt, the margin was still insufficient to gain passage. The amendment was rejected Aug. 25, 1970, by a 35-52 roll-call vote.

Support for improvements in the soldier's life (i.e. pay increases), whether the improvements led to an all-volunteer military or not, was the unanimous expression of witnesses appearing before the Armed Services Committees in 1971. The Nixon administration, anticipating the need for improvements, began modifying some of the stricter military regulations in January in an effort to make service more appealing. *(Military morale p. 22)*

Nixon Message. In a Jan. 28, 1971, message to Congress, the President said, "We should begin moving toward the end of the draft and its replacement with an all-volunteer force." In the same address, however, Mr. Nixon said, "No one knows precisely when we can end conscription." He said that "even the most optimistic observers agree that we would not be able to end the draft in the next year or so without seriously weakening our military forces."

Two alternatives for the length of a draft extension were proposed. The administration bill (S 427, HR 2476) requested a two-year extension and the Hatfield joint resolution, S J Res 20, (identical to H J Res 345 sponsored in the House by Rep. Bella S. Abzug (D N.Y.)) proposed repeal of the draft by Dec. 31, which would be the same as a six-month extension. Another alternative, which required no formal proposal, was for Congress to allow the President's induction authority to simply expire June 30.

Administration Proposals. Three bills included in the administration's two-year draft extension and volunteer army package were designed to improve conditions in the military in anticipation of the day when draft calls no longer would be needed. The three bills totaled a $1.5-billion program.

The administration bill (S 496, HR 3496) to increase pay was estimated to cost an additional $908-million in fiscal year l972. The proposal requested that a recruit's pay be increased by 50 percent or from $134 to $201 per month.

An estimated $79-million increase in quarters allowances for low-grade enlisted men (E-l through E-4) with dependents was requested in the bill. During fiscal 1971, cash expenditures for quarters allowances were $l.48-billion, according to the Pentagon.

An enlistment bonus for combat soldiers was requested in the second administration bill (S 495, HR 3498). Although the bonus specified in the proposal was a maximum of $6,000 for a three-year enlistment, Assistant Defense Secretary Kelley told the Senate Armed Services Committee that a $3,000 bonus would be used initially.

The third bill in the package (HR 3497, S 494) requested a 71-percent increase in the military recruiting budget for fiscal 1972. The proposal was designed to allow the recruiting officer a larger expense account when out in the field. The military recruiting budget in fiscal 1971 was $156-million. The proposed budget for fiscal 1972 was $267-million or an increase of $111-million.

Included in the $1.5-billion total for the three bills was $100-million to be held in a contingency fund.

Gates Commission Bills. The major differences between the administration package and the Hatfield-Goldwater bill (S 392) and (HR 4450), were implementation date and cost. Where the administration bills set no specific date for allowing the all-volunteer army to replace the conscripted force, but aimed for mid-1973, the other two bills sought to put the draft on a standby basis almost immediately, removing the element of presidential discretion. Where the administration bills requested $l.5-billion to move toward a zero draft, the two bills that closely mirrored the Gates Commission recommendations estimated costs of $3.1-billion during fiscal 1972. The bulk ($2.7-billion) of the $3.1-billion was for pay increases. The administration bill raised a recruit's pay by 50 percent and these two bills requested the recruit's salary be hiked by 124 percent, or from $134 to $301 per month.

Rather than offer an enlistment bonus to make combat duty more attractive, the two bills proposed raising the monthly dividend paid to soldiers working under "hostile fire" from $65 to $200. Under this proposal, a soldier stationed in a hostile fire zone could make $2,400 in addition to his regular salary in one year.

The two bills requested broader educational programs for military personnel, increased ROTC scholarships, higher pay for military doctors, increased quarters allowances and improved barracks conditions.

Committee Bill. The portion of the House Armed Services Committee bill (HR 6531), reported March 25 (H Rept 92-82), that dealt with the all-volunteer army went further than the administration bill in requesting pay raises ($1.87-billion), but did not include any type of

incentive for enlistment in combat units. Charman F. Edward Hebert (D La.), who repeatedly voiced skepticism about the possibility of attaining the voluntary force, told reporters March 22 that the committee bill put no obstacles in the way of attaining the all-volunteer force. Assistant Defense Secretary Roger T. Kelley told a press briefing the same day that without the enlistment bonus, "it will be very, very difficult" to achieve the voluntary force by mid-1973.

The committee bill requested twice as much money for pay increases as the administration proposal. The $1.87-billion requested in the committee proposal for wage hikes would increase a recruit's pay from $134 to $268 per month.

For quarters allowances, the committee requested 10 times more money than the administration bill. Where the administration bill requested $79-million, HR 6531 proposed $830-million for increases in quarters allowances. The administration bill emphasized enlisted men with dependents while the committee bill spread additional

---

Draft Extensions

Before 1971, the draft had been extended four times since 1951. Each extension has been for four years. The closest margin on House passage of any military draft bill since World War II had been in 1951 when the House first approved legislation establishing the current authority to induct men into the armed forces. The vote that year was 372-44.

In the Senate, no more than five votes were ever cast against a draft bill during the period 1951-1967.

1971 (two-year extension)
House—Passed by 293-99 roll-call vote; three days of debate; 23 amendments offered, 5 adopted.

Senate—Passed by 72-16 roll-call vote; over a month of debate; 60 amendments offered, 24 adopted.

1967 (four-year extension)
House—Passed by 362-9 roll-call vote; one day of debate; 13 amendments offered, 3 adopted.

Senate—Passed by 70-2 roll-call vote; one day of debate; 7 amendments offered, none adopted.

1963 (four-year extension)
House—Passed by 388-3 roll-call vote; one day of debate; 3 amendments offered, none adopted.

Senate—Passed by voice vote; one day of debate; no amendments offered.

1959 (four-year extension)
House—Passed by 381-20 roll-call vote; one day of debate; three amendments offered, none adopted.

Senate—Passed by 90-1 roll-call vote; one day of debate; two amendments offered, none adopted.

1955 (four-year extension)
House—Passed by 394-4 roll-call vote; one day of debate; 5 amendments offered, 2 adopted.

Senate—Passed by voice vote; one day of debate; one amendment offered, one adopted.

1951 Universal Military Training and Service Act
House—Passed by 372-44 roll-call vote; four days of debate; 34 amendments offered, 16 adopted.

Senate—Passed by 79-5 roll-call vote; seven days of debate; 17 amendments offered, 3 adopted.

compensation through all ranks of military personnel. The total committee request for wage increases and quarters allowances was $2.7-billion.

House Floor Action

The House April 1, after three days of debate, by a 293-99 roll-call vote approved a two-year extension of the military draft.

The bill (HR 6531) increased the pay for first-term enlistees at an additional cost of $2.7-billion, eliminated undergraduate student deferments and extended the period of alternate service for conscientious objectors (COs) to three years from the two-year period required by existing law.

During floor debate, the House rejected amendments to reduce the length of the draft extension, restrict duty in Vietnam to men who were not draftees, continue the existing two-year term of alternate service for COs and make the statutory language for acquiring CO status conform to previous Supreme Court decisions.

Only five amendments were adopted during the entire debate. Accepted were amendments to reverse the committee action which had abolished the deferment for

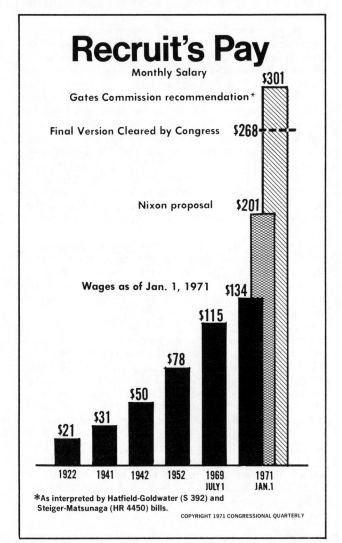

Recruit's Pay
Monthly Salary

Gates Commission recommendation* — $301

Final Version Cleared by Congress — $268

Nixon proposal — $201

Wages as of Jan. 1, 1971 — $134

$115

$78

$50

$31

$21

| 1922 | 1941 | 1942 | 1952 | 1969 JULY 1 | 1971 JAN. 1 |

*As interpreted by Hatfield-Goldwater (S 392) and Steiger-Matsunaga (HR 4450) bills.

COPYRIGHT 1971 CONGRESSIONAL QUARTERLY

divinity students, to require draft boards, clerks and records to be established in each county, to include private non-public hospitals, in addition to public institutions, as places where COs could meet their service requirements and to exempt from induction all male members of an immediate family in which one member had been either killed, totally disabled, a prisoner-of-war or missing in action.

Support for the concept of an all-volunteer military service was expressed throughout the debate. Differences of opinion were expressed, however, as to when the volunteer force could begin replacing draftees and draft-motivated volunteers, who were supplying about 48 percent of the manpower for the Army.

Four attempts were made on the floor to reduce the period of the draft extension to less than the two years recommended in the committee bill.

During the House debate on the military draft extension bill, new attitudes by a significant number of House members toward the draft and U.S. military involvement in Vietnam became evident.

Although HR 6531 dealt specifically with manpower needs of the military for 1971-73, the three days of debate March 30-April 1 comprised the most extensive review of U.S. policy in Indochina ever allowed by the House leadership. A new element in the debate was the March 29 conviction of Lt. William L. Calley Jr. *(p. 25)*

Not since passage in 1951 of the Universal Military Training and Service Act, which reinstated the draft as a part of the American way of life, had the House spent more than one day debating the draft.

The 1971 extension was opposed by 99 members. This was the largest protest vote against the draft in the House since before World War II. Nine House members voted against the 1967 draft extension.

DEBATE

General debate on HR 6531 was held March 30 and was limited to four hours under the resolution (H Res 350) adopted by the Rules Committee for consideration of the bill. Throughout the first half hour of debate. There was never more than 30 (out of 433) Representatives on the floor. A request for the quorum call during the first hour of debate temporarily brought all but 62 House members to the floor.

Explaining the committee's rejection of an all-volunteer army, Hebert said: "I think members of the House should keep very clearly in mind that the President did not recommend an immediate attempt to move to an all-volunteer force. What the President asked for was a two-year extension of the induction authority and the vehicle with which to be in a position to move to an all-volunteer force in 1973."

Leslie C. Arends (R Ill.), Republican Whip and ranking minority member on the Armed Services Committee, said that "all of us would like to end the draft, but to do so without being sure that sufficient volunteers would be available would be taking grave risks with our national security. I would point out that though the induction authority is extended for two years, there is nothing to prevent the termination of induction prior to that time if sufficient volunteers are forthcoming."

Discussing the issue of a one-year versus a two-year extension of the draft, Charles W. Whalen Jr. (R Ohio) *(Continued on p. 51)*

Volunteer Army or the Draft: The Issues

At issue in the draft-volunteer army debate were matters of morality, of economy, class inequities and control of foreign policy.

Mercenary Force. Some of those who opposed the all-volunteer army said that such a force would be a band of "professional killers" with little in common with civilian society. Those supporting the measure discounted such arguments by telling critics that the military was largely an all-volunteer force already.

Rep. Paul N. McCloskey (R Cal.) told the House Armed Services Committee: "There are men who love to kill, but it seems to me the nation is far safer when its army is made up of reluctant citizen-soldiers than by men who take pride in being professional killers."

Dr. Harry Marmion, representing the American Veterans Committee (AVC), testified before the House committee: "There is the danger than an isolated military establishment will be a potential political force in American life that must not be underestimated. Instead of the present picture of a mammoth military-industrial complex dominating our society, we can expect an even greater establishment which will have little stake in civilian society, and will seek a larger budget and more wars to perpetuate itself."

Army of Poor. Opponents of the all-volunteer army claimed that military enlistments would be predominantly from lower socio-economic backgrounds than the men touched by the draft. Why should the poor fight this country's wars? the critics asked. Supporters relied on the Gates Commission projections when answering the question. The commission's findings, they said, predicted only a slight increase in blacks and underprivileged would be noticed if the program were implemented.

Sen. Edward F. Kennedy told the Senate Armed Services Committee: "I would support a volunteer army in peacetime. But when American men are dying in Vietnam, Cambodia and perhaps Laos, I believe a volunteer army is both unwise and inequitable. I frankly do not want to insulate middle- and upper-class Americans from the horrors of war."

Assistant Defense Secretary Roger T. Kelley: "The alleged pitfalls of the voluntary military organization— that it will be dominated by mercenaries or be all black—are gratuitous and false claims. They should be knocked down hard lest the American public be misled by them."

Control War-Making. If there had not been a draft, Vietnam never would have happened, argued some opponents of draft extension. They said the draft provides the President with an unlimited supply of manpower which tends to perpetuate American "adventurism" abroad, and that the draft is eroding the power of Congress to control the nation's destiny. Supporters of draft extension called the claims "sheer speculation" and urged a two-year extension. Supporters of the draft said draftees were crucial in permitting a withdrawal from Vietnam.

Before the House committee Rep. Bella S. Abzug (D N.Y.) testified: "The draft has made possible the escalation and continuation of the war in Indochina. As an important step toward ending the wretched war, the President's power to induct men into the armed forces must not be extended beyond June 30."

Sanford Gottlieb, director of an anti-war group known as SANE, told both the House and Senate committees: "To suggest that we need draftees to generate anti-war pressures is to suggest that the burden of halting the war should be placed upon the men who are being shot at rather than exercised by the elected representatives of the American people."

Kennedy took an opposite view: "There are some who argue that we never would have become involved in a large-scale war in Indochina if there had been no draft. This is sheer speculation. Some suggest that if the draft were ended, American involvement in Indochina would have to come to a grinding halt. This is also speculation. In any event, if the Congress wishes to end the war, it can do so by legislation aimed directly at that goal."

Money-Saver. Critics and supporters of the all-volunteer army agreed that in the long run, such a force probably would be more economical. Opponents argued, however, that the country can ill-afford the initial expense of launching the program.

Testifying in support of the all-volunteer army, Kelley said such a force would be more efficient because it would be functioning in "a free environment" and would be more effective and economical because it would consist of fewer people than its conscripted counterpart.

Kennedy said: "In wartime, a society can least afford the extra cost of trying to achieve a volunteer army. When compared to pressing domestic needs, the extra costs of a volunteer army become highly questionable."

American Way. The draft is unfair, argued opponents of extension, because it interrupts a young man's life, forces him to fight in unjust wars and goes against the tradition of volunteerism in the United States. Supporters of the extension asked: Who would volunteer if the draft is eliminated?

"As a conservative," Goldwater told the Senate committee, "I believe that the most precious and fundamental right of a man is his right to live his own life. When force is used to tell a young man how he shall spend several years of his life, I consider this to invade his basic personal liberty." Hatfield called the draft "involuntary servitude that is contrary to every value and tradition that has made our country strong."

Director Curtis W. Tarr of Selective Service said: "I've talked with countless numbers of young people who would have gained a great deal personally by interrupting their college work so they might understand better their motivations for study and how better they might orient their lives." He said the draft might provide just such an interruption.

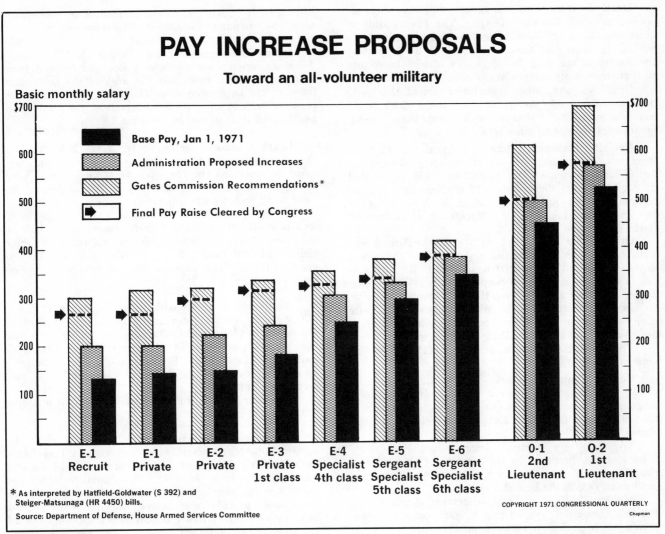

PAY INCREASE PROPOSALS

Toward an all-volunteer military

Basic monthly salary

Legend:
- Base Pay, Jan 1, 1971
- Administration Proposed Increases
- Gates Commission Recommendations*
- Final Pay Raise Cleared by Congress

Categories: E-1 Recruit, E-1 Private, E-2 Private, E-3 Private 1st class, E-4 Specialist 4th class, E-5 Sergeant Specialist 5th class, E-6 Sergeant Specialist 6th class, 0-1 2nd Lieutenant, 0-2 1st Lieutenant

* As interpreted by Hatfield-Goldwater (S 392) and Steiger-Matsunaga (HR 4450) bills.

Source: Department of Defense, House Armed Services Committee

COPYRIGHT 1971 CONGRESSIONAL QUARTERLY

Chapman

(Continued from p. 49)

said that if the draft could be reduced to zero before mid-1973, why extend it for two years? He said the committee's bill "fails to pursue the objective which I think many of us here in this body seek; namely, that of an all-voluntary military service." Whalen urged support for his one-year extension amendment, asserting that it would give the Defense Department an added incentive to make the transition to an all-volunteer force and would give Congress an opportunity for reassessment in 1972.

"This House will pass an extension of the draft," Parren J. Mitchell (D Md.) said: "We know that you have got your forces lined up so that you will end up continuing the draft. All that we can do is stand and argue and articulate against this kind of senseless action which will perpetuate a senseless, bloody, dirty war in Southeast Asia in which we should never have become involved."

AMENDMENTS

The House March 31 began consideration of numerous floor amendments. HR 6531 offered the first opportunity to put into effect a provision of the 1970 Legislative Reorganization Act (PL 91-510) allowing 10 minutes of debate on any amendment offered on the floor so long as it

had been printed in the *Congressional Record* at least one day before being considered. (Formerly, debate on an amendment could be cut off by majority vote without receiving any explanation at all. A request to cut off debate by the chairman of the committee responsible for a bill before the House was usually respected.)

Selective Service Repeal. Bella S. Abzug (D N.Y.) offered the first amendment to HR 6531. Her proposal sought to repeal the draft effective Jan. 1, 1972. It was rejected by a standing vote of 11-73.

Discussing her amendment, Mrs. Abzug said: "I am unalterably opposed to military conscription. I believe that the draft in this country not only violates the concepts of the American tradition of freedom and creates a system of involuntary servitude, but also I believe the draft has made possible the escalation and the continuation of the war in Indochina."

Chairman Hebert replied: "If the amendment were to be adopted, we would have absolutely no machinery, no mechanism in the government to induct or to acquire or to maintain any necessary manpower pool in the defense of this country. In these times the only way to get sufficient manpower is by the mechanism of the draft, as obnoxious as it may be to most of us. I wish we did not need it."

Draft Boards. Two companion amendments were offered by Jack Brinkley (D Ga.). The first would require the office of the clerk of the draft board to be within the county of the state served. It would require the records of the draft board to stay within the county so that intercounty records would not be pooled together.

Brinkley's companion amendment stated that only persons living in the county of a particular draft board could be members of that county's board. Both amendments were adopted by voice votes.

Divinity Students. James A. Byrne (D Pa.) offered an amendment to restore existing deferments for divinity students. The committee's bill eliminated divinity student deferments. "The Selective Service System has not justified the need for termination of the exemption for divinity students or seminarians," Byrne said.

Otis G. Pike (D N.Y.), a member of the Armed Services Committee, opposed the amendment: "The whole thrust of this bill and everything we try to do with this bill is to make it apply to people equally. We are after justice and we are after equality. Of course, divinity students are worthy but so are biologists and so are chemists and so are physicists and environmentalists and teachers and almost anything you want to name."

The amendment was adopted by a 114-29 standing vote.

Conscientious Objectors. Robert L. Leggett (D Calif.) offered an amendment to make the statutory language defining conscientious objectors conform with the 1970 Supreme Court decision in *Welsh v. United States. (Box p. 53)*

"What I have offered," Leggett said, "is merely a restatement, prepared by the counsel for the Office of the Director of Selective Service, of what the existing draft practice is in the United States today."

William G. Bray (R Ind.), a member of the Armed Services Committee, replied that it would open up "Pandora's box by trying to work out another rule as to what is a conscientious objector. I am against opening up a Pandora's box here." John E. Hunt (R N.J.) called the amendment superfluous. The amendment was defeated by voice vote.

CO Service. David W. Dennis (R Ind.) offered an amendment to keep the existing two-year term of civilian service for conscientious objectors. The committee bill extended the term to three years. The Dennis amendment also sought to change a section of HR 6531 that provided for the automatic induction of a CO doing unsatisfactory work in his civilian job. "The constitutionality of this provision which assigns a conscientious objector to the armed services is certainly doubtful, to say the least. On the other side of the coin, I cannot imagine any way you could get a more inefficient, unwilling and unsatisfactory soldier," Dennis said.

The Dennis amendment was rejected by a 132-242 recorded teller vote.

National Service. Jonathan B. Bingham (D N.Y.) offered an amendment to substitute a universal service plan for the draft whereby all males would be required to give two years of service to their country in either the military or in civilian service organizations. Hebert opposed the amendment, saying such a proposal would require extensive committee study and that Bingham

had failed to appear before the committee to explain his plan. The amendment was rejected by voice vote.

Police Deferments. Frank Horton (R N.Y.) introduced an amendment to defer police and firemen from military service. Horton said the work of the police and firemen was as dangerous as that of a soldier and the need for more men in these career areas was great. The amendment was rejected by voice vote.

Legal Counsel. Lester L. Wolff (D N.Y.) offered an amendment "to insure that every young man classified or processed (by the selective service) would have the right to be accompanied by a lawyer before his local board and at every stage of any appeal proceedings.

"In my judgment," Wolff added, "one of the most serious flaws in our current draft system is the lack of assurance that registrants will be informed of their rights and that they will have sufficient information to exercise them." The amendment was rejected by voice vote.

Academic Year Consideration. Clarence D. Long (D Md.) offered an amendment to allow a student to finish the academic year when drafted rather than just his current semester as recommended in the committee bill. Long said: "Breaking up a year's academic program creates a psychological hardship" as well as a financial burden.

The amendment was rejected by a 37-70 standing vote.

One-year Extension. Charles W. Whalen Jr. (R Ohio) offered an amendment to extend the President's authority to induct men into the armed forces for one year, through June 30, 1972. The committee's bill requested a two-year extension. Whalen said his amendment would provide an incentive, "lacking in the present bill," by which the Defense Department could work toward an all-voluntary military service. "The amendment establishes an objective, or a target date" and would put "pressure on the proper authorities to attain this goal."

Whalen's amendment was supported on the floor by 19 members; nine spoke against it. Among the opposition, however, were the minority and majority leaders as well as Arends and Hebert.

Gerald R. Ford (R Mich.), minority leader: "For the life of me I do not understand why the people who want an all-volunteer army do not accept the best of two worlds, which is the committee's recommendation.... I do not think we ought to gamble with the possibility of a crisis by weakening our military."

After an hour's debate, the amendment was narrowly defeated by a 198-200 recorded teller vote. The conservative coalition—defined as a majority of Republicans and southern Democrats opposed to a majority of northern Democrats—prevailed on the vote: Republicans 65-105; northern Democrats 116-35, southern Democrats 17-60. Freshmen members—those elected in November 1970—split 37-17 for the amendment.

June 30 Deadline. Michael Harrington (D Mass.), also a member of the Committee, offered an amendment to end the draft June 30, 1971, while holding the Selective Service System on standby. Debate on the amendment was allowed to extend for two hours and was then rejected by a 62 to 331 recorded teller vote.

Harrington: "I suggest it is time to cut through the accumulated inertia and speculative myths and return to the people of this country their birthright of personal freedom." He said the draft "enables the President to turn peaceful, free men into unwilling instruments of war."

John F. Seiberling (D Ohio): "We should ask ourselves, in the context of the My Lai situation and the Calley trial, whether we, too, as a nation are in the process of becoming Prussianized." He said he could think of no better time to end the draft than June 30.

Bray: "Sure, a lot of people will agree that it is a grand idea to stop the draft to make our country helpless. Anyone who believes that America can survive without defense is naive."

Joe D. Waggonner Jr. (D La.): "How many of you people are willing, in an election year (1972), to stand up here and advance these arguments all over again?...Do you really believe the merit of the issue would prevail, or would we simply be making campaign speeches? What would you do to the national security of the country?"

18-Month Extension. After earlier attempts to repeal the draft law, to let the President's authority to induct expire June 30, 1971, and to extend the draft for only one year, to June 30, 1972, were unsuccessful, Charles J. Carney (D Ohio) offered an amendment to extend the draft 18 months to Dec. 31, 1972. The committee bill requested a two-year extension. Debate on the Carney amendment lasted three minutes and was rejected by a 170-200 recorded teller vote.

Student Deferments. An amendment to keep student deferments was offered by Bingham. His proposal sought to allow those persons already enrolled in college to maintain their exempt status. "The purpose of my amendment is to delete this ex post facto effect of the committee bill," Bingham said.

"All this will do is to reinstate the college deferments which we have taken out," Pike said. "We are seeking to eliminate the privilege of the rich and the people who can manage to go to college. We are trying to treat all Americans equally."

The amendment was rejected by voice vote.

Non-profit Institutions. Stewart B. McKinney (R Conn.) offered an amendment to broaden the definition of what was to be considered a suitable place for a conscientious objector to serve his term of civilian service. A CO would be allowed to work in a private nonprofit institution if it were approved by the Selective Service director. The committee bill stated that a conscientious objector could work only in public nonprofit institutions.

The amendment was adopted by voice vote.

Statute of Limitations. The committee bill made a person who failed to register for the draft at 18 liable for prosecution until he reached 31. Abner J. Mikva (D Ill.) offered an amendment to strike out this clause in the bill. He said the statute of limitations on the crime of failing to register for the draft should be five years after the person reached 18, not five years after he was 26.

"I do not think people who fail to register under the draft law ought to be treated more harshly than those people who fail to file their income tax returns, those who commit burglaries, or those who commit a host

Conscientious Objectors

More than 100,000 applications were filed with local draft boards for conscientious objector (CO) status in 1970, Assistant Defense Secretary Roger T. Kelley told the Senate Armed Services Committee. Of that number, only 19,000 were granted conscientious objector status—equal to a rejection rate of 81 percent. For all of World War I, 13 percent of the CO applicants were rejected; in World War II, 28 percent of the applicants were denied exemptions. There were more applications for CO status in fiscal 1970 alone than during either of the world wars.

Decisions by the Supreme Court in 1965 and 1970 eased some of the qualifications necessary to obtain the CO exemptions, but some members of Congress felt the Court had not gone far enough.

The bill (HR 6531) extending the Selective Service System, reported from the House Armed Services Committee in 1971, extended the length of a CO's alternate term of service to three years from two. Rep. Michael Harrington (D Mass.), who cast one of the four dissenting votes when HR 6531 was reported by the committee, called the alternative service extension "harsh and punitive." Before Congress cleared the draft bill, however, the three-years of service was reduced to two years at the Senate's insistence.

The committee bill defined a CO as one who, "by reason of religious training and belief, is conscientiously opposed to participation in war in any form." The bill specifically excluded from the definition of religious training and beliefs "essentially political, sociological or philosophical views or a merely personal moral code."

In the 1970 Supreme Court majority opinion in *Welsh v. United States,* Justice Black wrote: "What is necessary for a registrant's conscientious objection to all war is that this opposition to war stem from... (his) moral, ethical or religious beliefs about what is right and wrong and that these beliefs be held with the strength of traditional religious convictions."

"We certainly do not think," Black continued, that the draft law's "exclusion of those persons with 'essentially political, sociological or philosophical views or a merely personal moral code' should be read to exclude those who hold strong beliefs about our domestic and foreign affairs or even those whose conscientious objection to participation in all wars is founded to a substantial extent upon consideration of public policy."

of other federal crimes, all of which are subject to a five-year statute of limitations. Under the committee proposal, the statute of limitations for failing to register for the draft will be 13 years," Mikva said.

The amendment was rejected by a 36-85 standing vote.

Sole Surviving Son. James T. Broyhill (R N.C.) offered an amendment to broaden the sole surviving son deferment. Under existing law, the last son in a family that had had all other male members killed in military service was exempt from the draft. Broyhill's amendment provided that once a single member of a family was killed in military service, totally disabled in service, missing in action or a prisoner of war, no other members of the immediate family could be drafted unwillingly.

Broyhill's amendment was adopted by a 130-41 standing vote.

Manpower Ceiling. The committee bill provided for an over-all 2.6-million manpower ceiling on active duty military personnel. Mikva offered an amendment providing for a 2.35-million man ceiling by June 30, 1972.

"I am still not sure how the force levels found their way into this bill, even though I have read and reread the report several times," Mikva said.

"This force level (2.6-million men) has been recommended by the Commander in Chief," Hebert argued, "who is responsible for the force levels."

The amendment was rejected by voice vote.

No Murder Indictment. John R. Rarick (D La.) proposed that no member of the U.S. military could be indicted for murder as a result of combat action anywhere in the world unless the person murdered was a member of U.S. or allied forces. "I dedicate this amendment to Lt. Calley," Rarick said. "His statement—putting country above self—most certainly must be considered as that of a true soldier and a great American. It should touch everyone who wonders where our country is heading and how all of this will stop." The amendment was rejected by voice vote.

Senate Committee Action

The Senate Armed Services Committee conducted hearings in February on the administration bill (S 427) to extend the draft two years to July 1, 1973, repeal deferments for divinity students and grant the President authority to end undergraduate deferments.

Other bills under consideration by the committee were: S 483, sponsored by Sen. Edward M. Kennedy (D Mass.), two-year extension of draft, removal of student and occupational deferments and additional legal rights for registrants; S 392, sponsored by Sen. Mark O. Hatfield (R Ore.), Voluntary Military Act; S J Res 20, sponsored by Hatfield, repeal of the Military Selective Service Act of 1967.

The committee May 5 unanimously reported HR 6531 (S Rept 92-93).

As reported by the committee, the only major provision in HR 6531 that was identical to the House-passed version was the administration's requested two-year extension, to June 30, 1973, of the President's induction authority.

Although both the House and Senate committee versions eliminated deferments for undergraduate students, the Senate-reported bill denied the President discretion to remove student deferments retroactive to April 23, 1970. The administration had previously announced its intention to abolish student deferments as of April 23, 1970, if such authority was enacted.

The committee restored the conscientious objector requirement in existing law of two years alternate service. The House-passed bill set a three-year obligation.

Increased compensation (pay, quarters allowances, subsistence pay, recruiting expenses for members of the armed services) provided by the Senate committee totaled $1-billion, which was $1.7-billion less than that in the House-passed version. The major committee cuts were in pay hikes and quarters allowances for enlisted men and their dependents. The Senate committee's bill, unlike the House version, included an enlistment bonus program designed to increase voluntary enlistments in combat units.

The reported bill also included a 150,000-man annual ceiling on the draft and a 2.55-million manpower ceiling on total military personnel for each of fiscal 1972 and 1973.

Supplemental Views. In supplemental views, Senators Harold E. Hughes (D Iowa), Richard S. Schweiker (R Pa.) and Stuart Symington (D Mo.) said: "We believe there should be only a one-year extension of the President's authority to induct and that the Senate should adopt the higher pay provisions passed in the House." The three-man statement argued that higher pay increases would make an all-volunteer armed force more easily attainable.

Peter H. Dominick (R Colo.) also included a supplemental statement in which he said he reserved the right to change his vote on the two-year extension when the bill reached the Senate floor.

Senate Floor Action

The Senate by a 72-16 roll-call vote June 24 passed and sent to conference with the House its version of HR 6531 extending the draft for two years and raising military pay $1.75-billion over the amount passed by the House.

The bill as passed by the Senate also contained the controversial amendment introduced by Sen. Mansfield setting a national policy of withdrawing troops from Indochina nine months after the bill's enactment. During consideration of the bill the Senate acted on 60 amendments. Major proposals rejected by the chamber were a bid by Mansfield to reduce by one-half the number of U.S. troops in Europe, attempts to eliminate or shorten the draft authorization and a 1971 version of the 1970 McGovern-Hatfield "end the war" amendment. *(Vietnam debate p. 70, 76)*

The Senate considered the bill from May 6 to June 24 during which time it was the subject of vigorous debate and lobbying. And passage of the bill came only after the Senate had voted to end the debate on a 65-27 cloture vote.

Debate on the bill began one day after it was reported by the Armed Services Committee amid complaints that the leadership was trying to force the proposal through the Senate without allowing proper time for opponents of the draft to brief themselves.

Many Senators indicated they would use the draft bill as a vehicle for proposing amendments to end the Vietnam war and to cut military spending.

Mike Gravel (D Alaska) announced during the first day of debate that he intended to talk the draft to death if proposed amendments to do the same were rejected. Gravel, the first senator on the floor, said that the President's "induction power...will expire June 30." He asked for support to filibuster the bill.

John C. Stennis (D Miss.) chairman of the Armed Services Committee was the first to rise in opposition to Gravel's tactic. "I believe that failure to renew this induction authority, whether by vote or by the inaction resulting from extended debate, would be calamitous. It would be particularly disruptive to make such a fundamental change in our procurement policy for military manpower in such an abrupt fashion."

Gravel protested the speed with which the bill was brought to the floor after it was reported by the committee. "I think it should be noted that the bill was laid before the Senate yesterday afternoon and the bill is being taken up today," he said.

DRAFTEE IN COMBAT

Gaylord Nelson (D Wis.) offered an amendment which prohibited the assignment of a draftee to a combat role in Southeast Asia unless the draftee either volunteered for the duty or re-enlisted. The Nelson amendment would have become effective Dec. 31, 1971.

"The central issue of the draft is the issue of Vietnam," Nelson said. "The draft feeds the war. The war becomes the argument for continuing the draft."

"No one relishes the idea or likes to draft these men," Stennis said. "No one wants to re-enact this law. All of us want the war to end. However,..we are in the war and we cannot abruptly cut and run."

The Nelson amendment was rejected May 25 by a 21-52 roll-call vote. *(Other Vietnam-related amendments, p. 70, 76)*

Tunney Modification. John V. Tunney (D Calif.) offered an amendment to the Nelson proposal which extended the limits imposed on the President's discretion to commit draftees to combat. The Tunney modification prohibited the assignment of a draftee "to duty in any combat area outside the United States" unless the draftee volunteered, re-enlisted or Congress enacted a law to provide for such placement.

Tunney said it had been clearly stated by Stennis "that it would be impossible over a long period of time to fight a war in Vietnam without draftees. I agree with that statement. That is one of the reasons I think this amendment is important. If there are no draftees in Vietnam, we will be required to scale down that war and get out."

"We would not only lose the influence of potential intervention," Stennis countered, "but also we would have a direct mandate of law known to all the world that a great number of our men were not eligible to go into a combat area....We would not have any chance to be of any influence in a crisis."

The Tunney modification was rejected May 25 by a 7-61 roll-call vote.

No Combat Bonus. In the committee version of HR 6531, a bonus, ranging up to $6,000, was provided to enhance enlistments in Army combat units. Edward M. Kennedy (D Mass.) offered an amendment to remove the combat bonus section from the bill.

"I cannot but feel," Kennedy said, "that a proposal to pay young men a $3,000 or $6,000 bonus to enlist in combat units is neither wise, nor just, nor fair. It reflects the underlying philosophy of any mercenary army."

Stennis opposed the Kennedy amendment: "This is a period during which great effort is going to be made in this experiment (all-volunteer military)....If some young fellow thinks he would like to join (a combat unit) and if

he is willing to go in and take the training...I am not objecting to paying him a bonus to do it. I say that even if he is a so-called poor boy."

The Kennedy amendment was rejected May 25 by a 25-49 roll-call vote.

Humphrey Amendment. Hubert H. Humphrey (D Minn.) offered an amendment June 24 which sought to prohibit the use of draftees in any foreign combat area. The proposal, which would have gone into effect June 30, 1972, stipulated that the President could override the provision temporarily in case of an emergency, but required him to provide Congress with acceptable justification or withdraw the troops within 30 days.

Stennis characterized the proposal as "the most crippling amendment that could be conceived for the units of our military."

The Humphrey proposal was rejected June 24 by a 23-66 roll-call vote.

PAY RAISE (I)

An amendment offered by Harold E. Hughes (D Iowa), which would have more than doubled the pay increases provided in the committee version of the bill, was rejected May 26 by a 31-42 roll-call vote.

Hughes argued that his amendment was nothing more than a telescoped version of what the administration was asking for. "Why should the pay increases come now?" Hughes asked. "I know that there are many other demands on the federal budget. But I also know that continuing one economic injustice is no more acceptable than continuing another. I reject the argument for delay. I do not believe that we should deny to men under fire what we believe is just in a future time of peace."

Defeat of the Hughes amendment, which was the first part of a one-year draft extension package, was considered a major blow to the campaign aimed at reducing the draft extension to a single year.

Stennis led opposition to the amendment. "Somewhere, sometime, the Senate is going to have to turn down a pay increase. If we do not, there is going to be a revolt of the taxpayers at the polls," he said.

Stennis produced a letter dated May 26 from the Joint Chiefs of Staff in which they said the Hughes amendment would "severely disrupt defense programs and substantially impair our capabilities to meet national security requirements."

"Is there a possibility," asked Mike Gravel (D Alaska), "that the administration may have secured from the military an agreement not to push for the total pay increase because this might support the logic of not extending the draft? Is there a possibility that there might be a conspiracy afoot here to maintain the draft?"

"I think the answer is yes," said Richard S. Schweiker (R Pa.), cosponsor of the Hughes amendment. "There is no question in my mind that if we adopted the two-step pay proposal which they suggested, in one step, we obviously could end the draft a year sooner."

18-Month Extension. Peter H. Dominick (R Colo.) offered a compromise amendment May 26 which requested an 18-month draft extension, placing it between the two-year extension requested by the committee and the one-year proposal to be voted on June 4. The Dominick amendment was rejected by an 8-67 roll-call vote.

The argument advanced by Dominick in support of his compromise was that when Congress next considered a draft extension, the 1972 elections would be over.

Stennis opposed the 18-month extension for the same reasons he opposed the one-year extension—not enough time would be allowed for the all-volunteer army to prove itself. Stennis was joined in opposition to the Dominick amendment by Schweiker and Hughes, who rejected anything but the one-year proposal.

PAY RAISE (II)

The Senate June 8 reversed itself and adopted a $2.7-billion military pay-increase amendment to the draft extension bill (HR 6531) after rejecting a similar measure two weeks earlier.

The pay-increase amendment, which was offered by Gordon Allott (R Colo.), was adopted by a 51-27 roll-call vote. *(Comparison of proposals, box p. 51)*

The passage of the proposal stood in sharp contrast to the Senate rejection by a 31-42 roll-call vote May 26 of a $2.7-billion amendment for pay increases and other types of compensation offered by Harold E. Hughes (D Iowa).

The Hughes pay-increase proposal was considered as part of a one-year draft extension package. The Allott amendment was not. Therefore, the Allott amendment was supported not only by those who had voted in favor of the Hughes proposal, but also by a contingent of Senators who had favored higher pay increases, but would not support a one-year extension of the draft.

While the Hughes amendment had the support of just nine Republicans, the Allott pay-increase proposal had 22 Republicans voting "yea." Twenty-two Democrats had supported the Hughes amendment and 28 favored the Allott proposal (ND 26-3; SD 2-12).

The only difference between the Allott amendment and the pay provision of the bill reported by the Senate Armed Services Committee May 5 was in the portion dealing with basic pay increases (amendment requested $2,667,000,000; committee version, $908,000,000). Related areas of compensation—quarters allowances, dependents' allowances, enlistment bonus—were identical.

In his drive to defeat the amendment, Stennis cited opposition to the proposal by President Nixon, Defense Secretary Melvin R. Laird and the Joint Chiefs of Staff.

Allott, who had opposed the Hughes amendment, said, "I wanted to ensure that we enter the next two years of conscription under circumstances which will enable us to improve our knowledge of the factors which will determine whether or not an all-volunteer army is feasible." He said that his amendment would best provide for such a determination.

"There are 95,000 soldiers doing nothing but KP argued Stennis, "no tax bills coming in that would raise it (the revenue) and no present taxes on the books that would raise it."

The amendment was adopted June 8 by a 51-27 roll-call vote.

ENDING THE DRAFT

Immediate Termination. Hatfield sponsored an amendment which would have eliminated the draft on June 30, 1971, thereby forcing the military to convert to an all-volunteer system. The amendment was rejected by a 23-67 roll-call vote June 4.

Hatfield said his amendment would tell the military that it must provide for its manpower needs without the draft and that "with other reorganizations they could meet the administration's end strength recommendation of 2.5 million (men) for fiscal year 1972."

"There are 95,000 soldiers doing nothing but KP duty and mowing lawns," Hatfield argued. "There are many more who are bartenders in officers clubs and who are driving as chauffeurs for admirals and generals. Those duties could be turned over from the military to civilians and those men who are trained for military duty could perform military functions."

Stennis led the opposition to the Hatfield amendment. "The main issue here is what kind of men we are going to have to maintain our security here at home," he said.

One-Year Extension. The Senate rejected the second part of a one-year draft extension package June 4. The first part of the proposal, the Hughes amendment, was defeated May 26.

Although the 43-49 roll-call vote on the amendment was the largest supporting vote for a one-year extension proposal in the Senate since World War II, the vote was not as close as supporters of the amendment had predicted.

The House turned back an identical proposal by a two-vote margin March 31 (198-200 recorded teller vote).

Richard S. Schweiker (R Pa.), principal sponsor of the amendment and a member of the Armed Services Committee, said during the debate that he was "somewhat perplexed by official and unofficial opposition to the amendment." He said, "The administration has taken the lead...to work toward and express a general commitment toward the eventual all-volunteer army. My amendment for the one-year extension of the draft is designed to be totally in keeping with that general commitment."

Minutes after his amendment was rejected by a six-vote margin, Schweiker appeared in the Senate press gallery and told reporters that only four hours earlier his amendment had been within two votes of having majority support. He credited last-minute administration arm-twisting with successfully widening the margin during the hours prior to the vote.

Schweiker cited two arguments against the one-year extension proposal that he said were crucial in defeating the amendment: a one-year extension would bring the issue up for a vote again in the middle of an election year (June, 1972); many senators desired to give the administration a chance to convert to an all-volunteer army without being forced into it by a mandate from Congress.

"But I'm satisfied," Schweiker said. "This means we're going to end the draft in two years because when this comes up again the administration won't have these arguments to use."

DRAFT CEILING

Draft Ceiling. Included in the committee version of the draft extension bill was a section which set a 150,000-

man ceiling on the number of men the President could order to be drafted during each of fiscal years 1972 and 1973. The President could exceed the ceiling by issuing an executive order citing urgent national security reasons for his decision.

Kennedy offered an amendment which sought to remove from the committee version what he described as an "escape clause" for the President. The Kennedy amendment made the troop ceiling a statutory provision. Under the Kennedy amendment, the President would have to get the consent of Congress if he decided that additional draftees were needed (above the ceilings).

No one spoke against the amendment although one modification which sought a lower ceiling than 150,000 men annually was offered. *(Stennis Modification)*

The amendment was adopted June 9 by 78-4 roll-call vote.

Stennis Modification. Stennis said he had introduced the provision dealing with the 150,000-man draft ceiling and the "escape clause" at the time the committee drafted the bill.

"I am still very strong for the ceiling," Stennis said, "but the facts have changed some as to the number since this bill was written up and reported by the committee." Stennis also said that he did "not think the escape clause as to the inductees is of major importance any more."

Stennis supported the stiffer requirements imposed on the President in the Kennedy proposal and offered a modification to the Kennedy amendment which sought to set the induction ceilings below 150,000—at 130,000 men for fiscal 1972 and 140,000 men for fiscal 1973. The Stennis modification was adopted June 9 by a 67-11 roll-call vote.

Unsatisfied with the 130,000 and 140,000-man draft ceilings which were adopted in the Stennis modification of the Kennedy amendment, Robert Taft Jr. (R Ohio) offered an amendment which sought to set the limitation at 100,000 for fiscal 1972 and 60,000 for fiscal 1973.

Taft argued that the Stennis modification, which had already been adopted by the Senate, "would not in any way require the Department of Defense or the administration to move in the direction of an all-volunteer army. They could continue the current operation under the draft without any inconvenience."

The Taft amendment was rejected June 9 by a 25-54 roll-call vote.

Explain Troop Request. Birch Bayh (D Ind.) offered an amendment which requested a detailed explanation and justification for the troop levels sought annually by the defense secretary and the President. The amendment requested information concerning each unit's mission and capability, the strategy the unit supported and the area of deployment. The defense secretary was also requested to detail the effects of a hypothetical 10-percent cut in the authorized troop strength.

Stennis supported the Bayh amendment. It was adopted June 24 by voice vote.

REGISTRANTS' RIGHTS

Procedural Rights. Kennedy offered an amendment June 24 which added five procedural requirements to the process of registering and appealing the draft. Kennedy's amendment allowed each registrant to appear in person before his local or appeal board, to present witnesses in his behalf and be accompanied by counsel. It required that a quorum of the local or appeal board members be present when the registrant appeared in person and that in the event of a board decision against the registrant, the board, upon request, had to provide a written statement explaining its decision.

Sam J. Ervin Jr. (D N.C.) opposed the amendment: "I think that the most patriotic people in the United States are those who now serve upon the Selective Service boards.... I cannot conceive of any good purpose that could be served by this amendment. It seems to me that it would have a deterent effect upon the willingness of persons to serve on Selective Service boards."

"This amendment has laudable purposes," said Stennis, "and it looks good on paper. But say what you will, this amendment creates a judicial procedure for a nonjudicial body of laymen to try to follow."

The Kennedy amendment was adopted June 24 by a 46-41 roll-call vote.

Induction Notice Timing. Cranston offered an amendment June 24 which sought to allow a person the right to be considered for conscientious objector status by his local draft board after he had received his induction notice. Existing Selective Service regulations specified that once the induction had been mailed, further claims by the inductee for change of status were to be handled by the armed forces, not the Selective Service System.

Stennis objected to the amendment, but agreed to take it to the House-Senate conference committee as part of the Senate bill. The amendment was adopted June 24 by voice vote.

Written Record. Gravel offered an amendment which would have required draft boards to keep a written record of the proceedings which a registrant appeared before the board in person.

Ervin opposed the amendment: "The underlying theory (of the amendment) is that when the government... undertakes to secure military personnel through the draft, it is imposing punishment on those who are called upon to serve their nation...."

Ervin added that the amendment "would require a court reporter to be employed in every draft area of the United States."

Gravel argued that because no clear records had been kept by draft boards, many registrants had been misrepresented when they took their cases to court.

John G. Tower (R Texas) moved to table the Gravel amendment and the Senate adopted the motion June 24 by a 67-20 roll-call vote, thus killing the amendment.

Statute of Limitations. An amendment sponsored by Gravel, which sought to remove from the committee version of the bill an extended statute of limitations clause for persons failing to register for the draft, was rejected June 8 by a 15-63 roll-call vote.

Gravel argued that the five-year statute of limitations should begin after a person first failed to register (at age 18) instead of when he reached age 26. Under the provision in the committee's bill, a person was liable for prosecution for failing to register with his draft board until he was 31 years old. A similar amendment was rejected by the House.

EXEMPTIONS, DEFERMENTS

Sole Surviving Son. The first amendment to the draft extension bill that was adopted by the Senate over the opposition of Stennis was a proposal offered by Robert W. Packwood (R Ore.) to expand the definition of draft exemptions provided to males of a family that had suffered the loss of an immediate family member while serving in the armed forces. A similar amendment was added to the House-passed version.

Stennis said the amendment would impair the military's ability to acquire manpower by exempting too large a portion of the eligible males in the draft pool. "Most important," Stennis said, "the amendment does not seem to be needed in view of the fact that the Department of Defense already has a policy of assigning members of families who have lost a member in the armed service—since Jan. 1, 1961, in Vietnam—to non-combat assignments."

The amendment was adopted by a 59-9 roll-call vote June 7.

Conscientious Objector. Existing law provided that one must conscientiously object to all wars in any form in order to receive a CO deferment from the draft.

Philip A. Hart (D Mich.) offered an amendment to expand the definition for COs by granting CO deferments to a person conscientiously opposed to a particular war—selective conscientious objection.

"In this amendment," Hart said, "we are attempting to respect the conscience of the individual who has a deep conviction central to his personal belief that a particular war is, for him, morally wrong to engage in.

"I am not suggesting that the burden of proof on that young man will be light or easily carried," Hart continued, "but I am pleading that, if he can carry it, if he can prove that, to him, this is an unjust war, that we respect his conscience and not confront him with the incredible dilemma of doing what his conscience tells him to be wrong."

Stennis replied: "I believe we had better stay by what we have and leave well enough alone." He said the amendment would lead the nation to the point where it could no longer defend itself.

The Hart amendment was rejected June 8 by a 12-50 roll-call vote.

Callups After Expiration. Cranston offered another unsuccessful amendment June 24 which would have provided that after the draft law expired June 30, 1973, the President would not be able draft persons whose deferments were still in effect. Existing law gave the President authority to cancel deferments after the draft law had expired enabling draft to continue.

"If, as the pending measure provides," Cranston said, "the draft law is extended until June 30, 1973, but is not renewed at that time, the President will still have the authority to draft millions of Americans for many, many years. The President, under present law, would have broad powers to terminate deferments held then by millions of young Americans."

Strom Thurmond (R S.C.) opposed the amendment: "If the pending Selective Service Act (HR 6531) should expire, the only way manpower needs could be met would be through the callup of men previously deferred."

The amendment was rejected June 24 by a 29-61 roll-call vote.

Draft Age 18-45. Gravel offered an amendment June 22 which sought to raise the maximum draft age from 26 to 45. The amendment stipulated that age groups be drafted equally.

"I do not think we need the draft," Gravel said, "but if we are going to have it, I think we can have an equitable draft.... Essentially, wars are initiated by older men and are fought by younger men."

Stennis argued against the proposal: "The disruptive effect on the nation's economy would be devastating.... Any military man will tell you that, for training purposes, it is best to get a man into the service in his earlier years, that after that, he becomes less acceptable to the right kind of military training that will enable him to accept discipline."

Gravel's amendment was rejected June 22 by a 5-73 roll-call vote.

Doctor Deferment. Robert P. Griffin (R Mich.), minority whip, offered an amendment, which was approved, giving doctors who promised to practice in "doctor shortage areas" for four years an exemption from the draft.

"This amendment seeks to ease a domestic crisis of grave proportions," Griffin said, "a growing shortage of doctors in our rural areas and in our inner cities. This shortage has been aggravated by the draft, which has been siphoning off more than half our newly qualified doctors each year."

The Griffin amendment was adopted June 23 over Stennis' opposition by a 50-38 roll-call vote.

DRAFT BOARDS

Tenure On Draft Board. Although the Senate Armed Services Committee had reduced the maximum length of time a person could serve on a draft board from 25 years to 20, Gravel offered an amendment to restrict individual tenure on a local board to no more than four years.

"I think most Americans would agree," Gravel said, "that it is inherently unfair and dangerous to vest board members with what amounts to a lifetime appointment to perform a quasi-judicial function." Gravel cited from an un-named national survey which indicated the average age for board members was 60 years and that one-fifth of all those serving on local boards were 70 years old.

William B. Saxbe (R Ohio) told Gravel the amendment would cripple the Selective Service System. Saxbe said that a four-year limit on individual tenure "would hardly permit him (the draft board member) to become acquainted with the operations of Selective Service."

Stennis added, "I don't think that senators want to take a meat ax and knock that system in the head and just obliterate the entire system against the unanimous recommendation of the 16 members of the Armed Services Committee..."

The Gravel amendment was rejected June 7 by a 20-48 roll-call vote.

Boards Reflect Community. Cranston offered a third amendment to HR 6531 June 23 which stated the President "shall appoint the membership of each local draft board" so that the board reflected the racial and religious complexion of the community the board served. Cranston agreed to a slight modification "requesting" the President to take such action.

"There have been too many cases reported," Cranston said, "of browns or blacks or Indians or Puerto Ricans going before boards where they find only white faces representing their own groups."

The Senate June 23 adopted the modified Cranston amendment by voice vote.

Selective Service Test. Cranston offered an amendment June 23 which would have restricted membership or clerkship on local draft boards to persons who could score a 65 or better on a Selective Service examination prepared and administered by the Civil Service Commission. The proposal also sought to limit appointees to the position of state director of the Selective Service to those who scored at least 75 on a similar test.

Gordon Allott (R Colo.) opposed the amendment: "I would say we are depending here on people who are good citizens and usually have to be asked to serve. If we put it on the basis of whether a man passes a competitive civil service examination, it seems to me what we do is change the system from the type of man who is willing to do this as a public service...to a system in which the man is looking for a job on the board and that would be most unsatisfactory."

The proposal was rejected June 23 by a 9-79 roll-call vote.

Voting Registration. Under the provisions of an amendment offered by Thomas F. Eagleton (D Mo.), a person could register to vote for federal elections when he registered for the draft at the local board just after his 18th birthday. The governor of each state would have the option of vetoing the amendment's application to his state by writing a letter to the director of the Selective Service System within 30 days after the enactment of the draft extension bill. State legislatures were also provided the option of making the registration for federal elections applicable to state elections if they passed an enacting measure and it was signed by the governor.

The Eagleton amendment was adopted June 8 by a 47-31 roll-call vote.

Conference Action

House Rejects Vietnam Amendment. Following Senate passage June 24 of the draft extension bill, the House June 28 refused, by a roll-call vote of 219-175, to instruct House conferees to the military draft extension bill (HR 6531) to accept a Senate-passed Mansfield amendment declaring it U.S. policy to withdraw troops from Indochina within 9 months. *(Mansfield amendment, p. 70, 76)*

The motion to instruct conferees was proposed by Charles C. Whalen Jr. (R Ohio). Whalen had earlier cosponsored with Lucien N. Nedzi (D Mich.) an amendment to the defense procurement bill (HR 8687) to cut off funds for military operations in Indochina as of Dec. 31, 1971. That amendment was rejected by the House June 17 on a recorded teller vote of 158-255.

The House June 28 killed the Whalen motion by adopting, by a 219-175 roll-call vote, a motion by F. Edward Hebert (D La.), chairman of the House Armed Services Committee, to table the Whalen motion. The House then sent the bill to conference.

The 175 members voting for the Whalen motion constituted the largest anti-Vietnam war vote in the House up to that time; the 43-vote margin was also the closest of any such vote. The number of representatives voting for such a measure had steadily increased through early 1971.

In early April, the House voted 122-260 against an amendment to HR 6531 to bar use of draftees in Indochina; at that time this was the strongest protest vote ever to come from the House on American Indochina war policy.

Of the 255 members who voted against the Nedzi-Whalen amendment, 22 switched positions June 28 and voted for acceptance of the Mansfield amendment. *(House action on Vietnam proposals, p. 76)*

One Month Deadlock. The bill was sent to conference June 28. Two days later the chief House conferee, Hebert, chairman of the Armed Services Committee, announced that only one provision of the bill remained in contention—the troop withdrawal amendment.

After meeting for 45 minutes July 12, the conferees postponed further attempts to reach agreement until July 20 which would give Hebert and his counterpart in the Senate, Stennis, time to confer with Defense Secretary Laird on the consequences of not passing the draft extension bill immediately and the implications to the Paris peace talks if the withdrawal date were forced on the President.

Hebert told reporters after the July 12 session that he was willing to accept a sense of the Congress resolution on ending the war but would not agree to the nine-month withdrawal deadline and the "declared policy" strength of the Mansfield amendment. Mansfield said he still favored his original language for the amendment.

No closer to agreement than in early July, conferees called off a scheduled session July 20, saying that a meeting would be fruitless, but announced they would try again July 26. The draft law had expired June 30. *(Box p. 60)*

CONFERENCE REPORT

When the conferees finally reached agreement on July 30, the compromise conference report contained the following major actions:

Vietnam Withdrawal. The Senate version contained an amendment introduced by Majority Leader Mike Mansfield (D Mont.) declaring it the policy of the United States government that a withdrawal of U.S. troops would be completed within nine months if, along with the phased withdrawal of troops, a phased release of U.S. prisoners was also implemented. The House had no similar provision. Conferees softened the Senate amendment, declaring it the sense of Congress that the United States terminate military operations in Indochina "at the earliest practicable date." The conference report urged the President to begin negotiations for an immediate cease-fire and for establishing a definite withdrawal deadline along with the release of U.S. prisoners.

Induction Ceiling. The Senate version provided draft ceilings of 130,000 and 140,000 men for fiscal years 1972 and 1973 respectively and provided that the ceilings could be exceeded only with the approval of Congress. The House version had no similar provision. The Senate version was adopted.

Troop Strength. The House version authorized a total active duty military manpower level of 2,609,409 men for fiscal 1972; the Senate version authorized a ceiling which was 56,000 men lower than the House provision. Conferees adopted the Senate authorized strength of 2,553,-409 men but made it clear that the ceiling would in no way inhibit the President from calling up the reserves to cope with civil disturbances and other national emergencies.

Conscientious Objector. The House version provided for three years of alternate civilian service for conscientious objectors (CO) and immediate induction if the CO failed to perform his civilian job satisfactorily; it specified that the alternate service program be administered by the Selective Service director (not the local draft board as in existing law). The Senate version required COs to be available for a third year of service only when the reserves were also called up because of a national emergency. Conferees dropped all language requiring a third year of service and providing authority for the induction of a CO who did not perform his civilian job satisfactorily. The alternate service program was removed from the immediate jurisdiction of the local draft, however, and placed under the Selective Service director.

Pay Increases. The over-all compensation package (pay increases, quarter allowances, subsistence allowances) which was adopted by the conference committee totaled less than either the House or Senate versions. The largest item was for basic pay increases for which conferees adopted the House provision which called for $1.8-billion.

Conferees compromised in the amounts passed by the House for quarters allowances and dependents' allowances, but the conference version was still substantially greater than approved by the Senate. In the allowances sections, the compensation tended to be spread through all levels of the military, not just the low-ranking personnel at which the pay increases were aimed. The House had failed to adopt a provision providing for an enlistment bonus, while the Senate had established a $6,000 enlistment bonus ceiling. Conferees settled on a $3,000 bonus maximum.

The following were amounts for each type of compensation increases provided for in the bill:

	House	Senate	Conference
		(in millions)	
Basic pay	$1,825.4	$2,667	$1,825.4
Dependents' allowance	184.1	79	105.9
Quarters allowance	640.1	0	409.8
Subsistence allowance	37.8	0	0
Enlistment bonus	0	40	20
Recruiter expenses	2.9	2.9	2.9
Optometrists special pay	.5	.6	.6
Dependents' allowance for reservists	20	0	20
Annual Total	$2,710.8	$2,789.5	$2,384.6

Student Deferments. Both the House and the Senate versions restored to the President discretionary authority over student deferments. The Senate version, however, stated that all students who had entered college before the summer of 1971 would be able to maintain their deferment until graduation or to age 24. The Senate stipulation was adopted by conferees.

Sole Surviving Son. Both the Senate and the House had expanded definitions of the sole surviving son exemp-

---

Draft Authority Expired

For the first time since 1948, the nation as of July 1, 1971, was without a military draft law. The law expired at midnight June 30. House-Senate conferees to HR 6531 failed to reach agreement on the Mansfield troop withdrawal amendment prior to a Fourth of July recess which began July 1.

White House Press Secretary Ronald L. Ziegler said June 30 that no men would be drafted until Congress completed action on the draft law extension. President Nixon would not exercise his emergency authority to call up men who had received deferments, he said.

The Selective Service System also instructed local boards to stop inductions, pre-induction physicals and classification actions, beginning July 1. The system had been given a call-up quota of 16,000 men for July and August. House Armed Services Chairman F. Edward Hebert (D La.) said that Curtis Tarr, director of the Selective Service, had assured that the nation could go for several months without inductions and without harm to its defense capabilities. Regular inductions began again in November 1971.

---

tion from the draft. Conferees adopted a Senate provision with minor changes which provided that no person could be inducted who had lost a member of his immediate family through service in the armed forces or who subsequently died as a result of injuries or disease incurred in the line of duty. Also included was Senate language giving an immediate discharge to those already in the military who became eligible for the new ruling. The section applied to family members lost after Dec. 31, 1959, and who were of "the whole blood" of the person exempted.

Divinity Students. Conferees adopted the Senate version declaring that divinity students would be provided a statutory deferment from the draft, not an exemption, and that divinity students would be eligible for the draft until age 35. If they should either drop out of divinity school or fail to become an ordained minister they would be subject to induction. The House bill had no similar provision.

Voter Registration. Contained in the Senate version was an amendment which sought to allow 18-year-olds who were registering for the draft to also register to vote in federal elections at the same time. The House had no similar provision and because the Selective Service director told the conferees that the amendment would cause administrative difficulties, the amendment was deleted.

Drug Control. The Senate passed an extensive drug and alcoholic treatment and control amendment while the House bill contained no such provision. New language was agreed to by conferees which was regarded as an interim measure. The conference provision stated that all practical methods for treating, identifying and rehabilitating drug addicts and alcoholics should be taken immediately for both men already in the service and those taking pre-induction physicals. The Defense

Secretary was ordered to report to Congress 60 days after the enactment of the bill on the department's programs and plans for drug and alcohol problems.

Procedural Rights. Although the House-passed bill contained no provision which expanded the procedural rights of draft registrants, the Senate version made five basic changes in existing law: 1) granted the right to appear in person before any local or appeal board; 2) granted the right to present witnesses before a local board; 3) required attendance of a quorum of any local or appeal board during a registrant's personal appearance; 4) required that a written report, upon request, be provided to the registrant by the local or appeal board when the board ruled against the registrant; 5) granted the right to be accompanied and advised by private counsel at a personal appearance before local and appeal board.

All the provisions above except that granting the right to have counsel were adopted by conferees.

Draft Board Regulations. Three provisions affecting the function of the local draft board were decided in conference. First, conferees limited to 20 years, the Senate-passed ceiling, the service of local draft board members. Existing law limited service to 25 years; the House had set a ceiling of 15 years.

Second, the Senate version provided that in making future appointments to local boards, the President should see to the "maximum extent possible" that the boards reflected proportionately the racial and religious breakdowns of the community they served. The House adopted a stricter provision specifying that all boards should reflect the community they served—the changes were to be made on all boards, not just in cases where new appointments were made to fill vacancies. The milder Senate language was adopted by conferees.

Third, the House-passed bill prohibited joint headquarters and consolidation of local draft boards within states. The Senate had provided that both practices were acceptable but only with the consent of the governor. The Senate version was adopted.

High School Students. The Senate version provided that a high school senior who reached the age of 20 during his senior year would be permitted to graduate before induction. The House had no similar provision. The Senate version was adopted.

Enlistment After Induction. The Senate bill provided that no person could enlist after an induction order had been issued for him. The House had no similar provision. The Senate language was adopted.

Studies. In the Senate-passed bill, there were four requests for studies relating to the military. The House version did not provide for any studies. House conferees accepted two of the study requests. Those accepted were a study of the Defense Department's and the Health, Education and Welfare Department's use of civilian medical facilities and a study of the effectiveness of the program for increasing voluntary enlistments. Those not accepted by House conferees were a study of military housing needs and a study of and detailed justification for requested manpower authorizations by the Defense Department which was to include an explanation of the impact of a 10-percent reduction in authorized strength.

Standby Draft. House conferees accepted a provision contained in the Senate version which provided that the Selective Service System would remain as an active standby organization if manpower needs were being met by volunteers instead of draftees.

Doctor Deferment. The Senate version provided that doctors who were practicing in doctor-shortage areas would not be liable for induction. The House-passed bill contained no similar provision. Existing law, however, provided for occupational deferments for doctors when their services were required in the national interest. Because the existing statute could be applied to cover the Senate's intent, the Senate amendment was deleted.

Student Induction. The Senate version provided that a college student could finish the semester or term or, in the case of a senior, the academic year, after receiving his induction notice. The House version was similar, but the Senate language was adopted.

FINAL ACTION

HOUSE. The House Aug. 4, two days before a month-long congressional recess, by a 298-108 roll-call vote, adopted a House-Senate compromise on the military draft extension bill (HR 6531), clearing it for final Senate consideration.

With adoption of the conference report, the House went on record for the first time in support of the withdrawal of all U.S. troops from Indochina at the earliest practical date.

After the conference agreement was reached, attention focused on Mansfield to see if he would support a Senate filibuster against the bill because of the conferees' modification of his amendment.

SENATE. The Senate Sept. 21, by a 55-30 roll-call vote, adopted the conference report on HR 6531, clearing it for the President's signature.

Adoption of the conference report occurred minutes after the Senate, by a roll-call vote of 61-30, the exact two-thirds majority required to invoke cloture and limit debate, blocked a filibuster attempt on the measure.

The Senate had discussed the possibility of adopting the conference report prior to its adjournment for summer recess Aug. 6. But during the rush of legislative business the week before the recess, the Senate, despite heavy pressure, did not act on the report.

With only Senate approval needed before the bill could be sent to the President for his signature, the Senate Aug. 5 was unable to take a vote on the conference report (H Rept 92-433) because several of its members objected to a time limit on the debate. The Senate agreed to again consider the report Sept. 13, but without a time limit on debate.

In contention were two points of the conference agreement: the pay increase provisions which conferees altered substantially from the Senate-passed version, and the Vietnam troop withdrawal proposal offered by Senate Majority Leader Mansfield in which the nine-month withdrawal deadline provision was deleted by conferees.

During the Aug. 5 deliberation, Stennis, leader of the Senate conferees, read a letter from President Nixon intended to prod the Senate into quick action on the bill.

The letter said the conference version of the draft bill "represents responsible compromise between differing viewpoints and remains consistent with the objec-

White House Lobbying

The White House and the Pentagon coordinated efforts Sept. 14-17 in applying heavy pressure on senators to defeat a proposal that would have further delayed passage of the draft extension.

The lobbying tactics included the rushed replacement of the late Sen. Winston L. Prouty (R Vt. 1959-1971), who died Sept. 10, by a man who said he supported the administration's position. The following is a chronology of the events:

Sept. 14—Secretary of Defense Melvin R. Laird announced he was canceling all his appointments to head the Pentagon lobby effort; Laird met with the Secretaries of the Navy, Army and Air Force to enlist their help; later in the day Senators John C. Stennis (D Miss.), chairman of the Armed Services Committee, and Margaret Chase Smith (R Maine), ranking minority member on the committee, met with the Joint Chiefs of Staff and the Secretaries of the Army, Navy and Air Force to discuss the prospects of the draft bill.

Sept. 15—Laird appeared on a nationally televised morning interview program and urged defeat of the proposed motion to table the draft bill; every senator received a hand-delivered letter co-signed by the Secretaries of the Army, Navy and Air Force urging defeat of the motion to table.

Sept. 16—Every senator received a personal letter from the White House, which was drafted by the White House Congressional Relations and National Security offices, outlining the administration's stance on the tabling motion; President Nixon announced he was ready to lend his personal support to the White House lobby effort; the President phoned Gordon Allott (R Colo.), who was opposed to the administration's position on the military pay provisions, and offered to support Allott's pay raise proposals in a later bill if the senator would support the President and vote against the motion to table; Allott announced he had reversed his position; George D. Aiken (R Vt.), the dean of Senate Republicans, announced that because of the Administration's "crash program" in lobbying against a second conference on the bill he would reverse his vote and oppose the White House; the White House confirmed that speechwriter William Safire had called selected newsmen and told them Senate Majority Leader Mansfield had threatened to cut off party campaign funds to any senator who did not support the motion to table the draft bill.

Sept. 17—After being appointed senator the night before by the governor of Vermont, Robert T. Stafford (R Vt.) was flown to Washington in a White House-dispatched jet in time to vote with administration supporters to defeat the tabling motion; Mansfield denied the rumor from the White House; the motion to table the draft bill was rejected by a 36-47 roll-call vote, with Allott absent on the roll call.

before the Congress takes its month-long summer vacation."

The President had been opposed to the Mansfield amendment when it was adopted by the Senate, but he was willing to accept the softened version of the withdrawal proposal drafted by conferees.

Mansfield, who was among the senators unwilling to put the conference version to a vote immediately, spoke bitterly about the war in Vietnam and the refusal of Congress to demand an end to the war.

"This is the longest war, I believe, in the history of this Republic," Mansfield said. "It is the second most costly war in the history of this Republic. This war has cost us around $120-billion to $130-billion conservatively speaking. Yet a Senate amendment (the Mansfield proposal) which the Senate adopted by a vote of 61 to 37... was vitiated in a conference between the two houses...."

The Senate Sept. 17, by a 36-47 roll-call vote, had rejected an attempt to send the military draft extension bill back to a House-Senate conference for a second round of negotiations with House conferees.

Both the White House and the Pentagon had been heavily lobbying senators the day before the vote, but it appeared likely opponents of the House-Senate compromise would succeed until Gordon Allott (R Colo.), who opposed the pay raise provisions of the compromise version and had led the effort on the Republican side to table, announced to the Senate late on the afternoon of Sept. 16 that he would support the compromise.

Instead of opposing the bill, which he said he fully supported except for the pay issue, Allott declared his intention to offer an amendment to the military procurement authorization bill (HR 8687) increasing the pay levels of enlisted men above that agreed to by the conferees.

Administration Lobbying. The Nixon administration stepped up its campaign of pressure Sept. 15. Every senator received a letter signed by the three military service chiefs warning that further delay "might jeopardize beyond redemption the prospects of achieving an all-volunteer force by July 1, 1973 (the Nixon administration's target date)." The letter was signed by Navy Secretary John H. Chafee, Air Force Secretary Robert C. Seamans and Army Secretary Robert F. Froehlke.

Then in rapid succession Sept. 21, the Senate voted to limit debate and adopted the conference report.

Up to the last minute of debate on the conference report, Gravel was charging that no case had been made by the administration for extending the draft. Gravel, who told the Senate on its first day of debate May 6 that he would filibuster if necessary, could not muster the necessary number of members to vote against cloture. Although Gravel's filibuster attempt was killed before he could get it started, those who were pushing for passage of the bill managed to cut off debate by the margin of a single vote.

On final passage of the bill, which came just minutes after the cloture vote although each senator was technically allowed one hour apiece for debate after adoption of cloture, Democrats split evenly (23-23). As on initial Senate passage in June, southern Democrats overwhelmingly supported passage (15-1) and northern Democrats opposed it 8-22. Republicans supported the President's position by a 32-7 margin.

tives sought by the administration in Southeast Asia." The President wrote: "I am hopeful that the Senate can quickly adopt the report so that I may sign it

EUROPEAN TROOP REDUCTIONS: TWO ATTEMPTS BY CONGRESS

Twice during 1971 the Senate considered proposals which sought to force reductions in the number of U.S. troops stationed in Europe. On both occasions, after heavy White House lobbying, the measures were defeated.

Although the House did not confront the issue of U.S. troops stationed in Europe in direct floor votes, the House Armed Services and Appropriations Committees both used strong language to urge that other North Atlantic Treaty Organization (NATO) countries, besides the United States, assume a greater financial burden in behalf of their own defense efforts.

The first debate in the Senate, which lasted nine days, came to a head May 19 with a series of roll-call votes ending just before midnight. The proposal, which was an amendment to the military draft extension bill (HR 6531—PL 92-129), was rejected in a final 36-61 roll-call vote. *(Draft debate, p. 46)*

The second attempt to force a reduction of U.S. troops in Europe came as a committee amendment to the defense appropriations bill (HR 11731—92-204). The Senate Appropriations Committee's provision requiring a reduction of U.S. troops garrisoned in Europe was rejected on the floor Nov. 23 by a 39-54 roll-call vote.

First Reduction Vote

The initial proposal introduced May 11 by Senate Majority Leader Mike Mansfield (D Mont.), which sought to impose a limit of 150,000 U.S. troops stationed in Europe (a 50-percent reduction) as of Dec. 31, 1971, was defeated by a 36-61 roll-call vote which came just before midnight May 19.

The intent of the Mansfield proposal was to reduce the U.S. balance-of-payments deficit and ease pressure on the dollar by authorizing funds for deployment in Europe of no more than 150,000 U.S. troops.

It would have forced the NATO allies to assume a greater portion of the economic burden for defending Central Europe.

During the nine days the Mansfield amendment was considered by the Senate, it drew severe criticism from the White House, the Senate Republican leadership and John C. Stennis (D Miss.), chairman of the Armed Services Committee and floor manager of the draft bill. The White House mounted an intensive lobbying campaign to defeat the proposal.

President Nixon had announced he would accept no amendments to the draft bill which dealt in any way with U.S. military commitments to Europe. Minority Leader Hugh Scott (R Pa.) said the President would veto the draft bill if the Mansfield amendment passed.

In the Senate, the proposal aroused intense interest which was reflected by the five other amendments introduced after Mansfield's initiative. The other amendments, which sought to soften the Mansfield proposal, were intro-

duced as compromise measures. They were all defeated by a coalition of Mansfield supporters, who wanted a record vote on the strongest possible version, and administration supporters, who felt the Mansfield amendment would be more difficult to defeat with the addition of more moderate language.

The Soviet Union watched the progress of the Mansfield amendment with interest. In a May 18 editorial in the defense ministry's official newspaper *Red Star*, the Soviets accused President Nixon of opposing the amendment for fear it would "encourage anti-militarist moods among the United States' European allies."

One of the major reasons cited in the defeat of the proposals to limit U.S. troop strength in Europe was the Soviet offer to negotiate a multilateral reduction in Central Europe of Warsaw Pact and NATO forces. The Mansfield amendment sought to force a unilateral reduction by the United States regardless of the Soviet position.

"Excess, waste or obsolescence in the U.S. troop commitments under NATO," said Mansfield, "are not bargaining chips in negotiations. They are as an albatross around the neck of the nation's basic policies."

Stennis and Scott argued that the current troop levels in Europe were not excessive but were vital minimal forces needed to defend Europe and the United States against possible Soviet aggression and to maintain the balance of power in the Middle East.

Before voting on the Mansfield amendment, the Senate first rejected five alternate proposals May 19. They were:

Mathias Substitute—introduced May 17 by Charles McC. Mathias (R Md.) and cosponsored by Jacob K. Javits (R N.Y.), Hubert H. Humphrey (D Minn.) and Adlai E. Stevenson III (D Ill.)—Requested the President to begin negotiations with NATO allies to achieve mutual troop reductions in Central Europe between NATO and Warsaw Pact forces; requested the President to also negotiate within NATO for a reduction of U.S. troop force levels and financial outlays consistent with the balance-of-payments problem in the United States; required the President to report to Congress on the progress of the negotiations on Sept. 15, 1971, and every ensuing six months. Rejected by a 24-73 roll-call vote.

Nelson Modification—introduced May 19 by Gaylord Nelson (D Wis.)—Struck the portion of Mansfield amendment dealing with funding and mandatory U.S. troop cuts and replaced it with a new schedule as follows:

Would cut U.S. troop strength to 250,000 by July 1, 1972; to 200,000 by July 1, 1973; and to 150,000 by July 1, 1974.

Declared it the sense of the Congress that the President should enter into negotiations with the Soviet Union and the other NATO and Warsaw Pact countries for a multilateral reduction in the armed forces stationed in Central Europe.

Provided that the schedule for U.S. troop withdrawals from Europe *(above)* would become inoperative if on or before Dec. 30, 1971, negotiations for a multilateral withdrawal of troops had begun. Rejected by a 26-63 roll-call vote.

Bayh Modification—introduced May 17 by Birch Bayh (D Ind.) and cosponsored by William B. Saxbe (R Ohio) and Abraham Ribicoff (D Conn.)—Declared it to be the sense of the Congress that the number of U.S. troops stationed in Europe could be reduced without endangering security and that deployment of the current level of U.S. troops in Europe had resulted in an added burden in the balance-of-payments problem; urged the President to negotiate with NATO allies for the assumption of no less than one-half of the balance-of-payments deficits resulting from U.S. troops stationed in Europe; required that if such an agreement were not completed by Dec. 31, 1971, no funds could be used for support of more than 225,000 troops as of June 30, 1972, or more than 150,000 troops as of Dec. 31, 1972. Rejected by a 13-81 roll-call vote.

Fulbright Modification—introduced May 19 by J. W. Fulbright (D Ark.)—Added three words, "unless hereinafter authorized," to the section of the Mansfield amendment setting a troop ceiling of 150,000 men; had the effect of giving the President an alternative to the statutory limitations. If the President could justify before the appropriate congressional committees the need for more than 150,000 troops stationed in Europe, more troops would be authorized. Rejected by a 29-68 roll-call vote.

Church Modification—introduced May 19 by Frank Church (D Idaho)—Altered the ceiling on U.S. troops in Europe to 250,000 from the 150,000 limit requested in the Mansfield amendment. Rejected by a 15-81 roll-call vote.

Issues Raised in Debate

Timing of Withdrawal. A frequently voiced criticism of the Mansfield amendment was that it was brought to the floor at the wrong time in light of world developments. Even before the Soviet offer (May 14) to negotiate a multilateral withdrawal, opponents of the amendment had cited the strategic arms limitation (SALT) talks in Vienna, Middle East negotiations on an Arab-Israeli settlement and the Bonn-East Berlin talks as examples of delicate international situations that would be adversely affected by any sudden withdrawal of U.S. troops. After the Soviet offer, critics of the amendment focused more intensely on the question of timing.

Mansfield (May 11): "Several times I have introduced resolutions making clear our belief in the need for a substantial reduction in our forces in Europe. Several times I have held off action because I have not wished to disrupt an allegedly delicate situation....The cautionary voices urging us to wait and see have raised a variety of reasons for inaction. Again and again we are told there can be no question but that the present level of American troops in Europe in time must be

---

European Troop Levels, Costs

According to the Pentagon, the United States as of Sept. 30, 1970, had approximately 300,000 troops with 250,000 dependents stationed in Europe.

Of the 300,000 troops, 215,000 were stationed in West Germany; 20,000 in the United Kingdom; 10,000 in Italy; 10,000 in Spain; 8,000 in Turkey; 3,000 in Greece, and 1,700 in Morocco.

Actual figures *(above)* on troop deployment provided by the Pentagon totaled 267,700 troops. A Pentagon spokesman in the legislative liaison office was asked why the breakdowns did not total 300,000. "I guess they're doing this on purpose because the exact number of troops is classified information," the spokesman said.

In addition to the troops actually stationed in Europe, the United States maintained a 188,000-man force in the Atlantic Fleet the spokesman said.

The Pentagon estimate as of Jan. 1, 1972, was that 310,000 U.S. troops were stationed in Europe with an estimated 218,000 dependents.

---

reduced substantially. But the cautionary forces keep murmuring that now is not the time."

Stennis: "I am not willing now to take such precipitate action as this and I think it would be a great mistake. Not only would it upset our allies over there by taking such action so abruptly, but I think great emphasis should be placed...on the SALT talks. We would be pulling the rug out from under the President."

Minority Whip Robert P. Griffin (R Mich.) (May 14): "The timing of the Mansfield amendment could not have been more unfortunate or inappropriate. The Senate is in danger of going down in history as the Senate which derailed the most promising disarmament talks of our times."

Monetary Crisis. In introducing his amendment, Mansfield stressed two fiscal matters—the balance-of-payments situation and the floating exchange rate of the German mark which caused a devaluation of the dollar in German markets.

Mansfield (May 12): "Because of the expenditures of this country abroad, in part in Europe, what happens when we come up against a crunch, when our economy is suffering, when we have problems of great importance at home? The dollar is no longer as sound....Others, like the guilder and the mark, are moving up on a floating basis. Well, they can float their money. They can give us a run on the dollar. They can make it difficult for us by increasing prices on American products exported to Europe. They can increase the cost for an American tourist taking a long-planned vacation in Europe. But they cannot do anything about living up to their pledges as far as NATO is concerned. Only two countries, to my knowledge, have lived up to their obligations in full or almost in full and they are Canada and the United States. And, Canada is now in the process of withdrawing half of its air complement and half of its brigade."

Strom Thurmond (R S.C.) (May 12): "Last year the U.S. balance-of-payments deficit in Europe hit $10-billion. I would be the first to agree this is an extremely serious problem and undoubtedly predicated the attack on the dollar last week. However, to propose to the Senate that our NATO commitment is causing these monetary upheavals is nonsense."

Isolationism. One of the recurring motifs used by the Nixon administration and its supports to describe proponents of total withdrawal from Vietnam had been to label them isolationists. During Senate debate on the amendment, Mansfield was accused of trying to lead the country into isolation by reneging on mutual-security agreements.

Thurmond (May 12): "This meat-ax approach in dealing with U.S. military commitments is another example of a rapidly growing rush toward isolationism. This is not to say that I oppose troop reductions in Europe. The international monetary situation concerns me as much as anyone and I favor strong steps to meet this crisis. One such step would be troop reductions in Europe, but such cutbacks should take an orderly and phased approach."

Mansfield (May 12): "The days of isolationism are gone forever...so I hope that the cry of isolationist, which has already been raised, neo-isolationist, and the like, will be put in the trash bin where it belongs because that is not a part of the present debate."

Balance of Power. Implicit in the arguments against the Mansfield amendment was the proposition that removal/of any U.S. troops from Europe would upset the balance of power and, consequently, open the door to alleged Soviet expansion in Western Europe.

Edward J. Gurney (R Fla.) (May 12): "The presence of substantial numbers of American troops in Europe is the stumbling block (for the Soviets). In my judgment, the new Soviet offensive is aimed at excluding the United States from Europe. That is, in my judgment, the real thrust behind the Soviet-West German draft non-aggression treaty. It is a calculated effort to destroy the alliance and to exclude the United States from Europe. We cannot and should not let that happen. It would be madness to help that scheme by a congressionally mandated American troop withdrawal at this time."

Alan Cranston (D Calif.) (May 13): "I reject the contention that American commitments can only be measured in terms of Army divisions stationed outside of the continental United States. It is a sad commentary on European faith in the alliance that after more than a quarter of a century of aid and the assurances of five Presidents they feel they must continue to hold 300,000 American troops hostage as assurance that we will live up to our word."

Committee Review. After the Mansfield amendment was introduced, Stennis said the proposal was not germane to the draft bill and that such a proposition should be considered by the Senate only after extensive committee hearings.

Stennis (May 12): "We are prepared to debate the draft bill and any phase of it...but the amendment offered by the Senator from Montana is another field, the activity of another committee, the Committee on Foreign Relations."

Mansfield: "It is true that the Mansfield amendment was not considered by the Senate Armed Services Committee...but I would point out that three years ago the Senate established a subcommittee composed of the

members of the Foreign Relations Committee and the Armed Services Committee to go into the matter. A number of hearings were held. I happened to be chairman of the combined subcommittee and Sen. Stennis happened to be the vice chairman."

Stennis (May 14): "One of the most important reasons why we should not vote as radical and rapid a cut as that included in the amendment proposed by the distinguished Majority Leader is that there has been no thorough study of this issue in the Senate for many years. I realize some Senators are under the impression that this issue has been thoroughly studied. I submit that this is not true. A good deal of discussion in one form or another has taken place here on the floor, but the Senate committee system involving hearings and reported legislation has not functioned in this matter."

Mansfield Speech

The following remarks were excerpted from Sen. Mansfield's final speech on his amendment to reduce U.S. troops in Europe. The speech was delivered in the evening of May 19 just before the midnight roll-call vote:

"Sometimes it takes a sledge hammer to make an imprint and place an issue on the table. I did raise this issue. I have been raising it for 11 years. I did not make the issue this time. But the issue has been made and regardless of the outcome of the vote tonight, it will not disappear. It will not return to the cobwebs where it has rested so peacefully for the past two decades and one year....

"What I have endeavored to do is to move from the past into the present and to look to the future. What I have tried to do is not to look over my shoulder in order to hang onto policies which were good two decades ago and think that despite the changing world, those policies are just as good and just as effective today.

"I am not a member of the old guard. There is a chronological gap between me and the great majority of the people of this nation who are under 30 years of age, but there will never be a credibility gap if I can help it because I want to join them in facing up to the world of reality today. I do not want to live in the past. I do not want to return to the 'golden old days.' I want to face up to the responsibilities which are ours, individually and collectively, today.

"In cutting by one-half the level of U.S. forces in Europe, the amendment is designed to put U.S. troop levels there into a contemporary perspective. Needless to say, I have been impressed by the intensity of comment which this proposal has prompted. It is a healthy sign of interest in our European policies—policies which have indeed suffered great neglect during these past several years of turbulence in Southeast Asia.

"At the outset, I would like to note my respect for the array of statesmen who have spoken out on this matter. Many of them will be judged exceedingly well by history. It was 20 years ago, in a time of ominous cold war tension, that many of them forged the powerful shield behind which West European recovery was allowed to proceed securely. Their voices spoke then to a world still shaken in the wake of a long and devastating war. Their voices have been revitalized today. But the world they address is quite different. *(Former officials, p. 66)*

(Continued on p. 67)

NATO Troop Cut: Massive White House Lobby Effort

The Nixon Administration, backed by two former Presidents and 24 high-ranking government officials from the last four Administrations, mounted a one-week campaign in May 1971 to defeat Senate proposals aimed at reducing U.S. troop strength in Europe.

Included on the list of those publicly supporting the Administration's effort to defeat the Mansfield amendment were two Democratic former Presidents—Lyndon B. Johnson and Harry S Truman—and two dozen high-ranking officials from past administrations, most of whom were Democrats.

Two former Secretaries of State—Dean Rusk, who served under Presidents Kennedy and Johnson, and Dean Acheson, who served in the Truman administration—were on the list. Acheson, who was one of the first former administration officials to throw the weight of his name behind Mr. Nixon's lobbying effort, was assigned May 13 to the job of collecting signatures of support for the President's position.

The morning of May 12, Dr. Henry A. Kissinger, the President's adviser on national security, met to discuss plans for defeating the amendment with the two ranking Republicans in the Senate—Minority Leader Hugh Scott (Pa.) and Minority Whip Robert P. Griffin (Mich.).

Later the same day in the Senate, Scott conferred with John C. Stennis (D Miss.), chairman of the Armed Services Committee and floor manager of the draft extension bill. With Mansfield's consent, the final vote on the troop cut amendment was delayed for one week (to May 19). Mansfield refused to withdraw his amendment or to replace it with a sense-of-the-Congress resolution which would not have been binding. Such proposals were included by other Senators in their substitutes for the Mansfield amendment.

Throughout the day, statements condemning Mansfield's resolution were issued from the White House.

By May 13, the White House had developed a hard line on the Mansfield amendment. No amendments and no resolutions dealing in any way with U.S. foreign policy and U.S. NATO commitments would be acceptable to the President, said White House Press Secretary Ronald L. Ziegler. Scott told reporters that he was "as sure as a man can be" that the President would veto the draft bill if it required a cutback of U.S. troops stationed in Europe.

At the White House the President convened the first of several strategy sessions. Included in the meeting were Acheson; Cyrus T. Vance, former Deputy Defense Secretary; George Ball, former Under Secretary of State; and Gen. Andrew Goodpaster, Supreme Allied Commander of NATO forces, and Robert Ellsworth (R Kan. 1961-67), U.S. ambassador to NATO, both of whom had arrived that morning from Europe. Ball assisted Acheson while working as a lobbyist on select members of the Senate. Secretary of State William P. Rogers also was meeting with a number of Senators individually.

Through Ziegler, the President announced May 15 that his opposition to Mansfield's amendment was supported by 24 high-ranking officials of past Administrations.

The list included Acheson and Rusk; three former Defense Secretaries, Robert Lovett, Neil McElroy and Thomas Gates; former Under Secretaries of State James Webb, Robert Murphy, Livingston Merchant, C. Douglas Dillon, Ball and Nicholas Katzenbach; former Deputy Defense Secretaries Vance and Roswell Gilpatric; former supreme allied commanders in Europe Matthew Ridgway, Alfred Greunther, Lauris Norstad and Lyman Lemnitzer; former NATO ambassadors Charles Spofford, W. Randolph Burgess, Thomas Finletter and Harlan Cleveland, and former military governors or high commissioners for Germany Lucius Clay, John McCloy and James Conant.

Later on May 15, former Presidents Johnson and Truman issued statements of opposition to Mansfield's proposal. Johnson, who was succeeded as majority leader of the Senate by Mansfield, said the amendment "would endanger what we have achieved in the past and shatter our hopes for the future."

According to Ziegler, only two of the persons who were asked to support the President's position declined to do so. They were Clark M. Clifford, Defense Secretary under Johnson, and James Douglas, Truman's Deputy Defense Secretary.

Former Defense Secretary Robert P. McNamara, who served during the Kennedy and Johnson Administrations, was included on the list with a footnote by his name which read: "Former Secretary McNamara declines to comment because of his position as head of an international institution (World Bank). He does not want this abstention to be interpreted as non-support of the statement (Nixon's position)."

Mansfield, who remained unyielding to requests for a compromise, was asked to comment on the President's array of supporters. "It looks to me like the resurrection of the Old Guard," he said. "It took me back 20 or 25 years when the NATO treaty was written)."

Soviet Initiative

Adding strength to the administration's campaign to kill the Mansfield amendment was a timely offer from the Soviet Union to discuss multilateral withdrawals from Europe. In a May 14 speech in Tiflis, the capital of Soviet Georgia, Leonid I. Brezhnev, Soviet Communist party leader, repeated an offer he had made March 30 to discuss mutual troop withdrawals along with disarmament negotiations.

Although the March 30 offer had stirred little attention in the White House, Brezhnev's May 14 announcement immediately was picked up by the White House, hailed as an initiative for multilateral withdrawals and used as ammunition by the President against the Mansfield amendment. Why should the United States make a unilateral withdrawal when the Soviets have offered us the chance to negotiate a multilateral settlement, asked administration spokesmen following the Brezhnev offer.

(Continued from p. 65)

"Europe's economic and social recovery has been remarkable; many of its members are in a stronger position than we, and all are capable of doing far more than their present effort if they really believe their security is in danger.

"A factor in Soviet reluctance to reduce its forces may actually be its assessment of the NATO threat. Many Soviet experts argue persuasively that Russia's foreign policy remains a mixture of aggressive and genuinely defensive attitudes. To the extent that this is a factor in Soviet reluctance to reduce its Warsaw forces, a unilateral reduction by the United States could be a positive factor in a Soviet willingness to make a suitable response.

"But it will be said by some, what of the deep fear of Western Germany? The argument goes that with a reduced restraining presence of American forces, Germany may seek to expand its own military power. It is this fear that would harden Russia's present position in Europe. This is pure speculation. Not only does it ignore the fact that Bonn has no financial stomach for substantial military enlargement, but it also denies the growing preeminence of West Germany in the Common Market and its desire to retain its strong ties to the West and its eagerness for trade ties with the East.

"As the Senate commences to vote on this issue, I would only ask that each Senator consider the effect of the outcome not in terms of what was right for yesterday but rather in the context of what is needed for today and tomorrow.

"I have asked no Senator, not one Senator, to vote for the pending amendment; nor do I intend to do so now.

"The Senate is made up of mature individuals who represent sovereign states. Each Senator is capable of making up his own mind on the basis of the issue which confronts us.

"I have no regrets and will have none, regardless of the outcome. I will have no alibis. I will admit no mistakes in this case. If the amendment is defeated, so be it. If otherwise, there will be no sense of personal triumph. The issue has been raised and the raising of this issue is a matter of monument for this body, for this government, for our people and for those of us who belong to the NATO organization."

Rebuttal. Leading the opposition to the Mansfield proposal were John C. Stennis (D Miss.), chairman of the Armed Services Committee, and Minority Leader Hugh Scott (R Pa.).

In Scott's final remarks on the amendment, he said: "This is a dangerous amendment. This is a mischievous amendment. This is an amendment which can cause more harm than any amendment or proposal I have seen in my 13 years in the Senate."

The following remarks were excerpted from the final Stennis rebuttal May 19 to Mansfield's proposal:

"This amendment totally upsets the entire structure of the position we have already taken and on which we have assured our allies for this calendar year.

"These nations (NATO allies) have become prosperous. They should have done more. But I have never been willing to withdraw our troops and leave ourselves exposed.

"I do not believe the Senate is willing tonight to withdraw to an appreciable extent and create the possibility of exposure of our own United States."

"The first thing I would advocate, if we were going to pull out, would be that we would, for a time, first build up our forces. But I do not believe we ought to do it that way. That is why I come back to the position that the President is bound to have been looking over this matter. He is no softie. He doubtless wanted to reduce it more. I have not talked to him about it. I am no expert on the subject, but I felt that I had enough of the facts and enough continuity of knowledge about this problem to be able to make a judgment in this matter and that is exactly what I have done."

Second Reduction Attempt

The Senate Appropriations Committee in marking up the fiscal 1972 defense appropriations bill (HR 11731—PL 92-204) added a provision which limited the number of U.S. troops stationed in Europe to 250,000 men.

The provision called for all funds supporting troops in excess of the 250,000-man ceiling to be cut off June 15, 1972.

When the Senate took up the committee's version of the defense appropriations bill, debate on the provision placing a ceiling on U.S. troop strength was limited to 80 minutes on the afternoon of Nov. 23.

John C. Stennis (D Miss.), chairman of the Armed Services Committee and an adamant foe of legislating U.S. troop reductions in Europe, produced a letter from President Nixon, dated Nov. 22, which said: "This week the Senate will once again consider a proposal to make a substantial unilateral reduction in United States armed forces maintained in Europe for the common defense. I believe passage of such a measure would be a great mistake.

"Passage of the proposed troop cut," the letter continued, "would with one stroke diminish Western military capability in Europe and signal to friend and adversary alike a disarray and weakness of purpose in the American government."

Majority Leader Mansfield told the Senate: "As for mutual, balanced force reductions, we negotiate and we talk and we thrash over these problems. We do not decide. We do not act. I wait now for it to be revealed right on this floor today that indeed, once again, we are on the brink of a decision that will accomplish mutual force reductions—that any action to affect a nominal U.S. pullback alone will destroy the last flicker of hope of achieving that end. It is a revelation, I must say, that will come as no surprise."

Mansfield argued that the United States had garrisoned troops in Europe since the end of World War II and it was time for the countries of the North Atlantic Treaty Organization to assume a greater role in defending themselves.

Opponents of the committee provision argued that any withdrawal on the part of the United States would substantially weaken—politically and militarily—the position of America's Western European allies. They also said that negotiations between the United States and the Soviet Union to mutually reduce troop strengths in Europe would be worthless if the United States acted first.

In a vote asking for confirmation of the committee's amendment, the Senate Nov. 23 rejected the provision by a 39-54 roll-call vote.

LAOS: GUERRILLA OPERATIONS AND SECRET U.S. INVOLVEMENT

While members of Congress could see a pattern toward total withdrawal of U.S. ground troops from Vietnam during 1970 and 1971, a reverse situation was revealed in U.S. dealings with Laos.

Throughout 1971 and early 1972 the United States stepped up its participation in the air war over Laos and the Central Intelligence Agency (CIA) continued to train and advise guerrilla forces.

The Senate met in secret session June 7, 1971, to discuss the Laos situation. Two months later a partial record of what was said during the closed-door session was printed in the *Congressional Record* (Aug. 3, 1971). The published transcript was riddled with deletions made by the executive branch.

Although the published version of the discussion was incomplete, the arguments which did emerge provided a picture of the difficulties encountered when members of Congress, who felt they had a right to know, attempted to obtain information classified secret by the executive branch and learned the position of the administration on disclosing such information.

Also revealed in the debate was the executive branch's explanations for congressional charges that secret U.S.-supported military operations had been carried out in defiance of the laws set by Congress.

The first attempt to acquire information that was mentioned in the censored floor debate was a letter written by Sen. J.W. Fulbright (D Ark.), chairman of the Foreign Relations Committee. The Jan. 27, 1971, letter was to Defense Secretary Melvin R. Laird and included a list of questions on Laos.

The April 14 Pentagon reply was signed by Assistant Defense Secretary G. Warren Nutter, who wrote: "I regret we are unable to comply with your request in this instance. It would not be at all appropriate to disclose outside the executive branch highly sensitive information on military combat operations of the kind your questions would elicit if answers were to be provided."

When the Senate met June 7 in secret session, members were briefed on the Laos situation by Sen. Stuart Symington (D Mo.) from a Foreign Relations Committee staff report. The staff report was censored by the executive branch and released Aug. 3.

Thai Guerrillas. Included in the censored staff report was a section dealing with Thai irregular forces fighting in Laos. "The CIA supervises and pays for the training of these irregulars in Thailand," the report stated, "and provides their salary, allowances (including death benefits) and operational costs in Laos.... The Thai irregulars are transported from Thailand to Laos by Air America (private airline sponsored by the CIA) and are returned to Thailand when their tours are up again."

Sen. Clifford P. Case (R N.J.), a member of the Foreign Relations Committee, had sent a letter to the State Department requesting information on any agreements between the United States and Thailand by which Thai troops were being imported into Laos against the provisions of United States law.

Assistant Secretary of State David M. Abshire replied to Case's letter May 19: "We believe that it has been made clear that this is not a question of U.S. support for regular Thai forces in Laos. The irregular forces involved, while raised and trained in Thailand, are all one-year volunteers who go to Laos to serve under the command of the Royal Lao government. These guerrilla forces are therefore considered to be local forces in Laos."

After reading Abshire's letter to the Senate, Symington said: "Common sense forces one to ask, how can these Thai irregulars in Laos be described as local forces? They are Thai, not Lao. They are recruited in Thailand, not Laos."

Sen. Robert P. Griffin (R Mich.), assistant minority leader, argued in behalf of the administration: "There is no question, I suppose, under the language here, that if the Thai government sent forces into Laos under a Thai military command and they fought, that there would be a violation (of the law)."

"But are we going to say that the Laos military command cannot recruit volunteers...should limit the recruiting of troops in its own country?" Griffin said.

Safe and Orderly Withdrawal. The justification advanced on the Senate floor for B-52 bombings in northern Laos and along the Ho Chi Minh trail in southern Laos was that it was part of over-all U.S. strategy to ensure the safe and orderly withdrawal of U.S. troops from South Vietnam. Symington said his staff investigators were told that the bombings were crucial to the withdrawal plans because they interrupted supplies coming down the Ho Chi Minh trial bound for South Vietnam and kept enemy forces pinned down in Laos when, if unharrassed, they would be an added force against the South Vietnamese.

"This," Symington said, "we are told, will buy more time for Vietnamization." Symington said that what his investigators were not told was how long the operations would continue in Laos. He conceded the bombings in southern Laos along the Ho Chi Minh trail might be of some help to the South Vietnamese and to the successful withdrawal of U.S. troops.

"But if anyone tries to justify the bombings and napalming of military and occasionally civilians up in northern Laos as a way to protect Americans we say are leaving Vietnam, in my judgment they are very wrong," Symington said.

CIA Budget. Symington, who was a member of the Armed Services Committee's CIA Oversight Subcommittee, said that he did not know about the details of the CIA-supported irregular army in Laos until the Foreign Relations Committee issued the staff report. "In all my committees there is no real knowledge of what is going on in Laos," he said. "We do not know about the cost of the bombing. We do not know about the people we maintain there. It is a secret war." *(CIA oversight p. 18)*

Sen. Jack Miller (R Iowa) said: "We should not leave the impression that the Senate somehow or other has been helpless in this matter. We are all mature individuals, and we know what we are doing."

Secret Staff Report

The Senate June 7, 1971, held a three-hour-23-minute secret session for a briefing on and discussion of the Foreign Relations Committee report which was at that time classified Top Secret.

A sanitized version of the staff report was released Aug. 3, 1971, and in it the government admitted that the Central Intelligence Agency spent about $70-million in 1970 to support an army of more than 30,000 irregulars in Laos.

The 23-page report, prepared for the Subcommittee on U.S. Security Agreements and Commitments Abroad by two of its staff members on the basis of a two-week trip to Laos, described the CIA-supported forces as the "cutting edge of the Lao military forces."

The irregular Laotian troops, called BG units (for the French term *Bataillons Guerriers)*, are the "most effective military force in Laos" and they are "trained equipped, supported, advised and to a great extent, organized by the CIA," the report stated. But the report said more than 60 percent of Laos is controlled by the Pathet Lao and the North Vietnamese.

Disclosure of the information contained in the report was released by Subcommittee Chairman Symington (D Mo.) after the material had been censored by the Defense Department, State Department and the CIA.

Expenditures. The report stated that the Laotian government budget for 1971 was $36.6-million and that U.S. expenditures in Laos for fiscal 1971 were estimated at $284.2-million, more than six times the total Laotian budget.

Not included in the estimates for U.S. expenditures in Laos were the costs of air operations or the cost of supporting and training Thai irregulars in Laos. The report estimated that expenses for fiscal 1972 would be approximately $374-million despite the decreasing number of U.S. air sorties over Laos.

"The Royal Lao government," the report stated, "continues to be almost totally dependent on the United States, perhaps more dependent on us than any other government in the world, and this dependence appears to be increasing as the war continues and the military situation worsens."

Air Operations. Although the total number of missions flown over Laos by U.S. military pilots declined in the first six months of 1971, the number of B-52 raids has increased. It was not not until April 29, 1971, that the subcommittee received confirmation that the United States was flying B-52 raids over Laos. The report disclosed, however, that missions have been flown since February 1970.

After a trip to Laos and South Vietnam in May, Rep. Paul N. McCloskey Jr. (R Calif.) returned to the United States claiming that civilian villages in Laos had been bombed by U.S. aircraft. The McCloskey report was denied by the Nixon administration.

Thai Mercenaries and the Law

The paragraphs below were excerpted from the 1971 Defense Department Appropriations bill (PL 91-668). The first section of this provision prohibits the United States from hiring mercenaries (from a third country) to fight in either Laos or Cambodia. The second provides the means by which such a practice could be justified.

"Nothing...hereunder shall be construed as authorizing the use of any such funds to support Vietnamese or other free world forces in actions designed to provide military support and assistance to the governments of Cambodia or Laos.

"Provided further, that nothing contained in this section shall be construed to prohibit support of action required to insure the safe and orderly withdrawal or disengagement of U.S. forces from Southeast Asia or to aid in the release of Americans held as prisoners of war."

The subcommittee report stated: "It is difficult to see how roads with civilian traffic, villages and groups of civilians could have been bombed, rocketed or napalmed." The report said that mistakes do happen, however, and that "there is a certain reluctance, especially on the part of the Air Force, to admit that mistakes have happened which tends to undermine the credibility of official claims." The report also said that "some pilots have deliberately violated the rules of engagement, expending ordnance (bombs) against unauthorized targets."

Irregulars. The CIA-supported irregular force in Laos was composed of Meo tribesmen and other soldiers for hire from Laos.

The BG forces, which prior to the release of the subcommittee report were thought to be located in limited regions of Laos, were conducting operations in four of the five military zones in the country in early 1971. In fiscal 1969, the BG forces numbered about 39,800 and the report stated the force was in April about 30,000 men.

Sen. Clifford P. Case (R N.J.) accused the government in a May 20 floor speech of hiring Thai soldiers to fight in Laos. The report confirmed the accusations.

The report indicated that an amount close to $35-million was being expended to support a force of 4,800 Thai irregulars who were trained in Thailand by United States military or CIA personnel, then flown to Laos to fight in a private airline's planes—an airline that was believed to be subsidized by the CIA, the report stated.

Outlined in the committee report were reasons why the United States government felt it necessary to maintain a shroud of secrecy around the activities of the CIA in Laos:

• If U.S. activities were publicized, the United States would be accused of violating the Geneva Accords of 1962.

• The CIA is a clandestine organization not used to operating in the open and its operations in other parts of the world might be compromised.

CONGRESS AND THE WAR: DIVISIONS AND LIMITATIONS

President Nixon's decisions in the spring of 1972 to resume bombing of North Vietnam and to mine North Vietnamese ports opened a new chapter in the long history of congressional frustration with the Indochina war. *(1972 decisions p. 79; bombing precedents p. 73)*

From 1966 through May 1972 Congress voted more than 100 times on measures aimed at restricting or ending U.S. involvement in Southeast Asia. Three of these proposals became law as riders to other bills. However, with the exception of restrictions on U.S. activities in Laos, Thailand and Cambodia, Congress did not adopt any binding measure dealing directly with Indochina. *(Key Vietnam war votes p. 73; charts, see appendix)*

Since the Senate adopted the Gulf of Tonkin Resolution in 1964, Congress has not been asked for its advice or consent prior to major policy declarations by the President on the conduct of the war. Congress repealed the resolution in 1970. *(Box p. 72)*

Two times during 1971 Congress went on record with votes urging the President to set a date for the withdrawal of U.S. forces from Indochina. When Nixon signed the bills containing these end-the-war provisions, he emphasized that he did not consider them binding in any way. *(1971 action p. 75)*

Despite a growing opposition to U.S. involvement in Indochina, Congress gave both President Johnson and Nixon full support in terms of funding military operations and aid. Although each defense appropriations request since fiscal 1967 was cut by Congress, no limits were set on the amount of money the Defense Department could funnel into Indochina for the war effort.

Congress and Indochina, Pre-1964

Early Criticism. U.S. military aid to Vietnam was begun by the Truman administration; by 1951, military aid alone amounted to more than $500-million. John F. Kennedy, a member of the House, said in 1951 "we have allied ourselves to the desperate effort of the French regime to hang onto the remnants of empire."

In 1953, President Eisenhower approved a recommendation to step up U.S. military aid. Sen. William F. Knowland (R Calif. 1945-59), majority leader, supported the decision. Sen. Mike Mansfield (D Mont.) said Oct. 26, 1953, the Viet Minh could be defeated if the United States continued its aid to Indochina.

Eisenhower barred a U.S. combat role in Vietnam in 1954, but the United States sent 200 Air Force technicians to aid the French. The Senate Foreign Relations Committee was reported Feb. 16 to have expressed concern at the lack of congressional approval. Acting Secretary of State Walter Bedell Smith pledged to take no further action of that nature without consulting Congress.

Sen. Richard B. Russell (D Ga. 1933-71) Feb. 10, 1953, deplored the use of U.S. Air Force men; and Sen. Arthur

V. Watkins (R Utah 1947-59) said Feb. 14 that sending the technicians might border on a violation of Congress' right to declare war. Sen. John C. Stennis (D Miss.) March 9 demanded that the technicians be withdrawn. He said: "For the good they do, the risk is too great. We are taking steps that lead our men directly into combat. Soon we may have to fight or run."

Congress Urges Caution. In March 1954—at the beginning of the disastrous 56-day battle of the French at Dienbienphu—the White House tentatively approved a plan for immediate U.S. air intervention. Senators Lyndon B. Johnson (D Texas), majority leader, Russell, ranking Democrat on the Armed Services Committee, and and others rejected the proposal.

The United States would have to send troops to Indochina if there were no other way to prevent its collapse, warned Vice President Nixon April 16.

On May 6, one day before the fall of Dienbienphu, Majority Leader Johnson delivered the first of a series of speeches criticizing the Eisenhower policy. "We have been caught bluffing by our enemies," he said.

By January 1955, the United States had taken over the training and equipping of the South Vietnamese army. On Feb. 1, the Senate ratified the Southeast Asia Treaty Organization (SEATO), 82-1.

When the Laos crisis erupted in 1959, J.W. Fulbright (D Ark.), John Sparkman (D Ala.) and other members of the Senate Foreign Relations Committee Sept. 8 commended the U.S. initiative for rapid United Nations Security Council action. But Mansfield Sept. 7 questioned the deepening involvement in Laos.

Kennedy Policy. President Kennedy said March 23, 1961, the United States had an obligation to protect Laos from Communist takeover. Mansfield had again warned against such a commitment.

After touring Vietnam in May 1961, Vice President Johnson told Kennedy the United States would have to undertake a "major effort" to meet the Communist challenge, or "throw in the towel."

Foreign Relations Committee Chairman Fulbright supported sending U.S. combat troops to South Vietnam and Thailand if necessary, but opposed intervention in Laos.

By the end of 1961, U.S. military advisers in Vietnam numbered more than 600. Large-scale American military aid began in 1962.

A Feb. 24, 1963, report to the Senate Foreign Relations Committee questioned the level of U.S. aid. The report—prepared by Senators Mansfield, J. Caleb Boggs (R Del.), Claiborne Pell (D R.I.) and former Sen. Benjamin A. Smith (D Mass. 1960-62)—stated: "there is no interest of the United States in Vietnam which would justify, in present circumstances, the conversion of the war...primarily into an American war to be fought primarily with American lives."

As U.S. involvement increased—there were about 15,000 advisers in Vietnam in early 1964—criticism intensified. On March 10, 1964, Senators Wayne Morse (D Ore. 1955-69) and Ernest Gruening (D Alaska 1959-69) demanded total U.S. withdrawal. (Morse and Gruening were the only two senators voting against the August 1964 Tonkin Gulf Resolution.)

On April 21, 1964, Senate Minority Leader Everett M. Dirksen (R Ill. 1951-69) and Rep. Charles A. Halleck (R Ind. 1935-69) charged that the Johnson administration was concealing the extent of U.S. involvement in the war.

Congressional Responsibility

Dr. Leslie Gelb, former head of the Defense Department's Vietnam task force, told the Senate Foreign Relations Committee May 9, 1972, that Congress was partly to blame for continuation of the war because Congress was responsible for funding it. "Congressmen and senators for years have hidden behind the President," Gelb said. "If the war continues, it will be as much the responsibility of Congress as of the President."

But Sen. John C. Stennis (D Miss.), chairman of the Senate Armed Services Committee, told the Senate May 3: "So far as the President is concerned, the Constitution puts the responsibility on him.... Let us keep the responsibility on him (for initiatives in the war). That is my doctrine with reference to any chief executive, to keep the responsibility on him."

Frustrations over U.S. involvement in Vietnam have not been the exclusive property of those supporting rapid withdrawal of U.S. forces. A number of senators and representatives argued for greater U.S. involvement as the key to ending the war.

After Nixon sent bombers deep into North Vietnam April 15, 1972, Sen. Barry Goldwater (R Ariz.) called Nixon's critics "weak-kneed" and "jelly-spined" in the face of a real war. "I would rather blow the living daylights out of Haiphong than to lose one more American life....If Russian ships are bombed, that's too damned bad. I hope they hit them all."

Reaction to Initiatives. Since the buildup of U.S. military forces in Indochina began in the early 1960s, Congress with rare exceptions played the role of a spectator to presidential initiatives—reacting with debate, seldom with legislative action. *(Box this page)*

As the war continued into the middle and late 1960s and no clear-cut victory was at hand, Congress and the public began a slow polarization process with an increasing number of senators and representatives switching to an end-the-war posture.

When Congress adopted the Tonkin Gulf Resolution in 1964, all but two members of the Senate voted for it. By 1970 and 1971 a majority of the Senate opposed the war on certain votes and in 1971 a high of 175 representatives unsuccessfully backed a Senate amendment setting a date for U.S. withdrawal from Vietnam. *(Charts on anti-war votes, see appendix)*

Congressional Power. Congress had little direct authority over the Vietnam war. The Constitution hardly mentions the conduct of foreign relations—with Congress and the President sharing limited powers over foreign affairs. *(War powers p. 40)*

Presidential Initiatives

Following is a chronology of major Indochina initiatives by U.S. Presidents from 1961 to 1972.

1961 (Kennedy)—Pledged substantially increased economic and military aid, including "military advisers," to South Vietnam, which he said was "under attack" by Communist guerrillas.

1962 (Kennedy)—Ordered 5,000 troops into Thailand in May to emphasize concern over Communist Pathet Lao forces in northern Laos. U.S. troops withdrew in December after Kennedy, to preserve Laotian neutrality, pressured Laotian government into coalition with Pathet Lao and neutralist forces in June.

1964 (Johnson)—Ordered retaliatory air strikes on Communist PT boat bases in August. After torpedo attacks on U.S. ships in the Gulf of Tonkin, Johnson called the air strikes a "positive reply" to "repeated acts of violence."

1964 (Johnson)—Turned down secret peace talks with North Vietnam, claiming later that North was not prepared for "serious talks."

1965 (Johnson)—Continued air strikes in hopes of forcing negotiations. Two bombing moratoriums May 12-18 and Dec. 24-Jan. 31, 1966, failed to elicit peace feelers. Johnson said Communists had "no readiness or willingness to talk."

1966 (Johnson)—Renewed air strikes because of North Vietnam's failure to respond to American peace drive and because of Hanoi's "aggression" during the pause in the raids.

1968 (Johnson)—On March 31, Johnson announced he would not run for re-election and placed restrictions on the bombing of North Vietnam in the hopes of getting peace talks started.

1968 (Johnson)—Ordered bombing halt on Oct. 31 and called for negotiations.

1969 (Nixon)—Offered on May 14 an eight-point peace plan based on mutual withdrawal.

1969 (Nixon)—Disclosed Nov. 3 that secret peace initiative to Ho Chi Minh had been "flatly rejected." Announced there was a secret timetable for withdrawal, depending on level of enemy activity and progress of Vietnamization.

1970 (Nixon)—Sent U.S.-South Vietnamese force April 30 into Cambodia to "clean out" Communist border sanctuaries.

1970 (Nixon)—Proposed Oct. 7 a four-point peace plan including cease-fire proposal.

1971 (Nixon)—Ordered in December the heaviest air raids on North Vietnam since 1968 in retaliation for Communist buildup and offensive.

1972 (Nixon)—Suspended Paris peace talks March 23 until North Vietnam showed willingness for "serious discussions." On April 25, he announced talks would resume April 28.

1972 (Nixon)—Ordered bombing of Haiphong and Hanoi April 15 in retaliation for the two-week-old North Vietnamese offensive.

1972 (Nixon)—On May 8 announced his decision to mine North Vietnamese ports and increase bombing of the North.

Congress was given power to "provide for the common Defence," to establish and maintain the army and navy and to declare war. The war power has proved useless in the Vietnam conflict, since no way has developed to use it negatively to stop an ongoing undeclared war.

None of the other foreign relations powers of Congress, such as treaty ratification, has proved applicable to the Vietnam war.

The principal power of the President in foreign affairs is not in the Constitution. It was exercised for decades by a succession of Presidents without serious challenge and finally articulated by the Supreme Court in 1936. Since then it has been known as inherent power— power that belongs to the executive in his exercise of national sovereignty. *(Court decision p. 42)*

Against this broad authority Congress could array certain powers but none of comparable scope in foreign policy. One is its power to investigate and gather information as a necessary part of the legislative process. Congress has used this power extensively in attempting to affect the conduct of the war. But both Johnson and Nixon have repeatedly frustrated congressional efforts to obtain certain kinds of information.

Congress regularly and repeatedly has been denied information about clandestine foreign operations, such as those in Laos. *(Laos, p. 68)*

Another congressional power is control of the "purse-strings" of government. Congress has not been able to use this power effectively. Efforts to cut into military appropriations to reduce the funds available for the war have not been successful.

Efforts to prevent use of funds for operations of certain types or in certain geographical areas—for example, a ceiling on U.S. expenditures in Laos—have been circumvented or ignored by the administration.

Presidential Consultation. Although President Nixon has met regularly with the leadership in Congress, he did not rely on that leadership for counsel in time of international crisis. In this respect, Nixon differed from his most recent predecessors.

President Lyndon Johnson, regarded by many of his critics as being excessively head-strong with regard to Indochina foreign policy, regularly consulted with the minority and majority leadership in Congress before announcing a bombing resumption in Vietnam or the need to send in additional troops.

President Nixon did not make a practice of asking for advice from Congress when he planned to make a major foreign policy move, although he often told Congress what he planned to do before he informed the nation. Congress for example, was told what the President planned to say May 8 one hour before Nixon went on national television to inform the nation. *(Congressional reaction p. 80)*

Reaching for Power. Frustrated in every attempt to legislate an end to the Vietnam war, antiwar forces in Congress during the first four months of 1972 turned their efforts toward assuring a larger foreign policy role for Congress in the future.

Although none of the measures considered bore directly on the Indochina fighting, it was clear that their intent was to "avoid future Vietnams." As in end-the-war efforts, the Senate Foreign Relations Committee led the way.

The measures were built upon the national commitments resolution (S Res 85) adopted by the Senate in

Tonkin Gulf Resolution 1964

Following is the text of the "Gulf of Tonkin" resolution (PL 88-408) enacted by Congress on Aug. 7, 1964, and signed into law Aug. 10 following North Vietnamese attacks on U.S. ships in the Gulf of Tonkin on Aug. 2 and 4. The Johnson Administration used the broad wording in this resolution as authority for expansion of the United States' involvement in the Vietnam war in 1965 and the following years. Whether the wording in fact gave the President authority to commit half a million American troops to a war without further Congressional approval was a highly controversial question. It was, at the same time, a moot question because the President considered he had the authority and ordered the troops to Vietnam without seeking further direct Congressional authorization.

"Whereas naval units of the Communist regime in Vietnam, in violation of the principles of the Charter of the United Nations and of international law, have deliberately and repeatedly attacked United States naval vessels lawfully present in international waters, and have thereby created a serious threat to international peace;

"Whereas these attacks are part of a deliberate and systematic campaign of aggression that the Communist regime in North Vietnam has been waging against its neighbors and the nations joined with them in the collective defense of their freedom;

"Whereas the United States is assisting the peoples of southeast Asia to protect their freedom and has no territorial, military or political ambitions in that area, but desires only that these peoples should be left in peace to work out their own destinies in their own way: Now, therefore, be it

"Resolved by the Senate and House of Representatives of the United States of America in Congress assembled, That the Congress approves and supports the determination of the President, as Commander-in-Chief, to take all necessary measures to repel any armed attack against the forces of the United States and to prevent further aggression.

"SEC. 2. The United States regards as vital to its national interest and to world peace the maintenance of international peace and security in southeast Asia. Consonant with the Constitution of the United States and the Charter of the United Nations and in accordance with its obligations under the Southeast Asia Collective Defense Treaty, the United States is, therefore, prepared, as the President determines, to take all necessary steps, including the use of armed force, to assist any member or protocol state of the Southeast Asia Collective Defense Treaty requesting assistance in defense of its freedom.

"SEC. 3. This resolution shall expire when the President shall determine that the peace and security of the area is reasonably assured by international conditions created by action of the United Nations or otherwise, except that it may be terminated earlier by concurrent resolution of the Congress."

The Tonkin Gulf Resolution was repealed in 1970 by an amendment to the Foreign Military Sales Act (PL 91-672). The Nixon administration did not oppose repeal and maintained that its authority to carry on the war in Indochina did not rest on authority granted by the 1964 resolution.

1969. S Res 85 stated the Senate's view that a national commitment by the United States could only be made by "affirmative action taken by the legislative and executive branches...by means of a treaty, statute or concurrent resolution of both houses...."

In general, the measures originated in the Senate and were designed to require congressional participation in decisions taking the nation to war or committing the nation to future action. Others attempted to make sure that Congress had adequate information with which to judge foreign policies.

Potentially most far-reaching among these measures was the war powers bill (S 2956) passed by the Senate on April 13. The bill, which had the support of the Foreign Relations Committee and of Armed Services Committee Chairman Stennis, would codify the President's authority to take armed action without prior congressional approval and give Congress an opportunity to overrule his judgment 30 days after the fighting started. *(War powers bill p. 40)*

Indochina Votes 1966-72

The following chronology shows the highlights of congressional action on proposals designed to limit or halt U.S. involvement in Indochina.

Since 1966 Congress has taken more than 60 roll-call or recorded teller votes on measures designed to curtail U.S. activities in Southeast Asia and at least another 40 voice or standing votes. Of the approximately 100 votes on such proposals, three measures were passed which broke new ground on restricting U.S. activities in Indochina.

During 1971 Congress twice adopted a proposal which urged the President to set a date for the withdrawal of U.S. troops; in 1970 Congress passed restrictions on U.S. activities in Cambodia and in 1969 restrictions were established on U.S. involvement in Laos and Thailand.

1972 VOTES (THROUGH MAY 1)

Senate. Early deliberations during the session were focused on preventing future Vietnams through a legislative proposal called the War Powers bill (S 2956). The bill was adopted April 13 by a 68-16 roll-call vote. It sought to force the President in future military conflicts to ask the advice and consent of Congress before committing U.S. troops on foreign soil. *(p. 40)*

House. By June 1 the House had not considered any proposals on the floor which dealt with the Defense Department or Indochina.

1971 VOTES

Senate. During the session the Senate took more than 20 record votes on proposals which sought to halt or restrict U.S. involvement in Indochina. Although the Senate did not adopt any measures which sought to cut off funds for U.S. involvement, two times floor vote amendments were adopted which set a specific deadline for the withdrawal of troops pending the return of POWs. In each case the House removed the deadlines and otherwise weakened the language.

Bombing Precedents: 1968 and 1972

President Lyndon B. Johnson on March 31, 1968, ordered a partial halt to the bombing of North Vietnam. No U.S. planes were to strike targets north of the 20th parallel, which was 61 miles south of Hanoi and 225 miles north of the demilitarized zone (DMZ).

Johnson announced on Oct. 31, 1968, that effective Nov. 1 the United States would halt all bombing of North Vietnam. He said the action was based on developments at the Paris talks and that the United States could "now expect...prompt, productive, serious and intensive negotiations in an atmosphere that is conducive to progress."

President Nixon maintained the Nov. 1, 1968, suspension through April 15, 1972. The United States did occasionally attack surface-to-air missile installations within North Vietnam, saying the attacks were necessary to protect U.S. reconnaissance planes operating over North Vietnam.

The Nixon administration contended that missile attacks against reconnaissance craft violated an understanding reached with the North Vietnamese in discussions leading to suspension of bombing and full-scale peace talks.

The administration justified the April 15 attacks on Hanoi and Haiphong on the ground that the North Vietnamese had violated another part of the 1968 understanding—that they would not move forces across the DMZ. *(Congressional reaction to renewed bombing p. 79)*

The following were key votes on the war:

June 16—McGovern (D S.D.)—Hatfield (R Ore.) amendment to draft extension bill—sought to cut off funds for U.S. military activities in Indochina effective June 1, 1972, pending the release of U.S. POWs. Rejected, 44-52. *(Vote 82, 1971 CQ Almanac p. 15-S)*

June 22—Mansfield (D Mont.) amendment to draft extension bill—sought the withdrawal of U.S. troops from Indochina nine months after enactment pending the release of POWs. Adopted, 57-42. *(Vote 100, 1971 CQ Almanac p. 17-S)*

Sept. 30—Mansfield amendment to defense procurement authorization bill—sought the withdrawal of U.S. troops from Indochina six months after enactment pending the release of POWs. Adopted 57-38. *(Vote 216, 1971 CQ Almanac p. 37-S)*

House. Each time the Senate adopted the Mansfield amendment, the House voted not to accept the amendment as written by the Senate. Later, the House accepted weakened versions of the Mansfield proposals as parts of various defense bills. There were 11 record votes on anti-war proposals and another 10 votes which were rejected by voice or standing majorities.

The following were key votes on the war.

June 17—Nedzi (D Mich.)—Whalen (R Ohio) amendment to defense procurement authorization bill—sought to bar use of funds included in the bill for U.S. activities in and over Indochina, giving the President the right to change the Dec. 31, 1971, fund cut-off date if he could gain the support of Congress. Rejected, 158-255. *(Vote 90(T), 1971 CQ Almanac p. 32-H)*

Oct. 19—A procedural motion, ordering the previous question, was offered which had the effect of blocking a direct vote on the Senate-passed Mansfield amendment. Adopted, 215-193. *(Vote 205, 1971 CQ Almanac p. 71-H)*

Nov. 17—Boland (D Mass.) amendment to defense appropriations bill—sought to cut off funds for U.S. involvement in Indochina effective July 1, 1972, pending the release of POWs. Rejected, 163-238. *(Vote 269(T), 1971 CQ Almanac p. 90-H)*

Dec. 16—A procedural motion to table (kill) a proposal which instructed House conferees on the Foreign Military Assistance authorization bill to accept the Senate-passed Mansfield amendment. Adopted, 130-101. *(Vote 320, 1971 CQ Almanac p. 105-H)*

1970 VOTES

Senate. On the 18 record votes taken during the session on matters related to the Indochina war, all but four dealt with Cambodia. The Senate adopted strict limits on U.S. military involvement in Cambodia (later weakened by the House) and after one unsuccessful attempt the Senate repealed the Gulf of Tonkin Resolution. The following were key votes:

June 30—Cooper (R Ky.)—Church (D Idaho) amendment to the military credit sales bill—sought to bar use of funds for U.S. military operations in Cambodia after July 1, 1970, unless authorized by Congress. Adopted, 58-37. *(Vote 180, 1970 CQ Almanac p. 33-S)*

July 10—repeal of Gulf of Tonkin Resolution by 57-5 roll-call vote. *(Vote 322, 1970 Almanac p. 39-S)*

Sept. 1—McGovern (D S.D.)—Hatfield (R Ore.) amendment to defense procurement authorization bill—sought to limit U.S. troops in Vietnam to 280,000 men by April 30, 1971, and to provide for the complete withdrawal of troops by Dec. 31, 1971. Rejected, 39-55. *(Vote 258, 1970 CQ Almanac p. 46-S)*

House. After refusing to accept even a modified version of the Senate-passed Cooper-Church amendment, the House finally relented after a six-month delay of several foreign assistance bills in conference.

Dec. 22—The House by voice vote adopted the foreign aid bill with provisions prohibiting the use of funds to finance U.S. ground combat troops or military advisers to Cambodia. The House refused to accept a Senate provision barring U.S. airpower over Cambodia.

1969 VOTES

Senate. Major votes during the session were directed toward defining the U.S. military role in Laos and Thailand. In riders attached to two defense spending bills, the Senate stipulated that the United States would not introduce combat troops into the two countries and that the United States would support only local forces.

Aug. 12—Fulbright (D Ark.) amendment to defense procurement authorization bill—adopted by voice vote—stipulated that the United States would support only local forces in Laos and Thailand. *(Floor action, 1969 CQ Almanac p. 274)*

Vietnam War Costs

The following chart shows Defense Department budget costs for the Vietnam war including assistance programs controlled by the department.

Fiscal Year	Costs (in millions)
1965	$ 103
1966	5,800
1967	20,100
1968	26,500
1969	28,800
1970	23,100
1971	14,700
1972 (estimate)	9,100
Total	**$128,203**

Source: Department of Defense

Dec. 15—Church (D Idaho) amendment to defense appropriations bill—barred the introduction of U.S. ground combat troops into Laos or Thailand. Adopted, 73-17. *(Vote 209, 1969 CQ Almanac p. 41-S)*

House. Although the House acquiesced to most of the amendments passed by the Senate concerning Laos and Thailand, it also adopted a series of resolutions which condemned North Vietnam's treatment of United States' prisoners of war and announced support of the House for President Nixon's programs in Southeast Asia.

Dec. 2. The House (H Res 613) "affirms its support for the President (Nixon) in his efforts to negotiate a just peace in Vietnam...affirms and supports the principles enunciated by the President that the peoples of South Vietnam are entitled to choose their own government...." *(Story and text, 1969 CQ Almanac p. 857)*

1968 VOTES

Congress. Although Vietnam was the issue credited with influencing President Johnson not to seek a second term in the White House, Johnson's move to bring about a settlement of the war in the spring of 1968 had the effect of pre-empting congressional action on the issue.

1967 VOTES

Congress. Debate focused on defense spending, but despite the heated words of Congress passed a $12.3-billion supplemental appropriations bill for the defense department as requested by the President and trimmed only $1.5-billion from a defense appropriations bill which represented an increase of $11-billion from the previous year. *(1967 CQ Almanac p. 78)*

1966 VOTES

Congress. There were no major votes on proposals to restrict United States' involvement in the war in Southeast Asia.

CONGRESS URGED WITHDRAWAL FROM VIETNAM

Opponents of the Vietnam war tried again in 1971 to assert the powers of Congress to force an early end to the U.S. role in the Indochina fighting.

Although they failed, Congress for the first time went on record urging the President to change his policy of gradual withdrawal of U.S. troops from South Vietnam.

Three times the Senate approved amendments by Majority Leader Mike Mansfield (D Mont.) declaring withdrawal deadlines. The House accepted two—in weakened form without firm deadlines—and the President signed the measures to which they were attached.

But the President was not moved. In signing a defense procurement bill bearing the weakened Mansfield amendment, the President declared that the provision "will not change the policies I have pursued."

Mr. Nixon continued his phased withdrawals throughout the year. His last 1971 announcement scheduled a reduction to 139,000 men by Feb. 1, 1972.

The President refused to set the deadline sought by Congress and said the United States probably would keep a residual force in South Vietnam indefinitely unless the war were settled by negotiations.

The President's refusal to accept the Senate's will on ending the war added intensity to congressional dissatisfaction with the way the United States conducted its foreign policy.

Unable to terminate "a war being waged without its consent or guidance," the Congress "has seemed almost impotent in its frustration," said Rep. Richard T. Hanna (D Calif.) during debate on an end-the-war measure.

Congress still found ways to show its displeasure with the President's handling of the war. And its actions promised a thorough re-examination of U.S. foreign policies that had led to costly commitments in Southeast Asia.

When the 92nd Congress ended its first session in December 1971 House-Senate differences over a third Mansfield amendment declaring a six-month deadline for withdrawal from Indochina had stalled action on the foreign aid bill. Early in the second session of the 92nd Congress (1972), however, Congress passed a foreign aid bill, but without the Mansfield amendment.

The bitter legacy of Vietnam also had been much in Senators' minds when they defeated an earlier foreign aid authorization bill—the first time either house of Congress had rejected a foreign aid bill since the program was launched after World War II.

Mansfield Amendments

As adopted by the Senate, all three versions of the Mansfield amendment declared U.S. policy to be withdrawal of all U.S. troops from Indochina by a certain date.

The first version, attached to the draft extension bill, set the withdrawal deadline at nine months after enactment of the measure; the other two versions allowed six months for withdrawal.

All three amendments made withdrawal contingent upon the release of all Americans held prisoners of war by North Vietnam and the Viet Cong.

All three amendments also urged the President to:
• Set a final date for withdrawal within the specified time frame.
• Negotiate with North Vietnam for an immediate cease-fire.
• Negotiate with North Vietnam for a series of phased withdrawals of U.S. troops in exchange for a series of phased releases of American prisoners, to be completed by the date set by the President but no later than the deadline specified.

Draft Bill. The Senate June 22 by 57-42 and 61-38 roll-call votes attached the Mansfield amendment to a bill extending the draft. The House, however, by a 219-175 roll call refused to instruct its conferees to accept the amendment. *(Box on debate, p. 76, 77)*

House-Senate conferees softened the Mansfield amendment, deleting the deadline and adding language declaring the sense of Congress that the United States should terminate military operations in Indochina "at the earliest practicable date."

By adopting the conference report by a 297-108 roll call Aug. 4, the House went on record for the first time in support of withdrawal from Indochina as early as possible.

Defense Procurement. The Senate Sept. 30 revived the Mansfield amendment with a six-month deadline by a 57-38 roll call that added the amendment to a bill authorizing appropriations for defense procurement.

The House leadership of both parties blocked a direct vote on accepting the second Mansfield amendment. Conferees on the bill again modified the amendment to remove the withdrawal deadline, replacing it with the language "at a date certain."

The House adopted the conference report including the Mansfield amendment by voice vote.

In signing the defense procurement bill, the President told reporters that in his opinion the amendment was "without binding force or effect and it does not reflect my judgment about the way in which the war should be brought to a conclusion. My signing of the bill that contains this section, therefore, will not change the policies I have pursued."

Foreign Aid. The Senate Foreign Relations Committee, in recent years a frequent critic of Vietnam policy, renewed its challenge to the President's policies in a series of amendments, including the Mansfield amendment, attached to the foreign aid authorization bill.

The third Mansfield amendment, identical to the six-month deadline amendment added to the defense

(Continued on p. 78)

1971 Selective Service Amendment Called...

The primary vehicle for end-the-war legislation during 1971 was the military draft extension bill (HR 6531—PL 92-129). The major amendment to that bill which dealt with the Indochina war was sponsored by Senate Majority Leader Mike Mansfield (D Mont.). *(Action on selective service p. 46)*

The nine-month withdrawal deadline in the Mansfield amendment became the center of controversy when the Senate took its version of the draft bill to the House-Senate conference committee to iron out differences. House conferees refused to accept the deadline and after a delay of more than one month, Senate conferees agreed to drop the deadline.

Before the Senate would pass the draft bill with its emasculated version of the Mansfield amendment, however, they stalled another two months causing the old draft law to expire and the induction process to be interrupted for nearly six months.

Although the original version of the Mansfield amendment was weakened before the draft bill cleared Congress, the fact that any end-the-war provision remained in the bill at all marked the first time Congress had expressed a desire to withdraw troops from Indochina.

House Debate

During House consideration of the draft bill, four amendments were offered that dealt directly with restricting U.S. troop deployment in Indochina or setting a withdrawal date for troops. All the proposals were rejected.

Donald M. Fraser (D Minn.) offered an amendment providing that no person drafted after Dec. 31, 1971, could be required to serve in Indochina. The amendment was defeated by a 122-260 recorded teller vote.

Immediately following rejection of Fraser's amendment, Henry B. Gonzalez (D Texas) offered a proposal to prohibit the use of draftees in any armed conflict outside the United States except during a war declared by Congress. The Gonzalez amendment was rejected by voice vote.

A similar amendment, offered by Sam Gibbons (D Fla.), provided that no person drafted after June 30, 1971, could be required to serve in combat outside the United States unless the President declared war or told Congress that an attack on the United States was imminent. The amendment was defeated by a 96-278 recorded teller vote.

Finally, William F. Ryan (D N.Y.) offered an amendment that called for the total withdrawal of U.S. military forces from Indochina and surrounding waters by Dec. 31, 1971. It was rejected by voice vote.

Opposition to the amendments was led by F. Edward Hebert (D La.), chairman of the House Armed Services Committee. "The Joint Chiefs of Staff came before our committee...and they said they could not live with it (manpower restrictions in Indochina), that it would destroy our ability to meet our commitment in Indochina," Hebert said.

Fraser said his amendment would serve as a "signal for the administration that we are determined to disengage from Vietnam."

"This amendment would provide the same reservation of power that Congress insisted on when it enacted the first peacetime draft," Gonzalez said when he introduced his proposal. "Under that law, no conscript could be sent overseas without the consent of Congress.... If a war is to exist, and if our citizens are to be drafted to fight it, then Congress must exercise its responsibility to declare that war exists."

Senate Debate

Twice during consideration of the draft bill the Senate came to major votes on end-the-war proposals, rejecting the tough McGovern-Hatfield amendment and one week later adopting the weaker Mansfield proposal with its nine-month troop withdrawal amendment.

McGovern-Hatfield. The Senate June 16 rejected by a 42-55 roll-call vote the anti-war amendment sponsored by senators George McGovern (D S.D.) and Mark O. Hatfield (R Ore.) after one week of debate.

The McGovern-Hatfield amendment sought to cut off funds for support of U.S. troops in Indochina for any purpose other than withdrawal as of Dec. 31, 1971. With one exception, the major issues debated were not appreciably different from those discussed prior to the 1970 vote on a similar proposal offered by McGovern and Hatfield.

Drug Addiction. The one major new topic which figured heavily in the presentations by supporters of the amendment was the soaring rate of drug addiction among soldiers and veterans who had served in Indochina. *(Drug problems, p. 28)*

Harold E. Hughes, co-chairman of a special Armed Services subcommittee on drug abuse in the military, said: "Opium can be bought as safely on the streets of Saigon and other cities of South Vietnam as one can buy chewing gum. It is sold by kids and in some instances (by) representatives of the police department.

"This is the government our men are fighting and dying for," Hughes said, "to support the type of government that allows this to go on."

'Remain Flexible.' One of the arguments advanced by President Nixon for not announcing a definite withdrawal date from Vietnam was the need to remain flexible with the hope of bringing the North Vietnamese to the bargaining table. The President's point of view was echoed by Robert Dole (R Kan.) during the debate:

"They would have us abandon the last remaining element of flexibility in our disengagement policy, the open-ended feature of our withdrawal timetable."

Hughes countered: "I suggest we are telling the enemy what we are doing anyway. He can read the last three announcements of the increased troop reductions and he can speculate about the next one in October as accurately as the rest of us can speculate...."

Prisoners of War. Always central to the debate on the amendment was the question of how to assure

...For Vietnam Troop Withdrawal Deadline

the return of U.S. POWs once the United States had withdrawn.

"The United States has left no avenue unexplored," Dole said, "for the release of all prisoners." The North Vietnamese "have not evidenced any willingness to commit themselves on the release of our prisoners and until they do make a commitment, the President will not and should not and cannot be taken in by their offers to discuss the fate of our men," Dole added.

"Our amendment," said Hatfield, "provides the vehicle for determining if the North Vietnamese are speaking in good faith. They have said they will negotiate on the release of prisoners and that this would be solved simply and easily."

Mansfield agreed: "If we agree to a termination date and the prisoners are not released, we still retain all our options and thereby lose nothing in the attempt."

Other Arguments. Repeatedly, opponents of the amendment argued that the United States was successfully withdrawing from Vietnam without a McGovern-Hatfield amendment. They referred to the Nixon administration's record of scaling down the war. Supporters of the proposal replied that withdrawal was not proceeding rapidly enough and that there was still a vagueness to the President's plans. Supporters cited the lower, but continuing, casualties of the war as an additional reason for expediting the withdrawal.

Opponents said a withdrawal date of Dec. 31, 1971, would endanger U.S. troops because the men would be left unprotected. The North Vietnamese would not waste their energy attacking a force that would soon be completely out of the country, especially when the withdrawing force possessed superior firepower, supporters asserted.

Mansfield Amendment. The Senate June 22, 1971, broke with historical precedents, reversed a position it had upheld six days earlier and adopted by 57-42 and 61-38 roll-call votes a proposal calling for the withdrawal of all U.S. troops from Indochina within nine months.

After a series of six consecutive roll-call votes on a tangle of troop withdrawal amendments and modifications considered during debate, the Senate adopted a withdrawal proposal offered by Mansfield.

The fifth vote of June 22, on which the Mansfield proposal was tentatively adopted by a 57-42 roll-call vote, was the crucial test for supporters of a withdrawal amendment. The final 61-38 roll-call vote, officially adopting the Mansfield amendment, was a procedural formality on which four additional senators voted "yea" when it became apparent the measure was certain to pass.

Mansfield termed his proposal a national policy declaration. It was adopted in lieu of an amendment sponsored by Marlow W. Cook (R Ky.) that had been weakened by modifications adopted on the floor prior to consideration of the Mansfield substitute. The Mansfield amendment declared it the policy of the United States that the withdrawal of all U.S. troops from Indochina would be completed within nine months of enactment of HR 6531. The amendment urged the President

to set his own date for complete withdrawal within the nine-month period set by the proposal, and that the President should begin negotiations for the release of all U.S. prisoners of war immediately. The withdrawal of troops, the proposal stated, was subject to the successful negotiation for the release of the prisoners.

The Mansfield proposal, which called for the phased withdrawal of all U.S. troops along with a phased release of U.S. POWs, was not legally binding. The policy declaration language, however, carried more weight than the standard sense of Congress resolution. If the Mansfield amendment had been accepted by the House en toto—which it was not—it would have acted as a policy directive for the administration although the President would have been within the rights granted to him under the Constitution to ignore it—which he did.

The six roll calls which resulted in the adoption of the Mansfield withdrawal declaration were preceded by a heated debate on the Senate floor and a last-minute lobbying effort by the administration to stem the growing support for setting a withdrawal date.

Vance Hartke (D Ind.) characterized the administration as trying to "perpetuate a deadly folly and willful blindness to decency—a folly and a blindness of leaders more concerned with geographical abstractions than with the national ideals they had sworn to uphold—leaders more concerned with their own place in history than with America's."

Stennis said: "Whether intended or not, let no one say that this (amendment) is not an attack upon the President of the United States and his handling of this unfortunate war."

Several times during the four-hour debate, senators supporting the withdrawal amendments referred to the disclosures released in *The New York Times* and *The Washington Post* about the early involvement of the United States in the Vietnam conflict.

"If there is one thing already evident from the Pentagon papers," said Birch Bayh (D Ind.), "it is that in the past some of our elected leaders, however highly motivated, misled the American people as to the direction they expected our policy in Vietnam to take."

F. Edward Hebert (D La.), chairman of the House Armed Services Committee, told reporters after the Senate adopted the Mansfield proposal that he would not allow the draft bill to be reported from conference containing a withdrawal amendment. As the Armed Services Committee chairman, Hebert served as the leader of the House conferees.

White House Press Secretary Ronald Ziegler told reporters after the vote June 22 the President would regard the amendment as a sense-of-the-Congress resolution and nothing more if it emerged from the House-Senate conference as part of the bill and was adopted by both chambers. Ziegler said the amendment was simply the view of 57 senators, not the will of the people.

Adoption of the Mansfield proposal represented the first time in modern U.S. history that either chamber of Congress had urged an end to a war in which the country was still actively involved.

(Continued from p. 75)

procurement bill, was adopted in committee by a 12-4 vote.

After the Senate defeated the foreign aid bill, the committee attached the Mansfield amendment to a new bill to authorize military aid spending. No floor votes were taken on the amendment, and the new bill was approved.

The House-Senate conference on the foreign aid bill deadlocked on the Mansfield amendment, preventing final action on the authorization legislation during the first session.

Mansfield, who had been angered by softening of the previous amendments and by the President's refusal to accept their recommendations, insisted that the House leadership permit a separate House vote on the amendment.

The deadlock was broken, however, after a surprise House maneuver. By a 130-101 vote, the House tabled a motion by Rep. William F. Ryan (D N.Y.) to instruct House conferees to accept the Mansfield amendment.

Mansfield interpreted the vote as a vote against his amendment, and the conferees quickly reached agreement on other provisions of the foreign aid bill.

The Senate then passed the conference version of the bill, but the House delayed a vote until the second session convened in 1972.

Other War Amendments

Both the House and Senate rejected attempts to amend the foreign aid, draft extension and defense appropriations bills to cut off funds for the conduct of the war.

McGovern-Hatfield. During debate on the draft bill, Senators George McGovern (D S.D.) and Mark O. Hatfield (R Ore.) failed to win approval of a proposal to force the Administration to terminate the U.S. role in the war by cutting off funds for any purpose other than withdrawal as of Dec. 31, 1971.

An attempt to attach the McGovern-Hatfield amendment to the draft bill on the Senate floor was defeated by a 42-55 roll-call vote on June 16.

When it became apparent that their amendment would fail, McGovern and Hatfield threw their support to a compromise proposal by Sen. Lawton Chiles (D Fla.).

The Chiles amendment set the cut-off date for funds at June 1, 1972, and added a provision that the cut-off would be nullified unless all Americans held prisoners of war had been released by April 1, 1972. It was rejected by a 44-52 roll-call vote.

Cooper-Church. In reporting the foreign aid bill bearing the Mansfield amendment, the Foreign Relations Committee also attached an amendment requiring that all funds authorized for U.S. forces in Indochina be spent only for the purpose of completing the withdrawal of all troops from South Vietnam.

The amendment, proposed by Frank Church (D Idaho) and John Sherman Cooper (R Ky.), was adopted in committee by an 11-5 vote. Under its terms, U.S. forces could not engage in fighting in North Vietnam, South Vietnam, Cambodia or Laos except to protect withdrawing Americans from "imminent danger."

Minority Leader Hugh Scott (R Pa.) raised the threat of a presidential veto if the Cooper-Church amend-

ment stayed in the bill. In a series of three close roll-call votes, the Senate deleted the amendment.

Laos-Cambodia. In an effort to limit U.S. involvement in Indochina, the Senate adopted amendments placing ceilings on foreign aid spending in Laos and Cambodia. Both amendments were offered by Stuart Symington (D Mo.).

A Symington amendment placing a $350-million ceiling on military and economic support of Laos was added to the defense procurement bill by a 67-11 roll call. The bill, which also included the Mansfield amendment, subsequently was passed by the Senate, accepted in conference and signed by the President.

The foreign military aid bill disputed in conference as the session ended included a Symington amendment placing a $341-million ceiling on aid to Cambodia.

Both ceilings permitted the exact amounts of aid planned for Laos and Cambodia by the Administration. But Symington offered the amendments to establish the principle that Congress should control U.S. assistance to those nations.

Armed Services Committee Chairman John C. Stennis (D Miss.) said continued aid to South Vietnam was required to fulfill U.S. goals in Indochina.

"Like it or not," he said, "I have reconciled myself... to the fact that for some two, three or four years more, at least, we will have to put up massive amounts of economic and military aid into South Vietnam if we are going to justify the blood we have already spilled there...."

Foreign Aid Debate

Consideration of the foreign aid bill brought to the surface the underlying frustrations in Congress over the Vietnam war and how the U.S. role should be ended.

Such frustration was among several factors that led the Senate to defeat the House-passed foreign aid authorization bill (HR 9910) by a 27-41 roll-call vote. (Another version of the foreign aid bill was at last adopted early in 1972.)

Such frustration also led some Senators to oppose the military assistance bill (S 2819) reported by the Foreign Relations Committee as part of a two-bill package to replace HR 9910.

The Mansfield amendment and Cambodian aid ceiling approved by the Senate when it passed S 2819 ultimately produced the conference deadlock that threatened the program's future.

Anti-war Senators did not take issue with the Administration's announced policy of withdrawing U.S. troops. They did question the rate of withdrawal and the President's unwillingness to set a deadline or to rule out a residual force of Americans to help the South Vietnamese continue the war.

They also expressed doubts about the Nixon Doctrine—the President's declaration that the United States would support friendly nations with money and arms but not American troops—and suggested that such assistance inevitably would create U.S. commitments requiring U.S. troops to back them up.

Calling attention to the "continuing intensity of the U.S. air war in Indochina," Fulbright said it was "difficult to escape the conclusion...that the President is still determined to control the future of Southeast Asia by the application of force."

THREE PRESIDENTIAL DECISIONS AND CONGRESS' REACTION

In the spring of 1972 President Nixon announced three major decisions concerning the Vietnam war. Each of these announcements stimulated renewed waves of congressional reaction in the form of statements, hearings and attempted legislation to control the course of the war. *(Reaction p. 82; hearings p. 80, 81; legislation p. 83)*

The Nixon initiatives were the following:

• His decision, announced April 16 by the U.S. command in Saigon, to bomb the Haiphong-Hanoi area in the wake of the North Vietnamese offensive into South Vietnam.

• A White House announcement April 25 that U.S. negotiators would return to the Paris peace talks, followed April 26 by President Nixon's televised address to the nation announcing the withdrawal of 20,000 more U.S. troops from Vietnam by July 1. In the speech, Nixon said the bombing of North Vietnam would continue until North Vietnamese troops were withdrawn from South Vietnam. The Paris peace talks had been suspended by the administration since March 23.

• His announcement May 8 in a televised address to the nation that he had ordered the mining of North Vietnamese ports and the interdiction of land and sea routes to North Vietnam in a move to cut off delivery of war supplies to that country.

Bombing Reaction

After President Nixon ordered U.S. planes to bomb Haiphong and Hanoi April 15, Congress came alive with a new round of heated debates over U.S. participation in the Indochina war.

A generally hostile Senate Foreign Relations Committee held open hearings April 17-18 at which members sharply questioned Secretary of State William P. Rogers and Secretary of Defense Melvin R. Laird on the meaning of the escalated air war over North Vietnam.

In both the House and Senate, Democrats led efforts to get anti-war legislation to the floor.

Senate Debate. Senators debated the war for more than five hours April 19, dividing along party lines. All Republicans who spoke on the floor supported the President's move, and all but one Democrat—James B. Allen (Ala.)—castigated the bombings. No liberal Republicans and just the one conservative Democrat joined in the debate.

"It is clear beyond peradventure," said Gorden Allott (R Colo.), "that the fuel that drives the Hanoi war machine, flows from the Soviet Union...the reckless rulers in the Kremlin." If the Soviets want to guarantee the safety of their merchant ships, Allott said, "they can take the sensible precaution of staying out of the war zone."

Barry Goldwater (R Ariz.) characterized those who didn't want to bomb Haiphong as "weak-kneed" and "jelly-backed." Goldwater said: "I would rather blow the living daylights out of Haiphong than to lose one

more American life....If Russian ships are bombed, that's too damned bad. I hope we hit them all. They have no business (being) in Haiphong."

Alan Cranston (D Calif.), who organized the debate, said: "It seems to me that Lyndon B. Johnson is back in the White House....We're seeing what almost amounts to a win the war attitude rearing its head again."

Thomas F. Eagleton (D Mo.) said: "After considerable contemplation as to the tactical value of our attacks on North Vietnam, the only conclusion I can draw is that we have embarked on a course of raw retaliation. The President's policy has been threatened and there is nothing more vengeful than the wounded pride of a king."

Democratic Caucus. The House Democratic Caucus April 20 passed by a 144-58 vote a resolution condemning as "a dangerous escalation of our role in the Indochina war and a direct contradiction of the administration's stated policy of winding down the war." The resolution also urged the President to set a date for the termination of "all U.S. military involvement in or over Indochina" subject to the release of U.S. prisoners of war.

The caucus also voted to ask the Foreign Affairs Committee to report out a bill within 30 days which would accomplish the objectives outlined in the resolution.

According to staff members polled by Congressional Quarterly, many House Democrats were pushing for at least one more record vote on the Vietnam war before they returned to their districts to campaign for re-election in the fall.

Peace Talk Reaction

President Nixon announced April 25 the return of the United States to the Paris peace talks, and followed April 26 with a television speech announcing withdrawal of 20,000 more troops from Vietnam by July 1. The Presi-

U.S. Troop Withdrawals

The table shows the eight announcements President Nixon had made concerning the withdrawal of U.S. troops from Vietnam through May 1972.

Announced	Number	Down To	Effective	Rate Per Month
June 8, 1969	25,000	524,500	Aug. 31, 1969	10,000
Sept. 16, 1969	40,500	484,000	Dec. 15, 1969	11,400
Dec. 15, 1969	50,000	434,000	April 15, 1970	12,500
April 20, 1970	150,000	284,000	May 1, 1971	12,500
April 7, 1971	100,000	184,000	Dec. 1, 1971	14,300
Nov. 12, 1971	45,500	139,000	Feb. 1, 1972	22,500
Jan. 13, 1972	70,000	69,000	May 1, 1972	23,300
April 26, 1972	20,000	49,000	July 1, 1972	10,000

dent said in his speech that U.S. bombing of North Vietnam would not be stopped until the enemy withdrew its troops from South Vietnam.

Divided Response. In Congress most criticism of the President's April 26 speech centered on his decision to continue bombing in North Vietnam. Sen. Frank Church (D Idaho) told the Senate April 27: "If the Nixon Vietnamization policy means we must interpose our Air Force and Navy to shield South Vietnam against each new attack from the North, then when will our pilots and sailors ever be freed from the bondage of this war?"

Sen. Jacob K. Javits (R N.Y.) said: "The President's decision remains the same because he has not given us the word on a residual force in Vietnam and implies our continued underwriting of the security of its (South Vietnam's) government.... The over-all position of the United States everywhere in the world is at stake and demands a complete withdrawal from Vietnam. We have done all any nation can be asked to do there."

Sen. Abraham Ribicoff (D Conn.) told the Senate that there were no new arguments advanced in the President's speech. "We must face up to the realities that a pro-American government in Saigon is impossible and that all of Vietnam—North and South—will most probably be united under a single flag....

"If we have learned anything from our deep involvement in Indochina," Ribicoff continued, "it is that all Vietnamese are united in their dislike of foreign interference.... Vietnamization cannot bring an end of direct American involvement in the conflict and the return of our prisoners.... We will not be able to get our prisoners back by dropping more bombs."

Supporters took the view that the President's efforts brought the end of the war closer. Sen. Robert P. Griffin (R Mich.), the assistant minority leader in the Senate, said: "If this courageous President gets the unified support he deserves here at home, the prospects for real peace now look brighter than ever.... This is the crucial testing period for the American people as well as the South Vietnamese."

Sen. James L. Buckley (Cons-R N.Y.) said that the announcement of withdrawing 20,000 more U.S. troops "is in itself excellent news because of the confidence which it reflects in the success of the Vietnamization program."

Mining Reaction

President Nixon's May 8 decision to mine the North Vietnamese ports evoked a denunciation by the Soviet Union, a bitter dispute in Congress and rejection of his peace terms by the North Vietnamese.

Nixon's action brought immediate opposition from Democrats in Congress and support from Republicans.

The North Vietnamese government declared May 9 it would never accept the President's conditions for ending the interdiction of shipping and increased bombing, which it called an ultimatum.

In his nationally televised speech, Nixon played down his escalation of the war, the risk of confrontation with the Soviet Union and the threat his action posed to his own global strategy for peace. He outlined a

Vietnam Bombing Hearings

The Senate Foreign Relations Committee April 17-18, 1972, questioned Secretary of State William P. Rogers and Secretary of Defense Melvin R. Laird on the resumption of U.S. bombing of North Vietnam, suspended in 1968. The April 15-16 bombing attacks were directed against military targets near Hanoi, North Vietnam's capital, and Haiphong, its major port.

Excerpts from the hearings:

J.W. Fulbright (D Ark.), committee chairman: "What is the purpose you seek to achieve by the intensified bombing of North Vietnam?"

Rogers: "We have three purposes in mind.... First,...to protect American troops that are in South Vietnam...(and) to make certain that the withdrawal program...can continue. And we're doing it to give the South Vietnamese a chance to defend themselves against the massive invasion by the North Vietnamese."

Fulbright: "Why was the Congress not consulted?"

Rogers: "The secrecy of this type of thing is very important. The President has told Congress from time to time he would take whatever military action was necessary."

Fulbright: "Does the policy of Vietnamization include the assumption that the United States will continue indefinitely to provide unlimited air and naval support whenever South Vietnamese forces are under pressure?"

Rogers: "The South Vietnamese are flying a good many of the tactical missions in South Vietnam .... We have every reason to think that they'll be able to continue the building up of their air capability."

Fulbright: "What do you think would happen if the United States removed its forces."

Rogers: "It probably would result in a blood bath. Secondly, I think it would destabilize that whole area."

Frank Church (D Idaho): "Why do you think a resumption of bombing of military targets...will succeed now when it failed (during the Johnson administration)?"

Rogers: "Because the facts are different. Before we were fighting what was sort of a guerrilla war.... Now it's a totally different concept militarily. There is a major invasion."

Fulbright: "Perhaps we should have known all along that the President's underlying objectives in Vietnam were identical to those of his predecessors.... Apparently, President Nixon believes that we can accomplish with air power alone what President Johnson failed to do with air power and more than 500,000 American soldiers."

Laird: "I cannot explain to you the reason that the North Vietnamese decided to invade across the DMZ. The 1968 understandings that led to the halt of bombing had been to a great degree lived up to by the enemy.

"At this time we are flying below the DMZ, in the DMZ and above the DMZ. We are also using air power in Cambodia and Laos."

plan of "decisive military action to end the war" and offered a peace plan. The military action was clear-cut:

• Entrances to Haiphong and other harbors were to be mined to stop the flow of Soviet, Chinese and East European supplies and equipment to Hanoi and prevent naval operations from the ports, a step long advocated by Vietnam "hawks" and proposed by Nixon himself as early as 1965.

• U.S. forces were to interdict the delivery of material in the internal and in the claimed territorial waters (12 miles offshore) of the North.

• Rail and all other communications were to be cut off to the greatest extent possible.

• Air and naval strikes were to continue against military targets.

• Ships in the ports had three daylight periods (ending at 7 p.m. May 11 Hanoi time, 6 a.m. May 11 Washington time) to leave safely, after which the mines were set to become active and ships trying to enter or leave the ports did so at their own risk.

Nixon said two conditions had to be met before the military plan would be suspended: Return of all American prisoners of war and an internationally supervised ceasefire throughout Indochina.

When those conditions were met, Nixon said, the United States would stop "all acts of force throughout Indochina" and would withdraw "all American forces from Vietnam within four months." The fixed withdrawal deadline in exchange for return of the prisoners was essentially what war opponents in Congress had been urging Nixon to offer.

Congress Ignored. In contrast to the Cuban missile crisis of 1962, during which congressional leaders were consulted before the major decisions were made, Nixon in reaching his decision ignored Congress.

An hour before his 9 p.m. television speech, Nixon met with the Democratic and Republican leadership of the House and Senate and the chairmen and ranking minority members of four committees of each chamber. "We were told after the fact," Senate Majority Leader Mike Mansfield (D Mont.) said of the President's decision, adding that he did not consider that as consultation with Congress.

Democratic Opposition. Senate Democrats reacted vigorously, although their votes did not guarantee similar action by the full Senate. In a series of three votes May 9 the Democrats in caucus:

• Condemned Nixon's escalation of the war, by a 29-14 vote.

• Determined to write the President's new peace terms into law by endorsing a cutoff of funds for all military operations in Indochina four months after North Vietnam agreed to release American prisoners. The vote was 35-8.

• Decided by a 44-0 vote not to postpone a vote on the funds cutoff until Nixon returned from his forthcoming summit conference with Soviet leaders.

Democratic members of the House Foreign Affairs Committee voted by a large majority May 10 to approve a resolution requiring withdrawal of U.S. troops from Indochina by Oct. 1 if prisoners were released, the missing in action were accounted for and safe withdrawal of remaining troops was allowed. Chairman Thomas E. Morgan (D Pa.) said he believed the committee, most members of

---

Origins of the Vietnam War

The Senate Foreign Relations Committee held hearings May 9-11, 1972, on the causes and origins of the Vietnam war.

Much of the material for discussion was provided by declassification and publication of the Defense Department compilation of "United States-Vietnam Relations, 1945-1967," known as the Pentagon papers.

Excerpts from the three-day hearings:

Leslie H. Gelb, chairman of the Defense Department Vietnam task force that prepared the Pentagon papers, now a fellow of the Brookings Institution, discussed U.S. involvement: "Given the constant goal of a non-Communist South Vietnam since the Korean war, Vietnam has presented the United States with a dilemma...the war could not be won with the United States nor without the United States. In full knowledge of these dilemmas, our leaders persisted nevertheless. Each successive group of leaders thought that they might just succeed where their predecessors had failed."

Arthur Schlesinger Jr., special assistant to the President, 1961-64. "In my view, the 'system' failed dismally. It failed to provide any systematic and serious assessment of American stakes in Vietnam.... It was terribly wrong in regarding Hanoi and the Viet Cong as the spearhead of Chinese aggression.

"The system, in short, did not offer Presidents intelligent or useful counsel; and it reinforced and compounded illusion. In my judgment, the Vietnam adventure was marked much more by ignorance, misjudgment, muddle and... stupidity than...by efficiency, foresight, awareness and calculation."

Noam Chomsky, professor of linguistics at Massachusetts Institute of Technology, traced U.S. involvement to opposition to nationalist movements: "One form of anti-communism motivated U.S. intervention namely, opposition to indigenous communist-led movements, under the assumptions of the domino theory. A second form of anti-communism was invoked to justify the intervention...fear of a Kremlin-directed conspiracy of Chinese aggression—as far as we know, a figment of imagination."

Abbot Low Moffat, chief of the State Department division of Southeast Asian affairs, 1945-47, reviewed U.S. policy toward the restoration of French rule in Indochina after World War II: "We are reaping today...the tragedy of our fixation on the theory of monolithic aggressive communism that began to develop at this time (1945-47) and to affect our objective analyses of certain problems. I have always been convinced that if the French had worked sincerely with Ho Chi Minh Vietnam would have evolved with a communist regime but a regime that followed the interests of Vietnam first.

"As (State) department concern about the communist domination of the Vietnam government became more apparent and more uncritical, we began... to allow our fears of such domination to overrule our better judgment...."

May 1972 Senate Reaction to Mining Vietnamese Ports

Opposition to the President

William Proxmire (D Wis.): The President's action "is both reckless and wrong.... It shoves this country into a direct collision course with the Soviet Union.... In doing so, it seriously jeopardizes the strategic arms limitation talks.... It will increase the killing and carnage and risk without any genuine likelihood that it can achieve a military success...."

Mike Mansfield (D Mont.), majority leader: "We were told about (the mining) after the fact, not before....What are we are witnessing is not a shortening of the war...but rather a lengthening of it...."

Frank E. Moss (D Utah): "We stand on the brink, linked to another escalation in Vietnam....The cornerstones of the President's Vietnam policy have failed....We are trapped by positions and policies that should have been reversed long ago."

Vance Hartke (D Ind.): The President "has thrown down the gauntlet of nuclear war to a billion people in the Soviet Union and China....Armageddon may be only hours away."

George McGovern (D S.D.): "The President must not have a free hand in Indochina any longer. The nation cannot stand it. The Congress must not allow it....The political regime in Saigon is not worth the loss of one more American life."

Jacob K. Javits (R N.Y.): "The President's announcement is the inevitable result of the gravely mistaken course of action our country has taken in Indochina."

Edward M. Kennedy (D Mass.): The action is "one of the most drastic steps America has ever taken in the entire history of the war....The mining of Haiphong is an escalation of a completely different order of magnitude.... (It is) a senseless act of military desperation by a President incapable of finding the road to peace."

Edmund S. Muskie (D Maine): "By taking these actions, the President is jeopardizing the major security interests of the United States.... This dangerous step...is not the road to peace."

Clifford P. Case (R N.J.): "For the last 7 years this course (mining) has been considered by our leaders too reckless and too dangerous. I know of no American interests or commitments which justify this risk."

Frank Church (D Idaho): "I disagree...with the military action the President decided to take. But the one thing that has been overlooked is that in the same speech he made a proposition for peace that needs to be given closer attention, not only by this body, but also by Hanoi and by Moscow...."

Support for the President

James B. Allen (D Ala.): "The President has made a bold and courageous move...."

Strom Thurmond (R S.C.): "Hanoi will abandon her goal of military conquest in the south only if this Congress shows a solid unified wall of support behind our President.... (He) wisely refused to follow those who would surrender when the stakes are so high."

Bill Brock (R Tenn.): "It seems passing strange to me that once again when the President makes a dramatic peace proposal, even before we get any response from Hanoi...his actions are criticized.... And yet...I hear no criticism of North Vietnam for endangering the world's peace."

John G. Tower (R Texas): "The step the President took was an eminently correct step."

Howard H. Baker Jr. (R Tenn.): "The new peace proposals and military actions...represent...a measured, courageous and necessary response to the overt military aggression of (North Vietnam)...."

Henry Bellmon (R Okla.): "The President's action has barred the duplicity of Soviet foreign policy for all the world to see.... The next move is plainly up to the USSR."

Robert Dole (R Kan.): "The policy of Vietnamization is being...severely tested. However, I am not willing...to conclude that our policy is a failure...."

Hiram L. Fong (R Hawaii): "The mining of Haiphong Harbor is a measure I have long advocated."

Robert Taft Jr. (R Ohio): "President Nixon has made a courageous choice. It is one best calculated to bring about a negotiated settlement.... It is now up to the Russians to join with us in a reasonable role to bring about an end to the flow of war materials and of hostilities...."

Gale W. McGee (D Wyo.): "I would urge all of us to give the President the chance to proceed in playing out his very mixed series of events that are all laced together...."

---

which had been supporters of Vietnam policy, would approve legislation cutting off funds.

Support for Nixon. Generally, Republicans rallied to Nixon's side on the new tactics while Democrats were critical. Exceptions in the Senate included Sam J. Ervin Jr. (D N.C.) and Gale W. McGee (D Wyo.), who urged the Democratic caucus not to act precipitously, as well as Chairman John C. Stennis (D Miss.) of the Armed Services Committee and Henry M. Jackson (D Wash.), who counseled against placing roadblocks in the

President's path though they did not approve of the new plan of action.

In the House, Speaker Carl Albert (D Okla.) expressed hope the action would shorten the war. Minority Leader Gerald R. Ford (R Mich.) praised the President's decision. The alternative, he said, would have been for the United States "to slink out of Vietnam like a beaten dog" and would have posed the danger of an unprotected evacuation of the remaining American troops.

Legislation

As it recessed June 30, 1972, for the Democratic national convention, Congress seemed likely to leave it to the American voters to decide in the November presidential election how the United States should end its involvement in the Indochina war.

Antiwar members continued to press during the first six months of 1972 for legislation terminating U.S. participation in the war. But neither the House nor the Senate was willing to challenge the peace terms set forth by President Nixon.

Even J.W. Fulbright (D Ark.), the Senate Foreign Relations Committee chairman and long-time advocate of end-the-war measures, was resigned to frustration of congressional attempts to set a deadline for U.S. withdrawal from the fighting.

"We have tried to stop the war," Fulbright told the Senate June 23, "but we have been unable to do it. It is up to the American people in November to make their choice as to whether they want to continue the war and to continue our sacrifices.

"If President Nixon wins re-election, we will continue to be there, I suppose," Fulbright added. "For what reason I do not understand."

Fulbright spoke during Senate debate of the fiscal 1973 foreign military aid authorization bill (S 3390), a measure including an end-the-war amendment approved by the Foreign Relations Committee. The foreign aid bill was left pending when the Senate adjourned.

An earlier Foreign Relations Committee amendment to the fiscal 1973 State Department-United States Information Agency authorization bill had been rejected with its sponsors' concurrence after the Senate watered it down.

In the House, the cautious Foreign Affairs Committee for the first time considered an end-the-war resolution after prodding from House Democrats. The final product of the committee's deliberations, however, was a Republican-backed measure that supported the President.

Senate Amendments. In its only key vote on the war from January to July, 1972, the Senate endorsed the Vietnam peace terms put forth by the President in his May 8 television address announcing the mining of North Vietnam's ports.

By a 47-43 roll-call vote on May 16, the Senate approved an amendment by Majority Whip Robert C. Byrd (D W.Va.) making an internationally supervised cease-fire a condition for U.S. withdrawal from Indochina.

Byrd's amendment modified an end-the-war proposal put forth by Frank Church (D Idaho) and Clifford P. Case (R N.J.) that would have prohibited the use of funds to maintain, support or engage U.S. forces in Indochina four months after an agreement was reached on return of all Americans held prisoners by the North Vietnamese and Viet Cong.

As modified, the Church-Case amendment in general was consistent with the President's May 8 peace terms: withdrawal of all American forces from Vietnam four months after return of the prisoners and implementation of an internationally supervised cease-fire throughout Indochina.

Byrd's amendment made the provision unacceptable to its sponsors, who wanted Congress to stake out an independent position on ending the war. They did not oppose its defeat by voice vote.

The Senate's action did not end antiwar efforts. Majority Leader Mike Mansfield (D Mont.) offered a two-stage withdrawal plan that was incorporated by the Foreign Relations Committee in the military aid bill.

Mansfield's proposal would treat separately the issues of withdrawing U.S. ground forces from South Vietnam and ending U.S. air and naval action in support of South Vietnamese troops.

Its first stage would forbid use of funds to keep any U.S. forces on South Vietnamese territory after Aug. 31, 1972. Its second stage would bar participation by U.S. forces in hostilities in or over Indochina upon completion of a cease-fire between U.S. and communist forces, release of all U.S. prisoners and an accounting for Americans missing in action.

Supporters of the administration's Vietnam policy were expected to attempt to strike Mansfield's amendment from the foreign aid bill when the Senate resumed floor consideration of the measure.

House Action. The House took one floor vote in the first half of 1972 on an end-the-war amendment, with antiwar forces falling short of the strength they demonstrated in 1971.

By a 152-244 recorded teller vote, the House June 27 rejected an amendment by Michael Harrington (D Mass.) that would have cut off funds for the war authorized by the fiscal 1973 defense procurement bill as of Sept. 1, 1972. The amendment was contingent on release of prisoners and accounting for men missing in action.

In 1971, the lowest House vote total in favor of an antiwar provision had been 158.

Another floor debate on the war was expected in 1972 when the House took up a resolution (H J Res 1225) reported by the Foreign Affairs Committee.

The committee, reluctant to challenge presidential conduct of the war, in 1972 for the first time gave full consideration to an end-the-war measure under prodding by the House Democratic caucus.

The caucus, responding to the resumption of bombing of Hanoi and Haiphong, had voted April 20 to request the Foreign Affairs Committee to report legislation setting a date for ending U.S. involvement in the war.

Although Chairman Thomas E. Morgan (D Pa.) supported the caucus request, the committee voted 19-18 on June 13 to report a Republican-backed substitute expressing support for the President's terms for ending the war.

The Republican resolution, offered by John Buchanan (R Ala.), stated the sense of Congress that U.S. troops should be removed from Vietnam not later than four months after an internationally supervised cease-fire, release of American prisoners of war and accounting for Americans missing in action.

Fourteen Republicans were joined by five Democrats—including the second-, third-, and fourth-ranking majority members—in voting for Buchanan's substitute. Only two Republicans voted against the substitute.

Antiwar Democrats were expected to try to amend the committee resolution on the House floor. Morgan, who voted against the Buchanan substitute, said there was "an excellent chance" that the resolution would be modified or defeated on the House floor.

CONGRESS SHARES RESPONSIBILITY FOR COST OVERRUNS

In five days of poorly attended hearings late in 1971, the Senate Armed Services Committee tried to find answers to the nagging questions of increasing weapons costs.

The unusual hearings, held in the final crush of legislative activity before the 92nd Congress adjourned at the end of its first session, were aimed at educating the committee and the public to the problems involved in the weapons acquisition process.

Sen. John C. Stennis (D Miss.), chairman of the committee, said the hearings were to explore the methods used in contracting for research and development of weapons and the methods employed in purchasing a tested weapon system.

The testimony showed that Congress was as much to blame for rising cost of weapons as either the Defense Department or defense contractors.

"The budgetary process has become a ritual with no content," said Dr. William B. McLean, technical director of the Naval Underseas Center, San Diego, Calif. "It occupies more than 50 percent of the productive time of our best technical people at the laboratory and the full time of large numbers of technical people in Washington."

Between McLean and an earlier witness—Gilbert W. Fitzhugh, chairman of the President's Blue Ribbon Defense Panel—the testimony showed that Congress:

• Caused costly delays in programs because the House and Senate were so slow in providing funds—often failing to appropriate defense money until the fiscal year was half over.

• Required people responsible for developing the weapons to spend too much time on Capitol Hill and not enough time in their workshops.

• Interfered too much during the research and design phase, then failed to challenge defense witnesses with sufficient vigor once they said a weapon was ready for production.

"One feels that life would be much more enjoyable if the amount of funding to be spent were known at the beginning of the year, whatever its amount," McLean told the committee.

Stennis regularly complimented his witnesses for their frankness. "It certainly is refreshing to hear your views," Stennis told two Rand Corporation witnesses. "Most of the witnesses we get in here are asking for money."

Pentagon Problems. While many witnesses implicated Congress as partially responsible for rising costs of weapons systems, they also indicated that the Pentagon:

• Had ignored the need to develop a weapon prototype (working model) before writing specifications on weapons which might be technically impossible.

• Allowed the services—Army, Navy and Air Force—to demand a weapon system that ignored cost implications and existing technology.

• Rewarded complex and expensive systems and penalized designers and manufacturers for developing simpler and less expensive weapons.

Dr. Pierre M. Sprey, a former Pentagon weapons designer, said that under the existing system at the Defense Department, "interesting technological possibilities become user requirements without any need for the user to concern himself with future cost."

Defense Contractors. The leading critic of the manufacturers who make weapons systems was Dr. F. M. Scherer, a University of Michigan economics professor and author. "The weapons industry is in its worst disarray since the late 1940s," he said. According to Scherer and other witnesses, defense contractors:

• Have devoted their primary resources to winning defense contracts, not to producing weapons.

• Were blindly optimistic on cost estimates when bidding for weapons contracts when they knew full well their estimates would be exceeded.

"One simply cannot expect weapons suppliers to devote their top resources to anything but winning new orders when their very survival depends upon such orders," Scherer told the committee.

Excerpts from the five days of hearings:

Testimony Dec. 3

John C. Stennis, chairman of the Senate Armed Services Committee, explained why he was holding the hearings:

"If the weapons we develop are so costly that we cannot afford enough of them and if they are so technically complex that they are unreliable and difficult to maintain, we have done the nation a disservice by developing and procuring them.... I am a lawyer by training and, quite frankly, the discussion of weapon systems in the Congress has seemed to me to be sadly deficient in its understanding of process and procedures....

"I hope that in these brief initial hearings we will be able to begin to understand some of the underlying problems of the weapon systems acquisition process: how the system functions, why individuals and institutions within it behave as they do, what their real incentives are, what sort of reforms in the process will give us a better product.

"We're getting into something I've been wanting to get into for a long time...down to the fundamentals, get the problem described...get it on the record for staff analysis as well as the press."

Gilbert W. Fitzhugh, chairman of the President's Blue Ribbon Defense Panel (1969-1970) and chairman of the board of directors, Metropolitan Life Insurance Company:

"One of the most urgent needs for improvement for the entire weapons systems acquisition process is more effective operational test and evaluation.... Operational testing is done to determine, to the extent possible, whether such systems and materiel can meet operational requirements. It must provide advance knowledge as to what their capabilities and limitations will be when they are subjected to the stresses of the environment for which they were designed (usually combat).... Funding throughout the Department of Defense has been and continues to be inadequate to support most necessary operational testing.... In fact, there is no agency that can even identify the funds that are being spent on operational testing.

"Evaluation type functions, including test and evaluation, should not be within the control of either those charged with the responsibility for acquiring weapons systems nor of those charged with the responsibility for using the weapon system as an end product. Dominance of the evaluation function by either the producer or the user has a strong tendency to weight any evaluation."

The services spend so much time "building up a file to defend the program (a weapon system) that they don't build the plane." Too many people in Congress are looking into the Pentagon's business. Committee inquiry, which is valuable in itself, should be limited to perhaps two or four committees. A completely new set of procurement regulations is needed. "They're so bogged down in paper work over there (Pentagon) they can't do the job they're supposed to do." Merely improving procedures has not and will not work as a solution to the problem. Rather, a systematic change in the acquisition process is called for.

Dr. John S. Foster Jr., director of defense research and engineering for the Department of Defense:

"From the outset, this Administration has been concerned about cost growth of weapon systems, the lack of authority and stature of program managers and shortfalls in performance or delay in some important systems. Since taking office, Secretaries Laird and Packard have placed heavy emphasis on improving procedures in these areas."

The "most important single element for ensuring the proper execution of programs is the selection of qualified program managers." Six months ago, only 12 flag officers were assigned as program managers; now, 20 of the 82 managers are of flag rank. A school—the Defense Systems Management School, Fort Belvoir, Virginia—is handling an increasing number of officers to participate in the weapons acquisition process.

The new position of Deputy Director of Defense (test and evaluation) was created to provide "over-all supervision of test and evaluation that heretofore had been lacking.

"The services have changed their organizations to ensure that a command independent of the developer participates in all operational testing and evaluation. This command renders a separate report, through a strong service focal point, to the chief of the service to assist him with his later decisions."

Dec. 6

J. A. Stockfish, member of the Rand Corporation, specializing in weapons acquisition:

"Since it is the military user who must assume the ultimate responsibility for commanding military operations in the field and in conducting war, it is their preferences that should dominate the decision-making process.... Since World War II the technicians have been making the decisions.... High technical precision has been equated with good weaponry. This is not true."

Stuart Symington (D Mo.), a member of the committee:

Why is the United States not getting more for the billions it spent on research and development?

Stockfish:

"A large part is all too frequently caused by overspecifying the system. The user is often as much at fault because he also insists on these specifications."

The committee should give the military an incentive to do more testing by placing greater budget restraints on the Penta-

---

Combat Readiness

The General Accounting Office (GAO) May 8, 1972, issued a report on the readiness capabilities of the Strategic Army Forces—general purpose forces relied upon for military actions short of nuclear war.

"It would be difficult for STRAF (Strategic Army Forces) units to deploy quickly at full strength because many units are not combat ready," the GAO report stated. More than one-third of the essential equipment for combat and combat-support operations was not functional.

The GAO report also found that:

- "About 83 percent of the M-60 tanks available to units of two divisions had deficiencies which seriously impaired their ability to perform effectively."

- Fifty-five percent of the tracked vehicles inspected were unable to perform their primary mission.

- In three of the divisions studied no stock was available for about 25 percent of the repair parts authorized for stockage.

- "No follow up actions were being taken on unfilled requisitions."

The GAO report concluded: "The high turnover of personnel, lack of qualified personnel and funding restrictions which were beyond the direct control of the divisions, prevented them from achieving and maintaining a high state of readiness. The two divisions were being manned almost entirely with Vietnam returnees who had only a few months of service remaining..."

The only portion of the GAO report which was released to the public was a four-page summary of their classified report.

---

gon. "Whenever you encounter assertions that this is the most cost-effective system...find out whether the model or theory was based on sufficient or valid testing.... Has the model been validated by some independent testing?

"I would not be too disturbed at a three-fold cost overrun if the system was good," but all too frequently the system overruns do not result in solid weapon systems.

Dr. F. M. Scherer, professor of economics at the University of Michigan, defense consultant and author:

The insecurity of defense contractors has been "a major source of incentive breakdowns and disfunctional behavior. Today, with the weapons industry in its worst state of disarray since the late 1940s, the problem is even more critical. One simply cannot expect weapons suppliers to devote their top resources to anything but winning new orders when their very survival depends upon such orders. One cannot expect them to estimate costs and technical risks accurately when optimistic estimates enhance the prospect of capturing a new program assignment. One cannot expect them to refrain from hoarding personnel under whatever contractual blanket they can find when long-run organizational viability demands that they keep the team together....

"Contractors must somehow be induced to maximize output given their limited resources, not to maximize the quantity of resources they can spread over a restricted array of programs.

"It must be made crystal clear through word and deed that organizations which consistently do a good job will be allowed to grow while those which repeatedly fail will find their support progressively withdrawn. This is admittedly a radical proposal. But I am convinced that unless we move in that direction, channeling the insecurity of national security contractors in constructive rather than counter-productive directions, we are not likely to eliminate the intolerable inefficiency and waste presently pervading the weapons acquisition process."

Dec. 7

Robert Perry, director of system acquisition studies and specialist on European aircraft acquisition, Rand Corporation:

"An analysis of programs of the 1950s and the 1960s has disclosed that in terms of schedules, cost and weapons performance which vary from those specified at program inception, the prediction and control of system acquisition programs in general did not significantly improve.... In the 1960s typical major programs in all three services continued to exhibit an average cost growth of about 40 percent (after corrections for inflation and changes in quantity of items purchased); schedule slippages of about 15 percent; and weapon system performance that characteristically deviated by 30 or 40 percent from original specifications.

"It appears that changes to system specifications imposed after programs had begun accounted for about half of cost growth.... Engineering difficulties encountered in the course of development accounted for at least an additional one third; and native (inherent) imprecision of cost estimating processes was responsible for the residual 15 to 20 percent."

"Separate the development phase of weapon system acquisition from the subsequent production phase, both sequentially and contractually...conduct the initial research and development for a new weapon in a highly austere manner, concentrating first on demonstrating system performance and deferring more expensive tasks of detailed production design and reliability demonstration until both the technical and the requirement uncertainties have been very substantially reduced."

Arthur J. Alexander, specialist on Soviet aircraft acquisition, Rand Corporation, described the Soviet Union's process:

"The competitive system of design and the importance attached to production have promoted a philosophy based on simplicity, commonality and inheritance. Simplicity implies an unadorned product which performs only what is required; commonality means the use of standardized parts and assemblies as well as the sharing of design features among different aircraft; design inheritance is an intergenerational concept which favors modification rather than introduction of entirely new products.

"Ironically, Soviet aircraft production is similar to the way the American industry operated before the government began to participate heavily in project management...."

Dec. 8

Dr. William B. McLean, technical director of the Naval Undersea Center (projects designer), San Diego, Calif.:

"Based on some 30 years experience with military procurement, I believe the weapon systems acquisition process is now dangerously inadequate because...the need for development prototypes to demonstrate technical feasibility before the writing of military requirements has been ignored; the total acquisition process rewards the design of complex and expensive systems and penalizes work of simpler and, therefore, less expensive ones; the budgetary process has become a ritual with no content, which is occupying more than 50 percent of the productive time of our best technical people at the laboratory level and the full time of large numbers of technical people in Washington."

The development and testing of prototype weapons prior to procurement and prior to the writing of detailed specifications for performance is essential to lowering the cost of

weapons development. "Requirements (for what a weapon should be able to do) written before the demonstration of a developmental prototype are worse than useless, because they have the effect of interfering with and even excluding, technically possible means of approach."

Dr. Pierre M. Sprey, systems manager of Enviro Control Inc. (water pollution devices); former systems analyst at the Pentagon, developing paper studies of light-weight fighters; consultant to Dr. Wayne Smith of Henry Kissinger's White House foreign policy staff:

"The weapons cost explosion has reached the stage where national defense is being severely impaired. Furthermore, I believe that the issues involved are so pervasive and fundamental that we cannot continue to treat this problem on a technical case-by-case basis; instead the issue must be raised to the level of national policy."

The military is requesting such complex weaponry that the development stages are taking years longer, the final product is produced in smaller numbers to cover cost overruns, the weapon produced is more likely to suffer mechanical breakdown than more austere versions of the same weapon. The military would get more weapons, better service at less money if the services were forced to write specifications which took into account existing technology and severe cost restraints.

PROCUREMENT POLICY. In a related inquiry, the Subcommittee on Priorities and Economy in Government of the Joint Economic Committee held one day of hearings April 28, 1971, on defense contract procurement policies.

Vice Admiral H. G. Rickover, director, division of Navy reactors, Atomic Energy Commission; and deputy commander for nuclear propulsion of the Naval ships system command:

"Today, the businessman who demonstrates acuity in business acquisitions, cash flow and financial manipulation gets more recognition in the business world than his counterpart who spends his time trying to manufacture high quality products efficiently. Consequently, many large companies today are virtually unmanaged while their officers are busy acquiring new businesses, lobbying for more favorable laws and regulations or devising new ways to make their actual profits look higher or lower depending on whether they are talking to stockholders, to the customer or to the Internal Revenue Service.

"Large defense contractors can let costs come out where they will and count on getting relief from the Defense Department through changes and claims, relaxation of procurement regulations and laws, government loans, follow-on sole source contracts or other escape mechanisms. Wasteful subcontracting practices, inadequate controls, shop loafing, and production errors mean little to these contractors since they will make their money whether their product is good or bad, whether the price is fair or higher than it should be, whether delivery is on time or late.

"The Atomic Energy Commission and the General Services Administration report that the computer industry as a whole refuses to provide the cost and pricing data required by the law, even though the government buys about $3-billion worth of computer equipment each year. I am told the same is true in the tire, ball bearing and communications industries. I am plagued by this problem in my work.

"This disregard for the law exists because the Defense Department does not enforce the Act. The Defense Department has been unwilling to require compliance from large defense contractors. Computer manufacturers, steel manufacturers, nickel producers, forging suppliers, divisions of some of the nation's largest defense contractors—whole segments of the defense industry—refuse to comply with the Truth-in-Negotiations Act."

CONGRESS BAILED OUT GIANT DEFENSE CONTRACTOR

The Senate Aug. 2, 1971, on a 49-48 roll-call vote, cleared for the President's signature a bill (HR 8432—PL 92-70) authorizing a federal guarantee of $250-million in bank loans for the Lockheed Aircraft Corporation, the nation's largest defense contractor.

The House had passed the bill in identical form by an equally close roll-call vote, 192-189, on July 30.

President Nixon signed the bill Aug. 9.

The Senate's action ended an effort which lasted almost six months and became one of the most controversial issues of the session. Opponents in the Senate survived three attempts to end a filibuster on the bill, but they could not muster support for damaging amendments to the bill.

The bill was passed in much the same form as it was proposed by the administration May 13. In the interim, to gain broader support, it had been broadened into a $2-billion loan-guarantee authorization for failing major businesses.

The House took up the bill July 30. With floor amendments, the House stripped the bill down to a $250-million guarantee authorization for Lockheed only and passed it by a three-vote margin. The Senate on Aug. 2 abandoned its own bill (S 2308), which it had been debating since July 21, and passed the House bill without amendment.

In the Senate, William Proxmire (D Wis.) led the opposition. John G. Tower (R Texas), ranking minority member of the Banking, Housing and Urban Affairs Committee, served as floor leader for the bill, supported by Chairman John Sparkman (D Ala.).

Chairman Wright Patman (D Texas) of the House Banking and Currency Committee and William B. Widnall (R N.J.), ranking minority member, led supporters of the amended bill in the House. Patman had originally opposed the Lockheed bill. Ten members of the committee filed individual views with the report, opposing both a broad bill and one limited to Lockheed. Five filed views opposing the broad version.

Background

The Lockheed issue developed soon after Rolls-Royce Ltd., the British manufacturer of jet engines for Lockheed's L-1011 Tristar airliner, declared bankruptcy Feb. 4, 1971. Reeling from large penalties assessed by the Defense Department for cost overruns on production of the C-5A military transport aircraft and under other defense contracts, Lockheed needed additional credit to go into production with its Tristar and needed the Tristar to stay in business. (*C-5A troubles, p. 88*)

The possibility of a government loan guarantee had been considered briefly in 1970 by leaders among a group of 24 banks which eventually agreed to lend Lockheed $400-million, without a guarantee, to complete development of the Tristar. The idea was raised again, soon after Rolls-Royce went bankrupt, when the banks indicated they would not extend further credit to Lockheed.

Cautious support and determined opposition met the legislation the Nixon administration sent to Congress May 13 to guarantee $250-million in bank loans to the beleaguered Lockheed Aircraft Corporation.

Treasury Secretary John Connally sent the draft bill to Congress.

"The failure of major business enterprises," Connally said, "can have serious national and regional consequences, including the causing of substantial unemployment, as well as other business failures. To provide for credit to avoid such consequences, government guarantees may be warranted."

Drafted in general terms, the bill did not mention Lockheed by name. If Congress increased the dollar total of guarantees permitted, the bill would have authorized the same kind of assistance to other major companies.

The Defense Department announced May 7 that it would start making progress payments to Lockheed from a $200-million contingency fund established in the fiscal 1971 federal budget to enable the company to meet its financing needs while continuing to produce the C-5A.

The employment aspect of the Lockheed loan guarantee made the administration's proposal difficult for many members of Congress to oppose. Yet a number hedged their support. Some posed conditions: that Lockheed be required to use American engines on the Tristar; that the legislation be broadened so that it would apply to future cases involving other companies or that Lockheed's management be required to resign.

Labor's position was crucial to many members. George Meany, president of the AFL-CIO, publicly announced support for the loan guarantee. But some influential labor spokesmen regarded Lockheed as a "runaway" because of its contract with Rolls-Royce.

President Nixon at San Clemente, Calif., May 5 told a news conference the major factor, in his view, was the unemployment that would be caused by a Lockheed bankruptcy and consequent abandonment of the L-1011 program. "Lockheed is one of the nation's great companies," Nixon said. "It provides an enormous employment lift to this part of the country, and I am going to be heavily influenced by the need to see to it that Southern California, after taking the disappointment of not getting the SST, which would, of course, have brought many, many jobs to this part of the country—that California does not have the additional jolt of losing Lockheed."

Connally said Lockheed had employed 17,000 persons in the airbus program, of whom some 7,000 had been laid off because of financial difficulties and the uncertainty of the project. The payroll for the 17,000, he said, was $5-million per week. In addition, the Secretary said, 14,000 persons were employed by the principal suppliers

(Continued on p. 89)

History of C-5A Controversy, Lockheed Involvement

In October 1965, the Pentagon drafted one of the most sophisticated "total package procurement" contracts ever awarded by the Defense Department. The contract, won by Lockheed, called for the development and construction of 120 giant transport aircraft—the C-5A Galaxy. The plane was to be nearly as long as a football field.

By setting a fixed-price on the project, the Pentagon hoped to eliminate the expensive cost overruns that had for so long inflated the defense budget. Yet, written into the fine print of the agreement was a web of complex mutual assurances designed to protect both parties from extraordinary financial penalties.

A Defense Department spokesman who had been involved over the years with negotiations between the Pentagon and Lockheed told Congressional Quarterly the total package procurement contract for the C-5A was "the most sophisticated we've ever done. We've never tied anything up like this one before." It was designed so "neither of us would lose our shirts."

Fitzgerald Testimony. The C-5A program remained in relative obscurity until the fall of 1968. The Air Force had given little indication that the program was already running far above original cost estimates.

On Nov. 13, 1968, the Joint Economic Committee heard testimony from a civilian accountant, A. E. Fitzgerald, who was deputy for management systems in the Office of the Assistant Secretary of the Air Force. In response to a question by Proxmire as to whether the C-5A program was running $2-billion above initial cost estimates, Fitzgerald replied that Proxmire's figure was "approximately right."

Fitzgerald was later dismissed from the position and became a consultant with the Joint Economic Committee.

New Contract. During 1969, the pressure exerted by the Joint Economic Committee and broad national publicity of the estimated cost overruns caused the Air Force to renegotiate its contract with Lockheed in an effort to bring costs down. In June, the Pentagon announced that the number of aircraft initially requested was being reduced from 120 to 81.

New cost estimates for Lockheed's share of total expenditures for producing the reduced number of aircraft were put at from $4-billion to $4.5-billion. Lockheed and Deputy Secretary of Defense David Packard continued to negotiate throughout 1969 and 1970, trying to reach agreement on who was going to absorb the losses on the program.

After 17 months of negotiation, Lockheed agreed Feb. 1, 1971, to take a $200-million fixed-loss on the C-5A contract. The agreement was reached with the understanding that still another contract might have to be negotiated if the company's financial stability continued to deteriorate.

Losing an Engine. Within minutes after the Senate Oct. 6, 1971, passed the $21-billion defense procurement bill (HR 8687)—which authorized funds for such weapon systems as the ABM, the F-14 jet fighter and the C-5A—the Air Force announced that eight days earlier a jet engine on one of the giant C-5A transport planes had dropped off onto a runway at Altus Air

Force Base, Okla., while the pilot was making routine checks before takeoff.

Pentagon spokesman Jerry W. Friedheim apologized to reporters for the delay in disclosing the incident and denied charges that the information had been released with an eye to the Senate's action.

When the announcement about the engine was first made at the Pentagon Oct. 6, seven of the 47 operational C-5As were already grounded. The following day 15 more were grounded pending safety tests and on Oct. 12 the entire fleet was prohibited from flying.

Two weeks before the Sept. 29 incident, the Air Force announced that a crack in the wing of another C-5A had been detected.

GAO Report On Lockheed. Investigators for the General Accounting Office filed a partial report with the Joint Economic Committee in March 1972, which documented charges that the Air Force knowingly made overpayments amounting to $1.1-billion to Lockheed Aircraft Corp. The report was released March 27.

According to the report, the money was turned over to Lockheed as progress payments on the C-5A jet transport, manufactured primarily at the Lockheed plant in Marietta, Ga.

(The report was not considered complete, according to Comptroller General Elmer B. Staats, head of the GAO, because it had not been reviewed by the Air Force or Lockheed for comment prior to release by the Joint Economic Committee.)

The GAO report calculated that an additional $705-million in overpayments also had been made. Proxmire said the $400-million overpayment by itself "exceeded the entire net worth of the Lockheed Aircraft Corp. as of Dec. 29, 1968."

Report On C-5A. Proxmire April 6, 1972, read into the *Congressional Record* the full text of a GAO report on the C-5A. The GAO report stated that:

• During one six-month period in 1971 there were 3,327 reported failures in C-5A landing gear.

• "The wing continues to be one of the major problem areas on the C-5A" and wing fatigue tests were not scheduled for completion until September 1974—two-and-one-half-years behind schedule.

• Final delivery of the 81 aircraft was scheduled for May 1973 which was a 13-month delay from the original schedule. Initially, 120 aircraft were to be delivered by April 1972.

• Of 15 aircraft that were accepted by the Air Force during eight months of 1971, each plane showed an average of 257 deficiencies in Air Force specifications.

Air Force Secretary Robert C. Seamans Jr. told the House Appropriations Defense Subcommittee Jan. 25 that training flights of the C-5A have been restricted to make the fleet last longer.

"Yes, I am disappointed in the airplane," Seamans said. "Not from the standpoint of its performance measured in terms of range, speed and the requirements for landing. But from the standpoint of the structure itself. It was designed too close to the margin."

Seamans' testimony was released April 6 after censoring by the Defense Department.

(Continued from p. 87)

for the L-1011. Lockheed—the nation's largest defense contractor—had 35,000 subcontracting companies, according to Connally, most of which were small businesses. If Lockheed went bankrupt, the Secretary said, the $1.4-billion invested in the L-1011 would be written off "as best it can be" by the investors, with a substantial loss in revenues to the government.

House Committee Action

STUDY. The House Banking and Currency Committee held hearings on HR 8432 in July. The committee July 8 received in executive session a staff report recommending rejection of the proposed Lockheed loan guarantee bill (HR 8432). The result of two months' work by the majority staff, the study concluded:

• There was substantial risk of default and loss to the government in the proposed guarantee.

• There would be great pressure to give Lockheed preferential treatment in defense contracts.

• There was doubt that lack of the guarantee would force Lockheed into reorganization under bankruptcy law and that severe unemployment would result.

• The guarantee would be fundamentally inconsistent with a free-enterprise system, would involve government favoritism toward Lockheed in relation to its competitors and might lead to similar guarantees for other aerospace firms.

• The request for the guarantee might rest on information not made available to Congress or might involve "a game of chicken" or a bluff.

The staff material included a year-old Defense Department study, previously classified, which said Lockheed would have to sell about 370 of its Tristars to break even. Lockheed's cost estimates had placed the break-even point more recently at 255 to 265 aircraft. At 252 aircraft sales, according to the study, the firm would lose at least $359-million. Lockheed predicted July 8 it would sell at least 400 of its airbuses.

REPORT. The House Banking and Currency Committee by 23-11 vote July 26 reported the bill (HR 8432—H Rept 92-379) authorizing the federal government to guarantee loans of up to $250-million to individual businesses, to a total of $2-billion in outstanding guarantees at any one time.

Prospects for passage of the bill in the House improved dramatically July 15 when Chairman Patman of the banking committee changed his position from opposition to support for a bill limited to a guarantee for Lockheed. Patman had announced his opposition to the bill May 4.

A source close to Patman said the chairman had decided reluctantly to support the limited bill. Patman was said to believe the bill should be brought to a vote in the House because the Administration regarded the Lockheed situation as an emergency.

House Floor Action

The House by a roll-call vote of 192-189 July 30 passed HR 8432 after accepting amendments whittling down its provisions to provide only a $250-million loan guarantee for the Lockheed Corporation, as originally proposed by the Administration, instead of the broader bill reported by the House Banking and Currency Committee.

Under an agreement among the majority and minority committee leadership, Chairman Patman and ranking minority member Widnall, four amendments were offered by Rep. Ashley to return the bill to a form similar to that of the original administration bill. The amendments were accepted as a package by a voice vote.

Ashley's amendments limited the loan guarantee authority to $250-million, the amount requested by Lockheed, and substituted the chairman of the Securities and Exchange Commission on the three-member Emergency Loan Guarantee Board for the president of the Federal Reserve bank of the district in which a firm applying for a guarantee was located.

The amendments required the board to limit interest rates on guaranteed loans to reflect the reduced risk to the lender and to charge a guarantee fee to the borrower that was at least equal to the difference between the interest cost of a guaranteed loan and prevailing interest costs. The amendments further struck out a provision for congressional review of proposed loan guarantees.

John D. Dingell (D Mich.) offered an amendment requiring the General Accounting Office to make a detailed audit of each applicant for a guarantee and report the results to the loan guarantee board and to Congress. The House accepted the amendment by a teller vote, 163-76.

The House rejected an amendment by Chairman William M. Colmer (D Miss.) of the Rules Committee to limit the government guarantee to 90 percent of the loans involved. The amendment failed by a recorded teller vote, 176-205.

A second Dingell amendment was rejected by a voice vote. This would have given the government the highest lien on the borrower's property and first priority for payment under bankruptcy law. The amendment failed on a voice vote. An amendment to Dingell's amendment, offered by Sam Gibbons (D Fla), previously was approved by voice vote. Gibbons' amendment explicitly preserved the priority of employees for their wages, which Dingell's amendment brought into question.

H. R. Gross (R Iowa) was unsuccessful in an attempt to kill the bill with an amendment to strike the enacting clause. Pointing out that the hour was late, Gross said, "By adopting the motion, we can settle this issue the way it ought to be settled—by killing this monstrosity—and go home promptly." His move failed by a voice vote.

Senate Committee Action

The Senate Banking, Housing and Urban Affairs Committee July 19 reported S 2308 (S Rept 92-270) authorizing the federal government to guarantee loans up to $250-million for individual businesses, up to a total of $2-billion in outstanding guarantees at any one time.

Proxmire Views. In a long dissenting statement, Proxmire charged that S 2308 was simply the original Lockheed guarantee bill in disguise. "It is apparent that the proposed Lockheed guarantee has practically no benefit and serious disadvantages," he said. "It is a big-business giveaway of the worst sort and should be rejected by the Congress."

(Continued on p. 92)

C-5A Overruns Demonstrated Congressional...

The massive cost overruns experienced by Lockheed Aircraft Corp. in producing the giant C-5A jet transport illustrate some of the difficulties Congress faces in trying to check rising defense costs. The following study of one phase in this cost overrun problem also highlighted some of the limitations of the General Accounting Office (GAO) in its role as Congress' investigative arm and watchdog agency.

Cost increases of more than $1-billion for procurement of 81 Air Force C-5A jet transports prompted the Joint Economic Committee in 1970 to request an investigation by the GAO of financially troubled Lockheed, developer of the C-5A. The committee asked for a thorough audit of the contractor's "cash-flow" statement (an account of expenditures and receipts for both defense and commercial programs). *(C-5A background, box p. 88)*

Without a thorough congressionally initiated audit of the company's books, said Senators William Proxmire (D Wis.) and Richard S. Schweiker (R Pa.) and Rep. William S. Moorhead (D Pa.), Congress would not have sufficient knowledge about Lockheed's shaky financial situation to make an evaluation on appropriating additional money for the project.

Proxmire said Lockheed could go bankrupt whether additional funds were provided or not. He also charged that some of the money appropriated for the C-5A had been transferred into the company's commercial airliner project—the L-1011 Tristar—and, consequently, that costs on the C-5A had gone up (from an estimated $31.8-million per plane in 1965 to $66-million in February 1971).

The GAO never conducted the thorough audit requested by members of the Joint Economic Committee. The Defense Department refused to allow it despite contentions by Proxmire and Schweiker that such an audit was within the statutory authority of the GAO.

Instead of a detailed audit, Comptroller General Elmer B. Staats, head of the GAO, announced Dec. 3, 1970, that the Pentagon was allowing only a "review" of the crucial cash-flow statement. Proxmire said that limitations on the "review" were so severe that the value of even bothering with the study was questionable.

According to the agreement reached with the Defense Department, GAO staff members were allowed to look at Lockheed's books, but they could not write down any figures, remove the material from the Pentagon or release to Congress any of the figures they saw concerning Lockheed's commercial problems.

The Pentagon restricted the GAO to an evaluation of whether or not Lockheed would be able to complete C-5A production if additional money were appropriated. No facts or figures about the interrelated commercial ventures of Lockheed accompanied the GAO report.

When Congress had to vote on the Lockheed loan guarantee six months later, they had no independent analysis of Lockheed's overall financial situation upon which to base their decision.

What Went Wrong. A detailed Congressional Quarterly study of a series of letters exchanged between the Defense Department, the GAO and the Joint Economic Committee, plus a review of various key statutes, showed several factors which contributed to the GAO's inability to conduct a full audit:

• Congress initially failed to demand a thorough GAO study—one which would have disclosed the full scope of Lockheed's dilemma. Long after it was known that the C-5A program had incurred cost overruns in excess of $1-billion, the Senate rejected a Proxmire-Schweiker amendment to the defense procurement authorization bill (HR 17123—PL 91-441) which, among other things, would have required a thorough GAO study. The amendment was rejected Aug. 26, 1970, by a 30-to-48 roll-call vote.

• The GAO failed to offer, over the years, an interpretation of the law thereby permitting the Pentagon to renegotiate the Lockheed contract without regard to normal contract procedures. The responsibility of interpreting contract laws affecting any government agency rests with the GAO.

• With regard to conducting an audit of Lockheed's cash-flow statement, the GAO failed initially to exert its statutory authority until pressed by the Joint Economic Committee. (Proxmire and Schweiker still questioned whether the GAO flexed its statutory muscles to the fullest.)

• The Defense Department refused to accommodate requests of the Joint Economic Committee and did not allow the GAO to gather detailed information for presentation to Congress.

Government Accounting Office

The Joint Economic Committee was the most aggressive group in Congress in seeking explanations for the C-5A cost overruns. But as Richard Kaufman, economic consultant to the committee, told Congressional Quarterly, "There's a limit to the number of times we can hold hearings on this one subject." Instead of more hearings the committee, in the spring of 1970, sought the aid of the GAO.

As an arm of the legislative branch, one of the GAO functions is to respond to congressional requests for investigative and evaluative audits of government agencies and programs.

The Joint Economic Committee (regarded as a study committee) does not have the authority to subpoena records such as those held by the Defense Department on the C-5A. Only legislative and investigative committees (the Armed Services Committees, for example) have this authority, and none of these committees used the power to investigate C-5A cost overruns.

Proxmire, who was chairman of the Joint Economic Subcommittee on Economy in Government during the 91st Congress, first requested that the GAO obtain information on Lockheed's financial status in a March 10, 1970, letter to the Comptroller General. In response to the request, Comptroller General Staats forwarded the Joint Economic Committee Lockheed's annual report and certain financial statements provided by the Air Force concerning expenditures on defense projects. On May 12, Staats wrote Proxmire, saying that "we

...Ignorance of Key Financial Data

have been informed by Defense on April 27, that Lockheed's legal staff had reservations about release of certain financial data which the company considers extremely sensitive."

Senators Proxmire and Schweiker signed the following letter, dated Sept. 14, to the Comptroller General:

"Lockheed Aircraft Corp. has refused to make public the fundamental facts about its financial position. We have only their word that they are in grave financial difficulties.... There is, in fact, an appalling lack of specific knowledge as to Lockheed's real financial condition and its causes."

Proxmire and Schweiker then requested the GAO to find out what the firm's financial capabilities were "to complete and deliver the 81 aircraft...and what is the total amount which would have to be expended to insure the complete delivery of the 81 planes."

In a Nov. 19, 1970, letter to Proxmire, the Comptroller General said: "We have been unable to conduct a study of Lockheed's financial capability to deliver C-5A aircraft because we have not been able to gain access to the necessary data."

Confidential Relationship. As an alternative to a full audit, the GAO suggested that it merely examine the data in the hands of the Defense Department without removing it from their offices. After examination the GAO would then furnish Congress "only with our opinion as to whether Lockheed has the financial capability to deliver C-5A aircraft." A spokesman for the Office of the Secretary of Defense refused the alternative, saying "it would constitute a violation of the confidential relationship existing between the department and the contractor."

When Proxmire received word that the GAO was not going to conduct an audit, he wrote Staats Nov. 20 saying that not only was he "deeply disturbed" by the Defense Department's actions, but also "by GAO's passive refusal to assert the statutory authority that clearly gives it access to the information desired." Proxmire was referred to the U.S. Code, Title 31, Section 54, which states: "All departments and establishments shall furnish to the Comptroller General such information regarding the powers, duties, activities, organization, financial transactions and methods of business of their respective offices...and the Comptroller General...shall, for the purpose of securing such information, have access to and the right to examine any books, documents, papers or records of any such department or establishment."

Proxmire then charged that the Defense Department was "in direct violation of the law" and asked Staats what the GAO planned to do about it.

Limited Review. Fourteen days after Proxmire's letter to the Comptroller General, Staats informed the Joint Economic Committee that the Secretary of Defense had changed his position. After further communication with Staats, the Defense Department decided to allow a GAO "review" of Lockheed's cash-flow statement.

A GAO representative would be allowed to look at the material but could "not copy or otherwise repeat data" about what he found. The GAO was not permitted "to disclose the reasons" for its opinion as a condition of the agreement with the Defense Department.

James H. Hammond, head of the GAO team that worked on Lockheed's cash-flow statement, said that if Congress wanted the confidential information on Lockheed's commercial difficulties, a subpoena would probably be necessary. Since neither the GAO nor the Joint Economic Committee had the authority to subpoena records, legislative committees would have to take the initiative.

The Senate and House Armed Services Committees and Appropriations Committees would probably be where such a subpoena would logically originate, Hammond said. As pointed out by a Joint Committee staff member, however, these four legislative committees have been "traditionally friendly" to the military services on these matters.

The Comptroller General subsequently issued a statement defending the GAO's position in the dispute with the Joint Economic Committee. He said that the GAO "has a proper concern" for the Defense Department's negotiations with Lockheed. He explained that the GAO has "no legal authority to demand from the contractors their records relating to commercial—that is, non-government—transactions. The fact that Lockheed's ability to make delivery is dependent upon its over-all financial situation has, therefore, complicated our ability to develop the data needed to reach such an opinion."

Interpretation of Contract Law

In dealing with another phase of the C-5A dispute, Comptroller General Staats turned back all queries concerning the legality of the Defense Department's authority to renegotiate the Lockheed contract, by citing a 1958 law (PL 85-804) that was broadly interpreted by the Pentagon.

PL 85-804 authorized department heads to modify defense contracts when it was determined that such action was necessary to "facilitate the national defense" in times of emergency. The Defense Department interpretation was used to renegotiate the C-5A contract several times since 1965 to cover unexpected costs totaling $1-billion and to set a fixed-loss of $200-million on Lockheed.

Prior to the C-5A controversy, the department had renegotiated a total of only $60-million in cost overruns between 1958 and 1969 under provisions of PL 85-804.

In lieu of any other interpretation of PL 85-804, the Defense Department was within legal boundaries in renegotiating the C-5A project. However, one of the GAO's important functions was to interpret statutes involving contracts with government agencies. Any GAO legal opinion, with certain exceptions, has the force of law and is binding on all government agencies unless decided otherwise in the federal courts.

No alternative interpretation of PL 85-804 was offered by the GAO, despite the latitude such a law gave the Department of Defense.

Senate Floor Action

The Senate by a 49-48 roll call Aug. 2 cleared HR 8432 for the President's signature.

Final action came after nearly two full weeks of debate on the Senate floor and after the Senate dropped its own bill (S 2308), which authorized emergency loan guarantees up to $2-billion to major business enterprises, in favor of the House bill for Lockheed alone.

The Senate debated its measure July 21-24 and 26-31, including Saturday sessions July 24 and 31. Proxmire and his allies sought principally to delay passage until Congress recessed Aug. 6. Supporters tried to shut off debate so the bill could be enacted before the recess.

The House, which initially had tried to stay in step with the Senate in order to avoid a conference or an impasse on differing versions of the bill, ultimately anticipated the Senate with passage of the limited version.

DEBATE HIGHLIGHTS

July 21. Proxmire moved to send the bill back to committee for further hearings, with instructions that the measure was to be reported back to the Senate not later than July 29. Sparkman moved to table Proxmire's motion. Proxmire urged delay in voting on the Sparkman motion, arguing that the printed record of hearings on the bill was not yet available and could not have been studied by Senators who did not attend them. Sparkman's motion carried by a roll-call vote, 56-36.

July 22. Majority Whip Robert C. Byrd (D W.Va.) announced that a motion would be entered July 23 to invoke cloture on debate on the bill. Proxmire said the bill deserved four to five weeks of discussion. Bennett and Brock argued that Lockheed would be in bankruptcy by the time the bill passed if debate continued that long.

July 23. Byrd announced that the first vote on cloture would be held July 26.

Proxmire displayed a half-page advertisement from *The Milwaukee Journal* in the form of an open letter attacking him for his opposition to the bill and threatening a boycott of Wisconsin products. The letter was signed by the National Group for the Preservation of the Aviation Industry, Marietta, Ga., which described itself as an organization representing aerospace workers.

July 24. Tower read President Nixon's and Defense Secretary Melvin R. Laird's statements issued earlier the same day in support of the bill. Weicker read Laird's July 23 statement in which the Secretary conceded that there was disagreement on the bill within the Administration.

July 26. The Senate rejected the first cloture motion by a roll-call vote, 42-47. A second motion was filed, and the vote was scheduled for July 28.

Stevenson argued that the bill, though broadened, was still designed primarily to accommodate Lockheed. He urged support for his amendment to eliminate the Lockheed exemption. By a roll-call vote, 38-45, a motion by Tower to table Stevenson's amendment was rejected.

July 27. Stevenson continued his case against the Lockheed exemption. Proxmire accused Tower of delaying a vote on Stevenson's amendment because of the surprising strength shown in the rejection of Tower's motion the previous day.

July 28. The Senate refused for the second time, by a 59-39 roll-call vote, to impose cloture and end debate on S 2308.

The cloture motion required a majority of two-thirds of those present and voting—66 votes—for adoption. Supporters of the bill thus fell seven votes short of thwarting the effort of opponents to debate the legislation until Congress began its summer recess Aug. 6. Proponents immediately filed a motion for a third attempt to close off debate. The vote was scheduled for July 30.

July 29. George McGovern (D S.D.) offered an amendment to double the loan guarantee authority of the bill (S 2308) by adding $2-billion for guaranteed loans for farmers and small businessmen. Congress could not justify assistance for major businesses, McGovern said, unless it provided similar help for others. The Senate rejected the amendment by a roll-call vote of 18-75.

Proxmire cited studies by the Transportation Department, the National Aeronautics and Space Administration and an unnamed group of executives and engineers employed by "a number of highly reputable aerospace firms," all of which, he said, showed that the airline market would not support both Lockheed and the McDonnell-Douglas Corporation, maker of the DC-10 airliner. Tower disputed Proxmire's conclusions. He referred to a study by McDonnell-Douglas and one by the Federal Aviation Administration (part of the Transportation Department), both of which showed the market was adequate, he said.

July 30. The third attempt to invoke cloture (end debate) failed by a roll-call vote of 53-37. A majority of two-thirds of those present and voting, or 60, was necessary to close off debate.

July 31. By unanimous consent the Senate agreed to take up the House bill (HR 8432) on Aug. 2 and limit debate to two hours plus 20 minutes for any amendment or motion. The order for the fourth cloture vote was withdrawn.

Proxmire argued that the loan guarantee was not necessary and that there would be more jobs in the aerospace industry if Lockheed left the commercial field. He said either the American banks that had already lent $400-million to Lockheed or British banks with a stake in Rolls-Royce were likely to lend Lockheed additional funds without the guarantee. Even if Lockheed went bankrupt, he said, the firm would continue at least the 85 percent of its work which was under defense contracts, though under new management.

Aug. 2. Ted Stevens (R Alaska) offered an amendment to create a $200-million emergency loan guarantee fund for small business. Stevens said he did not intend to have his amendment called up for a vote. After he was assured by Sparkman that hearings would be held on small business problems, he withdrew it.

Hubert H. Humphrey (D Minn.) offered an amendment to extend the existing unemployment compensation program by 26 weeks and provide federal financing. On Tower's point of order the chair ruled that Humphrey's amendment was not germane and thus was not in order.

Cranston said the government bore substantial responsibility for Lockheed's problems under defense contracts.

In the final roll call, the Senate passed the House bill without amendment, 49-48, thus clearing it for the President.

MALFUNCTIONS, RISING COSTS, SLOWING PRODUCTION

The Senate Armed Services Subcommittee on Tactical Airpower held hearings March 28, 29 and 30, 1972 to evaluate the Navy's F-14 (Tomcat) jet fighter-bomber program.

Production slippage, cost increases, test malfunctions and the manufacturer's request that the original contract be renegotiated spurred the subcommittee to review the aircraft's history and future in terms of cost, performance and need.

Howard W. Cannon (D Nev.), chairman of the subcommittee, opened the hearings, stating that the committee had in years past backed procurement of the F-14 "as essential to the Navy and to our national security."

"But," he continued, "there are some unique circumstances this year in that the Grumman Aerospace Corp., the prime contractor, has advised the Navy it cannot proceed with production of the 48 aircraft in this year's budget...unless the Navy restructures its contract."

"The important issue surrounding the F-14 today is its cost," said Cannon. The Navy's budget request for fiscal 1973 included $734-million for continued procurement, research and development of 48 F-14 jet fighter-bombers.

Background

In February 1969, the Navy signed a contract with Grumman Aerospace Corp. for the development of the F-14. The contract provided for the production of up to 469 aircraft, but the Navy estimated it would buy a total of 722 aircraft (which would require a second contract). By March 1, 1972, the Navy order for F-14s had been reduced to 313 aircraft; funds for 86 had been authorized prior to fiscal 1973.

When the House Appropriations Committee reviewed the first year's development of the aircraft Dec. 3, 1969, it said: "It is the considered judgment of the committee that the Navy is moving too fast into production on the F-14 aircraft. The committee does not share the optimism of Navy officials that the F-14 aircraft development represents a low-risk program."

During the aircraft's second test flight Dec. 31, 1970, the test plane crashed and was destroyed after its hydraulic systems failed.

For two years, 1969 and 1970, said a House Appropriations Committee report late in 1971, the Navy "virtually ignored" growing production problems of the F-14 and did not disclose any of the difficulties or rising costs to Congress. Yet Grumman officials, when questioned on the Navy's optimistic reports, documented several instances where they had told the Navy of production problems which would be passed along in higher costs.

The estimated production costs for each F-14 increased from $13.1-million to $16.8-million between the time the contract was signed in 1969 through early 1972, according to the F-14 project manager, Rear Adm. L. A. Snead.

Another problem with the F-14 was revealed when the second phase of the program was about to go into production. The Navy was originally scheduled during fiscal 1972 to purchase 28 F-14A aircraft and 20 of the advanced F-14B planes. The difference in the two models, according to the House Appropriations Committee, "was almost as great as the performance differences between the F-4 Phantom jet fighter and the F-14A," the plane scheduled to replace the Phantom as the Navy's top jet fighter. The fiscal 1972 program was revised, however, to include only the purchase of the F-14A model. The F-14B aircraft development program slipped almost a full year behind schedule.

The Navy was advised by Grumman in a March 31, 1971, letter "that present data demonstrates that performance of (the F-14)...contract is commercially impracticable under the existing terms and conditions." Under pressure from Congress and the Navy, Grumman backed down from its initial request for a new contract on the F-14 program during fiscal 1972. Further production during fiscal 1973, however, appeared unlikely without a renegotiated contract, according to staff sources on the Senate Armed Services Committee.

The Armed Services and Appropriations Committees of the House and Senate conceded the need for an aircraft to succeed the Navy's old F-4 Phantom jet fighter. Although all four committees expressed reservations about the F-14 program, they authorized and appropriated the necessary funds (prior to fiscal 1973) for continued development and production—despite rising costs—for fewer aircraft.

Testimony March 28-29

Adm. Elmo R. Zumwalt Jr., chief of naval operations:

"The F-14 is an all-weather, high performance, carrier-based fighter....It will carry the long-range Phoenix missile, the Sparrow and Sidewinder missiles as well as a rapid-fire cannon. In addition to its two fighter roles, it will perform admirably as a fighter-bomber.

"If we concede that citizens of the United States should be able to engage in ocean commerce and that the government of the United States should seek to enhance world peace and stability through mutual defense treaties with other governments, we then establish the need for a strong Navy....In the next decades as technology improves, the sea is certain to become a major source of world resources...not only for what can be extracted from it, but for the uses to which it can be put.... Sea-based tactical air (power) is the backbone of our sea control and force projection capabilities.

"The F-14 weapons system is one of the highest priority items in the Navy budget. The F-14's importance rests primarily upon its ability to track and fire on multiple targets simultaneously at long ranges. It will be capable of tracking and evaluating multiple targets and of controlling up to six independent Phoenix missiles simultaneously.

(Continued on p. 100)

NIXON TO CONGRESS: AN 'UNPARALLELED OPPORTUNITY'

President Nixon—back in the United States for less than half an hour from his mission to Moscow—reported June 1, 1972, to Congress and the American people on the results of his summit agreements with leaders of the Soviet Union.

The President had been in the Soviet Union from May 22-30. On May 26, he and Soviet Communist Party General Secretary Leonid I. Brezhnev signed a treaty limiting construction of antiballistic missile sites to two and an agreement limiting the number of offensive strategic missiles each side would have. *(Texts of the two accords, p. 109-111)*

He urged the assembled lawmakers to "seize the moment so that our children and the world's children live free of the fears and free of the hatreds that have been the lot of mankind through the centuries."

He assured them that "the present and planned strategic forces of the United States are without question sufficient for the maintenance of our security and the protection of our vital interests."

"No power on earth is stronger than the United States of America today," he said. "None will be stronger than the United States of America in the future."

He added: "It is clear the agreements forestall a major spiraling of the arms race—one which would have worked to our disadvantage."

The President encouraged "the fullest scrutiny of these accords," and said he was confident that "such examination will underscore...that this is an agreement in the interest of both nations."

Soviet Approval. As the President urged Congress to approve the accords, the Soviet news agency, Tass, reported that the Soviet Politburo, the Council of Ministers and the Presidium of the Supreme Soviet all had "entirely approved" the summit pacts.

The American system of endorsement promised to be slower moving. The Senate will have to ratify the defensive arms treaty by a two-thirds majority. Both the House and Senate would have to approve the offensive arms agreement by simple majorities. *(Box p. 97)*

Administration officials were quoted as saying they hoped Congress would complete action on the package by August 1972.

Presidential national security adviser Dr. Henry A. Kissinger, who was instrumental in arranging the summit and preparing the U.S. position on key issues, said: "What we did there (in the Soviet Union) is not a partisan issue and we will not use it in a partisan way."

But partisan feelings were evident in the House chamber as the President spoke. The American success in the strategic arms and other negotiations, the President said, "came about because, over the past three years we have consistently refused proposals for unilaterally abandoning the ABM (antiballistic missile),

unilaterally pulling back our forces from Europe, and drastically cutting the defense budget."

Nixon said Congress deserved "the appreciation of the American people for having the courage to vote such proposals down and to maintain the strength America needs to protect its interests."

Past Summits. The President alluded to past meetings of Soviet leaders and American Presidents. "One meeting after another," he said, "produced a short-lived euphoric mood—the spirit of Geneva, the spirit of Camp David, the spirit of Vienna, the spirit of Glassboro—without producing significant progress on the really difficult issues."

But this summit was different, he said. "This was a working summit. We sought to establish not a superficial spirit of Moscow, but a solid record of progress on solving the difficult issues which for so long have divided our two nations and the world." That goal was accomplished, the President added.

Seven Agreements. The first American President to visit Moscow, Nixon returned to Washington June 1 with seven agreements he had signed with Soviet leaders.

They included pacts on joint space missions, technology, the environment, medical research, trade, incidents at sea and the limitation of strategic arms.

But it was the arms accord that overshadowed every other aspect of the dramatic week in Moscow. The agreement was based on three premises:

• That development of offensive weaponry clearly was more advanced than the development of defensive weapons systems. Therefore, the freeze on both offensive and defensive weapons would leave both nations naked to a first attack.

• That both powers were confident they could survive a first strike to the extent they could retaliate with enough force to totally destroy the opposing nation.

• That the threat of nuclear obliteration—the "balance of terror" that had prevailed for almost a quarter century—was an adequate deterrent to all-out war.

Two Arms Agreements

There were two elements to the arms agreement worked out by the American and Soviet leaders: a treaty that would limit the deployment of antiballistic missiles (ABMs) and an executive agreement limiting the number of offensive weapons to those already under construction or deployed when the agreement was signed. The executive agreement also placed limitations on the number of missile-carrying submarines that could be constructed.

Under the defensive arms treaty, both the United States and Soviet Union would be limited to one ABM site for the defense of their capital cities, plus one additional site each for the defense of an ICBM (Intercontinental Ballistic Missile) field.

Defense critic Senator William Proxmire (D Wis.) argued that the treaty did not require construction of the two ABM sites.

Under the offensive arms agreement, the Soviet Union would be permitted to field about 300 of its new giant SS-9 missiles in silos occupied by older models. But the total number of the larger variety could not be increased.

Both sides would be able to construct new submarine-launched ballistic missiles (SLBMs) of the Polaris or Poseidon variety if they dismantle an equal number of land-based ICBM launchers or older submarine launchers. Thus, while the number of submarines could increase, the total of warheads would not.

Although the Russians were left with more land- and sea-based missiles in their arsenal, the United States—because it had developed systems whereby one missile delivers a number of independently targeted warheads—would have more than three times the Soviet number of deliverable warheads.

The Soviets had not yet tested a multiple warhead weapons system, although the treaty would allow them to do so.

The agreement did not provide for any on-site inspection. Both sides apparently were satisfied that satellite reconnaissance was adequate for monitoring the other's activities. But there was an unusual agreement whereby each side pledged not to interfere with the other's gathering of technical data. Both promised not to try and conceal their missile deployments or tests.

Debate in Congress

For both President Nixon and his Soviet counterparts, the road from the conference table promised a few more obstacles. Communist Party chief Brezhnev had to contend with some of the more reluctant members of the Soviet hierarchy.

President Nixon had to face the Congress.

The offensive arms agreement required approval by simple majorities in both the House and Senate; the ABM treaty must be ratified by a two-thirds majority in the Senate. *(Box p. 97)*

President Nixon had several advantages going into congressional hearings in the summer of 1972 on the nuclear arms pacts he negotiated with the Soviet Union. Though sentiment was mixed, the President hoped to avert an all-out battle like the one when the Senate ratified the 1963 nuclear test ban treaty. *(1963 CQ Almanac p. 248)*

By contrast with 1963, the 1972 agreements:

• Were produced by a President with a long record of anti-communism.

• Received early approval of the Joint Chiefs of Staff. In 1963 the joint chiefs qualified their endorsement with insistence on four safeguards eventually incorporated. In 1972 they insisted on weapons progress.

• Were supported by a secretary of defense (Melvin R. Laird) with a congressional record of backing a strong military posture. In 1963 Secretary of Defense Robert S.

FACT SHEET ON AGREEMENTS

Following is the text of a White House fact sheet, released May 26, 1972, on the strategic arms limitation agreement. *(Texts, appendix p. 109-111)*

The Current Agreements

The ABM Treaty

• Limits each side to one ABM site for defense of their national capital (Moscow and Washington) and one site for each side for the defense of an ICBM field.

• There will be a total of 200 ABM interceptors permitted each side, 100 at each site.

• Radars will be limited to Modern ABM Radar Complexes (called MARCs) six for each side within a circle of 150 km radius around the national capitals; (MARCs are a circle of 3 km diameter, in which radars can be deployed; in practice they can accommodate about one large radar or a few smaller ones).

• For the ICBM defense fields there will be a total of twenty radars permitted; two of them can be about the size of the two larger radars deployed at Grand Forks; the other eighteen radars will be much smaller.

• The Soviet ICBM protection site will be at least 1300 km from Moscow. Our comparable site will be at Grand Forks, North Dakota.

• Other large non-ABM radars that may be built in the future will be restricted to space tracking or early warning and limited in size so as not to create a clandestine ABM potential.

• The treaty will be of unlimited duration with withdrawal rights if supreme interests are jeopardized, and on six months notice.

The Interim Offensive Agreement

• Limits ICBMs to those under construction or deployed at the time of signing the treaty or July 1. (This will mean about 1618 ICBMs for the USSR and 1054 for us.) The USSR will field about 300 large SS-9s, but they will be prohibited from converting other ICBM silos to accommodate the large SS-9 types. Other silos can be modified, but not to a significant degree. Modernization is permitted.

• Construction of submarine launched ballistic missiles on all nuclear submarines will be frozen at current levels. The further construction of SLBMs on either side, can only be accomplished by dismantling of an equal number of older land based ICBMs or older submarine launchers.

• The Interim Agreement will run for five years (compared to the original Soviet proposal of 18 months), and both sides are committed to negotiating a permanent and more comprehensive agreement.

• Both sides will abide by the obligations of the agreement once it is signed, though formal implementation will await ratification of the ABM treaty.

McNamara was widely criticized by defense-oriented sources.

• Were negotiated in a period of comparatively relaxed tensions between the United States and Soviet Union. In 1963 the memory of the 1962 Cuban missile crisis was fresh in congressional minds.

On the other hand, Congress had not abandoned support for a strong military defense. Proxmire and others succeeded in trimming military funds by several billion dollars in 1969, but Congress in 1971 resisted defense-cutting attempts.

Many members of Congress who voiced basic approval of the 1972 pacts, as well as some who criticized them,

Laird: Savings from SALT ABM Treaty Offset by War Costs

Defense Secretary Melvin R. Laird told two congressional committees June 5, 1972, that the Strategic Arms Limitations Treaty (SALT) would save about $550-million in fiscal 1973 defense spending. But, he added, the escalating costs of the Vietnam war probably would require an additional $3-billion to $5-billion expenditure the same year. *(Controversy over SALT, p. 94)*

In separate appearances before the Senate and House Appropriations Committees, both in open sessions, Laird gave the administration's first budget appraisal of the SALT agreement and the Vietnam situation since the North Vietnamese began their offensive March 30.

"The ABM treaty," Laird said before the House committee, "will permit a reduction of about $650-million in fiscal 1973 ABM (antiballistic missile) funding requests. We propose to apply about $100-million of that to modification and initiation of other action in the strategic area to ensure maintenance of a realistic strategic deterrent." *(Text of agreements, p. 109)*

Information released by the Pentagon June 6 conflicted somewhat with Laird's fiscal outlook. The Defense Department summary stated that the SALT agreements would result in a savings of $711-million in fiscal 1973 as a result of cancelled ABM construction and deployment. The $711-million in savings would then be offset by $168-million used to accelerate other strategic weapon programs. Total savings, according to the Defense Department statement, would then be $543-million during fiscal 1973 as a result of the SALT agreement.

"Initial estimates of these program changes resulting from SALT," Laird said June 5, "indicate that additional savings over the next five years could amount to as much as $5-billion."

Although the administration had only been given congressional approval for full deployment at two ABM sites and approval for advanced planning at two additional sites, Pentagon planners maintained—prior to the SALT agreement—that a full ABM system would require 12 sites. The SALT agreement stipulated that only two ABM sites could be built—one to protect the national capital and another to protect an offensive missile site.

Two of the strategic weapon programs Laird stressed repeatedly during his appearance on Capitol Hill were the B-1 long-range bomber and the Trident missile-firing submarine. Laird said that both of these programs would be accelerated, but gave no figures for how much additional funding would be required. The initial budget request for the B-1 bomber program was $444.5-million for fiscal 1973 and the request for the Trident program (called ULMS until early 1972) was $942-million plus $35-million in deferred requests from fiscal 1972, making a total of $977-million for Trident.

"Although ABM deployments will be limited to two sites," Laird said, "...we will vigorously pursue a comprehensive ABM technology program." In addition to the Trident, B-1 and ABM technology programs,

Laird said stress also would be placed on "re-entry vehicle technology (MIRV war heads) plus some advanced technology to improve our command control communications capabilities and some increases in intelligence resources to augment verification capabilities."

Laird warned that since 1965 "the Soviet Union has far outstripped the United States in terms of numbers of weapons both offensive and defensive.... It is absolutely essential during this period (after the SALT agreement) that the United States be in a position that it can go forward with new weapons programs... and that the United States not take unilateral action."

If Congress forced the administration to disarm without mutual moves by the Soviet Union, Laird said, "I believe the opportunity to negotiate any kind of an agreement that is meaningful to ensure the safety of our people and peace of the world would be diminished greatly."

Vietnam Costs

Instead of requesting a fiscal 1972 supplemental appropriation to cover the increased costs of the Vietnam war, Laird warned the House Appropriations Committee that the fiscal 1973 budget request for $83.4-billion in new obligational authority would have to be amended.

Although cost estimates for fiscal 1972 spending on the war were not officially issued by the Pentagon, unofficial estimates placed the figure at about $7-billion prior to the North Vietnamese offensive which began March 30. The U.S. response to North Vietnam's offensive was a massive increase in U.S. firepower from the sea and air. Increased U.S. activities in Indochina since late March had nearly doubled the cost of the war for the United States on a month-by-month basis.

Robert C. Moot, Pentagon comptroller, accompanied Laird before the House committee and said that as a result of North Vietnam's offensive:

• An additional $3.3-billion would be needed by the Pentagon if enemy activities in South Vietnam continued through Sept. 30.

• An additional $5-billion would be needed to support U.S. and South Vietnamese efforts if the enemy's offensive continued through Dec. 31.

• About $400-million in munitions had been expended above the budgeted amount.

• About $300-million for operational costs (fuel and transportation) had been expended beyond the budgeted amount.

George Mahon (D Texas), chairman of the House Appropriations Committee, asked Laird if the Vietnam war could "go on for four or five years now with varying degrees of intensity?"

Laird said, "Yes."

"When could we cease our Air Force and Navy support," Mahon asked.

"It can be tomorrow if the enemy accepts our peace proposal," Laird said. "The only way this (war) can be finally solved is the negotiating route."

emphasized they would be influenced by disclosures at committee hearings. A chief complaint by early critics was the lack of details and lack of clarification of complex technical questions affecting U.S. security.

CONGRESSIONAL VIEWS. Reactions by senators and representatives to the strategic weapons agreements included the following:

Sen. Mike Mansfield (D Mont.), majority leader. Commended Nixon May 30 "for the substantial successes" achieved in Moscow, citing as "most important of all" the SALT agreements. "I do not intend to get euphoric over what was accomplished (by) this first step, but it could possibly lead to a diminution of the arms race and a stop to the spiral of arms expenditures...."

Sen. Hugh Scott (R Pa.), minority leader. On May 30 predicted Senate ratification and said SALT "is a strong step, a step that recognizes the balance of terror that has for too long frightened the rest of the world."

Sen. Robert C. Byrd (D W.Va.), majority whip. Said June 2, "None of the agreements...was entered into blindly and, in my judgment, none will endanger the military or economic security of the United States." He opposed the 1963 test ban treaty.

Sen. John C. Stennis (D Miss.), chairman, Armed Services Committee. "I hope that Congress will be able to support such a first step toward limitations," he said. While inclined to be favorable, he made it clear much would depend on the hearings. He voted against the 1963 treaty.

Sen. Henry M. Jackson (D Wash.), chairman Armed Services strategic arms limitation talks and nuclear test ban treaty safeguards subcommittees. "Far from curbing the arms race, the present agreements are likely to lead to an accelerated technological arms race with great uncertainties, profound instabilities and considerable costs. The agreements do not encourage a reduction in strategic spending and may well encourage an increase." He supported the 1963 treaty.

Sen. James L. Buckley (Cons-R N.Y.). "I fear that the announcement...will have the effect of lulling the nation into a totally unwarranted sense of security." He expressed "grave misgivings" concerning defensive missiles.

Sen. John Sherman Cooper (R Ky.) Said May 30 the SALT agreement was "one of the most unusual and significant agreements in the history of nuclear weapons— perhaps in the history of the world."

GROUP POSITIONS. Organizations interested in weapons and arms control matters concerning the SALT agreements had the following reactions:

American Legion. National Commander John H. Geiger May 31 wrote Nixon commending his efforts "in the cause of peace and better understanding" between the two countries. Geiger said legion veterans "are deeply aware of the desirability of reducing tension and increasing dialogue" between the great powers.

Noting the legion traditionally advocates strong military defense to enhance chances for peace, he said "our current policies advocate safeguards, such as on site inspection, to assure good faith on the part of both nations.

Veterans of Foreign Wars. The VFW took no immediate position. A spokesman said the group had questions but he had seen no indications of organized opposition.

Nuclear Pacts and Congress

Congressional approval was required on both the offensive and defensive aspects of agreements on nuclear arms reached by the President with the Soviets.

A provision in the 1961 law establishing the Arms Control and Disarmament Agency, which produced the pacts, specifies that any agreement to limit U.S. armed forces or armaments must be approved by legislation or treaty. *(1961 CQ Almanac p. 317)*

President Nixon June 13 submitted the two accords to Congress together with documents explaining U.S.-Soviet agreements and disagreements on interpretations of the accords. *(Appendix p. 106)*

The disagreements concerned mainly the ultimate size of nuclear submarine fleets and the size of certain offensive weapons. The explanation of the differences was designed to head off reservations on the part of the Senate to the treaty.

The President urged approval "without delay" promising that U.S. defense capabilities would remain "second to none." He called for "a sound strategic modernization program" as the nation moved to negotiate further arms accords.

The explanatory statements, drawn up in Moscow by U.S.-Soviet negotiators, emphasized U.S. concern over development of large Soviet missiles and envisaged future negotiations on nuclear limitations.

The document recorded a unilateral Soviet statement, not agreed to by the United States, that the Soviet Union increase the number of its nuclear submarines, if Washington's NATO allies increase theirs.

The President said the two Moscow agreements were "a significant step into a new era of mutually agreed restraint and arms limitation between the two principal nuclear powers." The agreements did not, he said, "close off all avenues of strategic competition." They "open(ed) up the opportunity for a new and more constructive U.S.-Soviet relationship, characterized by negotiated settlement of differences, rather than by the hostility and confrontation of decades past."

Arms Control Association. William C. Foster, head of the U.S. Arms Control and Disarmament Agency, 1961-69, and now chairman of the association, said the agreements were "the most significant step taken thus far" to slow the arms race. He said the proposed ABM limits would help to prevent war by leaving deterrent weapons credible.

American Conservative Union. Executive Director Larry Pratt said, "Our position is one of alarm and opposition." He said the group is concerned about the impact of the agreements on national security and also about the psychological effects. "We will be hoping as many people as possible on the Hill will oppose it,"

SANE. (Committee for a Sane Nuclear Policy) Executive Director Sanford Gottlieb said that of all the groups favoring arms controls, SANE was probably the most dissatisfied with the pacts because of what he called the failure to put a lid on offensive weapons. "It's hardly an arms control agreement," he said.

INVESTIGATION OF NON-APPROPRIATED FUND ACTIVITIES

After a worldwide investigation of more than two years, the Senate Government Operations Investigating Subcommittee issued a 300-page report Nov. 2, 1971, which documented "corruption, criminality and moral compromise" at all levels of the military in connection with nonappropriated fund activities.

The investigation implicated a limited number of armed forces personnel ranging from the joint chiefs of staff to low-ranking enlisted men, as well as the suppliers of such consumer goods as Carling Black Label beer and Jim Beam bourbon.

"Military personnel—both uniformed and civilian—stole, received kickbacks and gratuities and otherwise profited dishonestly from their association with clubs and exchanges," the subcommittee report stated. "But they could not have carried out their improprieties without the encouragement, support and complicity of vendors, brokers and salesmen who paid kickbacks and offered gifts.

"Too often, dishonest practices were considered the normal and customary means of operation," the report continued. "The military services failed to properly administer and police the operations of the nonappropriated funds which are used to finance military clubs and PX systems throughout the world."

The subcommittee investigation pieced together two major examples of corruption which spanned more than a decade—one involving a group of sergeants whose influence extended to the joint chiefs of staff and another which involved a powerful merchant who sold goods and

services to U.S. military facilities throughout Southeast Asia and the complicity of a brigadier general in the merchant's operation.

The Sergeants

"The Maredem Co. sold goods to NCO (noncommissioned officers) clubs in Vietnam. The officers of the Maredem Co. were Army sergeants who controlled the club systems Maredem sold to," said the report.

Seven Army sergeants who were stationed together in Augsburg, Germany, during the early 1960s were all involved in supervisory capacities with the club and open mess system. The Senate subcommittee report traced their activities together from Augsburg to Fort Benning, Ga., and finally to South Vietnam where they established the Maredem Co.

The subcommittee noted dozens of investigations which were started in connection with the sergeants' activities. Without exception, the military probes were frustrated. The subcommittee also found numerous instances where records had been tampered with or destroyed to protect the sergeants.

The five men who became shareholders in the Maredem Co. were Sgt. Maj. William O. Wooldridge, Sgts. Narvaez Hatcher, William Higdon, Seymour Lazar and Theodore Bass. Two nonshareholders who were cited as friends of the enterprise were Sgts. William Bagby and John Nelson.

Germany. The first record of the sergeants being investigated was in 1963 when a fellow sergeant noted questionable practices of clearing money from club slot machines. Sgt. Maj. Kenneth Parrent also found that the club had paid $50,000 to a nonexistent construction company without the approval of the club's board of directors of which Parrent was a member.

In Parrent's testimony before the subcommittee, he said that the sergeants appeared to be living in a style which was above their means. One of the group, Hatcher, was being chauffeured by a man with a higher rank than Hatcher had himself.

Parrent turned over his information to Maj. William L. George, who after observing the sergeants in action briefed Maj. Gen. William Cunningham about the situation. Cunningham was at that time the commanding officer of 24th Infantry Division in Europe and refused to launch a full scale investigation.

When Cunningham was reassigned from the European command, his successor called in the military's Criminal Investigation Division (CID). The CID agents were "immediately critical of the manner in which Gen. Cunningham had supervised—or not supervised—the club system operations," the subcommittee report stated.

During the CID investigation, the two agents who were working on the case "ran into a new roadblock" in July 1966. Sgt. Maj. Wooldridge, a prime suspect in

---

Nonappropriated Funds

Nonappropriated funds are self-generating supplies of money used by the military to finance major recreational and consumer programs within the armed forces. Nonappropriated funds supplement appropriated money in supplying these recreational programs. Two of the largest revenue-generating programs for the military's nonappropriated fund activities have been the post exchange (PX) system and open messes (restaurants and bars).

The armed forces exchange system ranked as the third largest American department store with gross sales of $3.3-billion for the year ending Jan. 25, 1972. Only Sears, Roebuck and Company with $10.9-billion in gross sales and J.C. Penney with $4.8-billion in gross sales were larger than the PX system.

Military clubs and open mess facilities, which provide the services of a bar and grill plus entertainment, had gross sales of $625-million in calendar year 1971.

SOURCE: Defense Department; Sears, Roebuck and Company, and J.C. Penney Company.

the Augsburg probe, was named sergeant major of the Army—the highest ranking enlisted man in the Army. In his new capacity, Wooldridge was serving directly under the Army chief of staff, General Harold Johnson.

"I encountered much resistance from officials who wanted the case closed and forgotten," said one CID agent on the case. "We were all aware of the sensitive nature of the case, particularly after Sgt. Maj. Wooldridge became sergeant major of the Army." The agent said there was also added concern that further inquiry might embarrass Gen. Cunningham or Army Chief of Staff Johnson.

The seven sergeants were never brought to trial for their improprieties at Augsburg and in fact, no investigation was ever completed because of interference from and lack of communications between some of the Army's highest ranking uniformed personnel.

Fort Benning. The name of Sgt. Maj. Wooldridge turned up in several investigations involving the illegal transport of liquor, first from Vietnam and then from Fort Benning to Washington where Wooldridge was stationed.

The CID agents assigned to the case were refused access to the files on Wooldridge involving the investigations in Augsburg and the CID men were ordered to delete any mention of Wooldridge's name from their reports.

Maj. Gen. Carl C. Turner, provost marshal general (chief law enforcement officer of the Army), told the subcommittee he had made the order to remove Wooldridge's name from the CID report, and that he issued the order because there was not sufficient evidence to warrant bringing the man's name into the inquiry.

The liquor transport investigation also involved four other sergeants who had been in Augsburg with Wooldridge and who were then stationed together at Fort Benning. Wooldridge, according to the report, "exercised undue influence in arranging new assignments for his associates" in moving from "one open mess system to another several thousand miles away."

Gen. Turner, who blocked the investigation of Wooldridge and the other sergeants, was subsequently indicted in the civil courts for income tax evasion and for violation of the Federal Firearms Act. Turner had received firearms from several police departments around the country on the assumption that the general would give them to the Army. Turner kept some of the weapons and sold them for about $7,000. He was sentenced May 13, 1971, to one year in prison and was fined $25,000.

Vietnam. Before Wooldridge was named sergeant major of the Army in mid-1966, he served for one year in Vietnam. Three months after he had arrived, Wooldridge helped Sgt. Lazar become custodian in charge of the 1st Infantry Division open mess system. Lazar was succeeded in his position by Sgt. Hatcher who was in turn followed by Sgt. Nelson as custodian of the division open mess. All three of the sergeants had served together in Augsburg and all three had been involved in several investigations for their handling of open mess and club funds.

It was during November 1967 that Wooldridge, Lazar, Hatcher and Higdon formed the Maredem Co. which became one of the major supply brokers for the open mess system in Vietnam. The company's initial capital was provided by selling the Army open mess system a walk-in freezer that it already owned for $13,000.

About the time Maredem Co. was formed, Lazar retired from the Army to become the company's chief salesman—selling primarily to his successor as 1st Division custodian of the open mess system, Sgt. Hatcher—a full partner in the business. By Dec. 21, 1967, Lazar's salary as Maredem's chief salesman was $2,000 per month.

During Maredem's first year in business, it sold more than $1-million in goods to clubs in Vietnam—80 percent of the sales going to clubs run by Higdon, Hatcher and Bagby.

In February 1969, the five partners in Maredem (Bass became a partner after Maredem was established) declared the following financial statements showing a combined worth of $318,026: Wooldridge, $49,212; Higdon, $115,000; Hatcher, $86,500; Lazar, $54,903; and Bass, $12,321.

When brought before the Senate subcommittee for questioning, the sergeants took the 5th Amendment, refusing to answer questions which might incriminate them. In an interview published by the Scripps-Howard newspapers, however, Wooldridge said: "If half what they tell about me is true, I've been able to control every general in the Army, including the chief of staff. I've been powerful enough to conceal and destroy records at Ft. Holabird (Md.), depository for the CID and direct the military assignment of personnel all over the world.... And I only got to the tenth grade in school."

Several months after the interview, in February 1970, a federal grand jury handed down a 21-count indictment against Wooldridge, Higdon, Lazar, Hatcher and Bass. The indictment charged conspiracy to defraud the United States, false and fraudulent claims against the United States, bribery of public officials and concealment of material fact. Higdon, the only one of the sergeants indicted by the Army, was convicted June 11, 1971, of larceny, fined $25,000 and dishonorably discharged from the armed forces.

With the trial of Wooldridge still pending in a federal court, the Army Feb. 1, 1972, allowed him to retire with full pension ($783 per month) with both him and his dependents eligible for medical benefits, commissary and post exchange privileges.

Asian Merchant

The second major part of the Senate subcommittee investigation concentrated on the business activities of William John Crum who was, according to the report, the "most successful businessman in Vietnam."

Crum, who was the third son of an American national, was born in Shanghai, China. His father was a river pilot on the Yangtze. Although Crum has led an active life, he was half-crippled by muscular dystrophy during childhood and had a glass eye.

During the Korean war, at least four military investigations were started on the sales activities of Crum and his liquor and slot machine concessions to military nonappropriated fund activities. Although he was at one time forced to leave Korea briefly to avoid prosecution, his business interests never flagged and he inevitably had friends in the command who saw to it that Crum was allowed to operate without undue interference from the CID.

In the early 1960s Crum switched his base of operations from Korea to South Vietnam where American military presence was becoming increasingly evident.

During 1965 and 1966 Crum helped establish and reorganize several companies that became the major suppliers of electronic amusements (i.e. juke boxes and pinball machines), slot machines and liquor to military clubs and messes in Indochina. Sarl Electronics sold and leased coin-operated gambling machines and amusement machines; Price and Co. handled liquor and packaged snacks; Vietnam Electronics did repair work on Sarl Electronic equipment and sold machines to Vietnamese-owned bars and hotels; Century Trading Co. supplied clothing and textile goods to the PX system. Crum was either part owner or full owner of all these enterprises, according to the subcommittee report.

" A benchmark in William Crum's rise to fortune in Vietnam occurred when his Sarl Electronics won a concession" with the Vietnam regional PX June 1966 to provide, install, maintain and repair amusements in exchange facilities.

The manner in which Crum won this contract was of particular interest to the Senate subcommittee. The subcommittee report described the events leading up to Crum's winning the contract as a typical example of the manner in which he operated in both Korea and Vietnam.

In late 1965 the Vietnam PX system was in the process of being transferred from Navy to Army-Air Force control. When the five men who were to take charge of system for the Army-Air Force arrived in Vietnam, Crum moved them into a villa he had rented and redecorated for them. One of the PX officials told the subcommittee he paid Crum $100 per month which covered only the food, not the maid, chef or the four-bedroom living accomodations. It was while these five men were living in Crum's villa that Sarl Electronics was awarded the $1-million contract with PX system.

In the years that followed, Crum built a massive trading empire in Vietnam and according to the subcommittee, he did it with the help of Brig. Gen. Earl F. Cole, who had administrative control over the service club system and the Army CID in Vietnam.

"Crum's success in monopolizing the business is attributable to the assistance and protection he received from...Cole...from senior PX officials and from other U.S. government personnel," the report said. Crum used Cole's friendship to bring merchandise illegally into Vietnam duty-free, to store some of the goods in Army warehouses and then to sell goods on the Vietnamese blackmarket which were not used by the club and PX system.

When various branches of the Army tried to investigate Crum, Cole stepped in, blocking their efforts and had troublesome CID agents transferred out of Vietnam.

"During the period while the subcommittee was investigating the conspiracy which involved Gen. Cole and Sarl Electronics," the report stated, "the Department of the Army continued to cover up and whitewash its investigation of Brig. Gen. Cole.... The attempt by the Army to cover up the Cole matter was a calculated plan to ease Cole out of the service with the least possible embarrassment to the Army."

In dealing with the PX system, Crum found willing allies in at least one the sergeants involved in the Maredem Company. Brig. Gen. Cole, in protecting Crum from investigation, also blocked the Army's efforts to gather information on the activities of Sgt. Higdon who was accepting gratuities from Crum in exchange for stocking the NCO club with Crum's products.

Under pressure by the Senate Investigating Subcommittee, Brig. Gen. Cole was relieved of his command Sept. 7, 1969, and was allowed to retire July 30, 1970, with the rank of colonel. Cole never faced a court martial and collects his Army retirement pay.

The elusive William Crum, who never appeared before the subcommittee, was barred from doing business with the U.S. military.

(F-14 Fighter continued from p. 93)

"The test program is proceeding exceptionally well. Ten F-14As have been delivered and are in a flight status. Over 250 flights have been made for an aggregate of almost 600 flight test hours. The last research and development aircraft (the twelfth) has been delivered and the first full production aircraft is scheduled for delivery next month (April).

"As you are aware, the prime contractor, Grumman Aerospace Corp., informed the Navy by letter Jan. 20, 1972, that Grumman was unwilling to perform the option for production of the 48 aircraft in Lot V (those planes scheduled for production in fiscal 1973) of the contract under the terms.

"The option to buy Lot V is exercised by the Navy until October 1972 by the terms of the contract. The Navy and the Defense Department are of the view that the F-14 contract with Grumman is valid and binding. It is our current intention to proceed within the framework of the existing contract....In the event a contractual dispute arises, the Congress will be kept informed of the Navy's actions in a timely manner."

Rear Adm. L. A. Snead, project officer for the F-14 aircraft and Phoenix missile:

"As you will recall when the Navy testified before you in late April last year we had only one F-14 flying, very little test flight data, but lots of high hopes. Now we have 10 aircraft flying...(and) we like the results we are seeing from our hardware in flight test."

Production milestones of the F-14A have slipped six months behind schedule, but the Navy now anticipates the production of one aircraft per month.

"Development of the F-401 engine for the (F-14) B model slipped so production of the F-14B has been delayed and our currently approved program is for 313 F-14As." Delivery date for the first production engines for the F-14B could take place in April 1974. "We could have our first F-14B delivered in July 1974."

March 30

Gerald J. Tobias, group vice president of aerospace systems group, Rohr Industries Inc., subcontractors to Grumman for structural components of the F-14:

The target price for Rohr's production of F-14 components for the 48 aircraft for fiscal 1973 was set at $218-million. With regard to the production of components already delivered to Grumman, Rohr considers the profit-loss situation less favorable to the company. "Frankly, Lots I through III (early shipments) have been less than satisfactory since we are in a loss position due to a combination of influences."

Regarding production of components for aircraft currently under negotiation, "we have the ability from a schedule standpoint....Although we are dissatisfied with the present and projected cost and profit picture, we will perform to contract...if Grumman requires us to do so."

APPENDIX

DEFENSE DEPARTMENT HISTORY, SIZE, THE PENTAGON

The position of the Secretary of Defense was created by the National Security Act of 1947. The law replaced the War and Navy Departments with a National Military Establishment consisting of separate departments of the Army, Navy and Air Force.

The Defense Secretary was to be "the principal assistant to the President in all matters relating to the national security." His duties were to "establish general policies and programs..., exercise general direction, authority and control" over the departments and "take appropriate steps to eliminate unnecessary duplication or overlapping in the fields of procurement, supply, transportation, storage, health and research."

The three department secretaries enjoyed substantial freedom to develop programs and to set policy under the act and they retained the right to "present to the President or to the director of the budget...any report or recommendation relating to his department which he may deem necessary." Moreover, the defense secretary was not permitted to "establish a military staff" and was restricted to three civilian assistants.

The Defense Department was established in 1949 as the successor to the National Military Establishment. The further reorganization was an effort to stem the high cost of national security and to eliminate the waste and duplication among the armed forces.

Under the National Security Act Amendments of 1949, the three departments, separately administered by their respective secretaries, were incorporated into a single department under the direction, authority and control of the defense secretary. However, the defense secretary was not permitted to transfer, abolish or consolidate any of the services' combatant functions.

In 1953, organizational shortcomings in the department and high military spending forced Reorganization Plan No. 6 to be adopted. It gave the defense secretary power to select the director of the joint chiefs of staff and gave the chairman of the joint chiefs the responsibility for managing the group.

More authority was concentrated in the defense secretary's office under the Defense Reorganization Act of 1958 which authorized the secretary to consolidate common supply and service functions, to assign responsibility for development and operation of new weapons and to transfer, re-assign, abolish or consolidate established combatant functions of the three services subject to Congressional veto.

Civilian Control. By law, the defense secretary must come from civilian life. Of the ten secretaries since 1947, two were attorneys (Louis Johnson and Clark M. Clifford); two were bankers (James V. Forrestal and Robert A. Lovett); four were business executives (Charles E. Wilson, Neil H. McElroy, Thomas S. Gates Jr. and Robert S. McNamara) and one, Melvin R. Laird, was a politician.

One secretary, however, Gen. George C. Marshall, was a career serviceman. Marshall had been President Truman's special envoy to China in 1945-46 and secretary of state in 1947-49. When Louis Johnson resigned as defense secretary after being blamed for initial U.S. reverses in the Korean war, Truman nominated Marshall.

Congress, after bitter debate, amended the National Security Act and permitted Marshall to serve.

President Eisenhower reflected his concern for efficient operation and civilian control of the Pentagon by naming three corporate executives to the post during his eight years in office. President Kennedy followed suit with the appointment of McNamara, a Ford executive. Clifford, appointed by President Johnson, was an attorney specializing in corporate cases.

McNamara, who served longer than any other secretary, centralized more control in the secretary's office than did any other man to serve in the position. He consolidated military and supply services and exercised almost complete control over military procurement decisions. Under his planning-programming-budget system, service budget requests were subject to analysis by function to enable comparison of relative cost and effectiveness of the Army, Navy and Air Force weapon systems. McNamara was severely criticized after leaving the Pentagon because he left a legacy of weapons programs that cost more than expected and performed less than anticipated.

Laird returned much of the decision-making to the military and sought to eliminate cost-overruns by developing working models of certain weapons systems before deciding whether to buy.

Dimensions

The United States pours nearly two times more money into defense than does any other nation on earth. U.S. defense expenditures are so large that only a handful of countries in the world have a Gross National Product (GNP) which is greater than this one portion of the federal budget. The GNP of Canada, for example, or the combined GNPs of the People's Republic of China and Nationalist China are about equal to the Pentagon's annual budget.

The fiscal 1973 Defense Department budget request was $83.4-billion (about 30 percent of the total federal budget). The Soviet Union had a defense budget of about $45-billion, the People's Republic of China was about $12-billion and Great Britain about $6-million.

Secretaries of Defense

The position of Secretary of Defense was established by the National Security Act of 1947, which made the secretaries of the three services subordinates of the Defense Secretary.

James V. Forrestal (9/17/47 - 3/27/49)
Louis Johnson (3/28/49 - 3/19/50)
George C. Marshall (9/21/50 - 9/12/51)
Robert A. Lovett (9/17/51 - 1/20/53)
Charles E. Wilson (1/28/53 - 10/8/57)
Neil H. McElroy (10/9/57 - 12/1/59)
Thomas S. Gates Jr. (12/2/59 - 1/20/61)
Robert S. McNamara (1/21/61 - 3/1/68)
Clark M. Clifford (3/1/68 - 1/20/69)
Melvin R. Laird (1/22/69 -   )

The United States maintains about 20,000 combat aircraft, 12,000 helicopters and 700 ships ranging from nuclear powered submarines and aircraft carriers to patrol boats. There is sufficient nuclear fire power in the U.S. arsenal of land-based and sea-based missiles, plus bomber-delivered nuclear explosives, to destroy every major target in the Soviet Union and the People's Republic of China several times over.

By mid-1972, the United States had a standing armed force of 2.3 million persons, a civilian Defense Department payroll of about one million persons and a reserve component force of about 900,000 persons. An additional 2 million persons were employed in private industry on defense projects ranging from construction of jet fighters to research on military satellites.

Although the United States spends more than any other country in the world to pay for salaries of its standing armed force of 2.3 million persons, the largest standing armies are maintained by the Soviet Union (3.3 million men) and the People's Republic of China (2.8 million men). Both the Soviets and the Chinese maintain large contingents of uniformed personnel on their mutually shared borders.

The United States maintains mutual security agreements with about 50 countries. The U.S. military stands behind those agreements. In fiscal 1972, Congress approved military construction projects in 16 different countries ranging from Sicily to Grand Turk Island (West Indies) to Australia.

The Defense Department is the third largest government landholder in the United States—behind the Bureau of Land Management (Interior Department) and the Agriculture Department. The Defense Department owns 28.8 million acres of land, 2 million of which is outside the United States. Territorial landholdings of the Pentagon are equal to the land covered by New Hampshire, Vermont, Massachusetts, Connecticut, New Jersey, Delaware and Rhode Island.

Since the end of World War II, Congress has appropriated about $1.2-trillion to the Defense Department which amounts to 41 percent of the total $2.9-trillion appropriated by Congress for all purposes.

Building the Pentagon

The idea of putting all armed forces headquarters personnel under one roof was not a new concept when it was presented to the House Appropriations Committee July 22, 1941, five months before Pearl Harbor. What did come as a surprise was that the military wanted to make their edifice the largest office building in the world, one that would last 100 years.

The speed with which the War Department presented its plans to Congress and the way the appropriations were rammed through both houses took not only many members of Congress by surprise, but also the President, the press and the public.

In a House Appropriations Committee hearing July 14, 1941, a War Department witness was asked if he had any ideas on how his department might consolidate its people who were then taking up office space in 17 buildings throughout Washington, D.C. The request was taken back to the War Department and eight days later Brig. Gen. Brehon B. Somervell appeared before the subcommittee.

The *Washington Star* reported: "Gen. Somervell was ready and must have been for some time. For he unrolled his maps and plans and displayed to the committee the site and architect's drawings of a building to be erected near the entrance to Arlington Memorial Cemetery (the building site was later moved one mile down the Potomac River to its current location).

During the hearings Rep. Clifton A. Woodrum (D Va.; 1923-1945) asked Somervell: "What will be the cost?"

Somervell: "$35-million."

Woodrum: "Will that complete the project, covering everything including the utilities?"

Somervell: "Yes, sir."

One year after Somervell assured the committee that the $35-million would cover everything, construction estimates were up to $70-million. The building which Somervell said would contain 4,000,000 square feet of office space in a building of 5,100,000 total square feet ended up with 6,000,000 square feet of total space of which only 2,336,000 was for office use. Both the increased cost figures and the decrease in office space were classified "confidential" by the War Department until they were read into the *Congressional Record* by an angry House member Oct. 1, 1942.

Congressional Action. Six days after Somervell made his debut before the House Appropriations Committee, the committee had reported a bill and was pressing for passage. The members of the Appropriations Committee took their bill to the Rules Committee to get a special ruling because they were attempting to push through an appropriation bill which contained a $35-million item that had not yet been authorized by the proper legislative committee.

Rep. Robert F. Rich (R Pa.; 1930-1943) told the House during debate: "If it is necessary to construct this War Department building...we ought to come in here in the regular way and argue the question pro and con and then vote on it. We should not permit the Rules Committee to come in here with a closed rule (allowing for no amendments), with 25 members of the House present and say you have got to take it or leave it, regardless of the merits of the question of whether the building is necessary or not."

The $35-million for the new War Department building was included in a $6-billion supplemental appropriation for the War Department to buy guns, planes and tanks. By getting a closed rule on consideration of the bill, House members were unable to single out the $35-million portion as perhaps being unwise or hasty.

The supplemental bill which sailed through the House in three days, got a somewhat more skeptical hearing from the Senate. Adding to the controversy was a letter from President Franklin D. Roosevelt to Sen. Alva B. Adams (D Colo.; 1933-1941) which said: "When this project was first brought to my attention, I agreed that it should be explored. Since then I have had an opportunity to look into the matter personally and have some reservations which I would like to impart to your committee." Roosevelt raised questions in his letter to the subcommittee chairman which focused on the location chosen for the edifice on the Virginia side of the Potomac.

The Future. Besides the location and cost arguments, some members of Congress were not willing to commit the nation to a building that would permanently house a work force of from 30,000 to 40,000 War Department employees.

Rep. Raymond S. Springer (R Ind.; 1939-1947) told the House July 28, 1941: "If we are not to become militaristic in the future, why the construction of this huge building for our War Department?... No one appears to know whose suggestion it was that brought this tremendous building into the pending bill....We do not want a militaristic nation in the future and therefore we do not need the largest office building in the world for our War Department."

In April 1917 when the United States entered World War I the War Department had 2,816 employees. One year later the War Department employed 37,400 persons who were provided office space in temporary buildings constructed on the Mall between the Capitol and the Washington Monument. By 1922 the War Department payroll had again dropped to a 4,900-person peace time force and the temporary buildings were torn down once the emergency conditions had passed.

What are we going to do with this building, asked legislators, when the war is over? Some people thought it might be converted into a hospital after the war. The *Washington Daily News*, March 13, 1947, carried a story stating that Rep. Thomas J. Lane (D Mass.; 1941-1963) wanted to convert the building into a co-educational college for veterans.

The voice of authority on the subject, however, was Somervell. The new five-sided building could be used to house other departments of the government when the time of emergency passed, Somervell argued. Unlike the period immediately after World War I, however, the War Department (renamed the Defense Department in 1949) did not drastically reduce the size of its headquarters personnel following World War II. The staffing level at the Pentagon has remained at about 25,000 to 32,000 employees since 1950.

An article in the *Washington Star* in mid-August 1941 said: "The Army's blitzkrieg on Congress and Washington with the largest office building in the world as its immediate objective has been so sudden, so overwhelming, that effective resistance has been scattered and left in total confusion. Nothing quite like it has ever happened in Washington before.

"Within a few days," continued the article, "the House and the Senate Appropriations Committees have approved not merely a $35-million building at the very gate of Arlington National Cemetery; they have approved a scheme so revolutionary in its ramifications and effect on Washington...that no one has had time even to attempt any careful appraisal of their full significance."

Rep. Everett M. Dirksen (R Ill.; House 1939-1949; Senate 1951-1969) was concerned about transportation costs. "You can ride to the present War Department for 20 cents," Dirksen said. "It will cost you at least 60 cents to go over there (to Virginia) in a taxicab and 60 cents back. Think of the expense."

Within a month, both the House and Senate passed the $6-billion supplemental appropriation bill with its $35-million item for construction of a new War Department building.

Construction. Work began Sept. 11, 1941, on what still remains the largest office building in the world. It was called "Somervell's folly" by the press. There was

Women: Military Minority

Of the approximately 2.5 million persons in the active duty armed forces, less than two percent are women.

Compared to other minority groups serving in the armed forces, women are well represented in the officer corps. Thirty percent (12,800) of the women in the military (44,350 total) are officers.

Six women in the history of the United States military have served at the rank of general or above. At the beginning of 1972, three women had the rank of brigadier general—Mildred C. Bailey, director of the Women's Army Corps; Lillian Dunlap, chief of the Army Nurse Corps; Jeanne M. Holm, of Women in the Air Force. They were all promoted to the rank of general after 1969. Alene Bertha Duerk April 1972 became the Navy's first female admiral.

Breakdowns at the beginning of 1972 for branches of the military were: Army, 17,200 women; Air Force, 15,700 women; Navy, 9,200 women; Marine Corps, 2,200 women (included both officers and enlisted personnel).

ROTC. The Army announced Feb. 16, 1972, that for the first time women would be admitted to college-level Reserve Officer Training Corps (ROTC) programs and they would be eligible for an officer's commission at the end of the program.

The experimental program was to be offered at 10 colleges and universities during 1972 to a limited number of females.

While the military opened up some of its ROTC scholarship programs to women, no parallel move was made to admit women to the three major military academies serving the Navy, Army and Air Force.

no ground breaking ceremony, no official hoopla as work began on the massive project.

Construction of the Pentagon took 16 months from ground breaking to completion—a job that normally would have taken four years. Work crews ranging up to 13,000 men labored round the clock to finish the building. Because of the need to channel most available steel into the arms industry, the Pentagon was designed to use a minimum of metal structural supports, relying instead on 40,000 concrete blocks. The finished structure was three times the size of the Empire State building and twice the size of the Merchandise Mart in Chicago. The Capitol building could fit into one wing. The Pentagon occupies 580 acres of land, 34 of which are devoted to the building itself and 67 acres to parking lots.

Although the building has 17½ miles of corridors, its pentagonal shape allows a person to walk to any part of the structure in about five minutes. The shape was also selected because it was reminiscent of several medieval fortresses in Europe. As reported by one visitor writing for the *Cleveland Plain Dealer* Oct. 13, 1943: "The Pentagon building is something to take your breath away. It is the concrete and bizarre symbol of the immensity of the war in which we are now engaged.

"There the Pentagon building stands," the report continued, "in all its massive and formidable dimensions and there it will continue to stand, like the pyramids of Cheops, immovable and incredible."

FISCAL 1971 DEFENSE PRIME CONTRACT MONEY BY STATES

Rank State	Population 1970 Census (in thousands)	Fiscal 1971 Percent (in millions)	Fiscal 1971 Amount (in millions)	Fiscal 1970 Percent	Fiscal 1970 Amount (in millions)	Fiscal 1970 Rank	Fiscal 1962 Percent	Fiscal 1962 Amount (in millions)	Fiscal 1962 Rank
1. California	19,900	18.5	$5,292	19.6	$5,824	1	23.9	$5,993	1
2. New York	18,200	11.8	3,370	10.3	3,076	2	10.7	2,669	2
3. Texas	11,196	9.5	2,722	9.3	2,774	3	4.0	1,006	7
4. Virginia	4,648	4.6	1,304	2.1	634	15	1.8	446	17
5. Massachusetts	5,689	4.5	1,284	4.0	1,200	5	5.2	1,310	3
6. Connecticut	3,032	4.2	1,195	4.2	1,237	4	4.8	1,213	4
7. Pennsylvania	11,794	3.6	1,015	3.9	1,174	6	3.8	952	8
8. Ohio	10,652	3.4	957	3.4	1,006	8	4.5	1,129	5
9. New Jersey	7,168	3.2	905	3.4	1,007	7	4.3	1,063	6
10. Missouri	4,677	3.1	880	3.0	898	11	2.2	546	14
11. Florida	6,789	2.9	821	2.9	849	12	2.6	646	11
12. Indiana	5,193	2.7	784	3.0	906	10	2.3	571	12
13. Georgia	4,589	2.6	730	3.2	949	9	1.4	337	19
14. Washington	3,409	2.5	707	1.3	384	21	3.7	921	9
15. Maryland	3,922	2.5	727	2.5	729	13	1.9	470	16
16. Illinois	11,114	1.8	511	2.4	721	14	2.1	531	15
17. Mississippi	2,216	1.6	461	1.7	509	18	.4	100	34
18. Michigan	8,875	1.6	449	1.9	563	17	2.7	678	10
19. North Carolina	5,082	1.5	427	1.5	449	19	1.1	296	22
20. Minnesota	3,805	1.4	407	2.0	605	16	1.2	297	21
21. Tennessee	3,924	1.2	334	1.3	399	20	.7	184	25
22. District of Columbia	756	1.1	319	1.1	316	24	.7	182	26
23. Arizona	1,772	1.1	299	.9	277	26	.6	153	29
24. Wisconsin	4,418	1.0	288	1.3	317	22	1.0	259	23
25. Alabama	3,444	1.0	282	1.1	316	23	.6	154	28
26. Louisiana	3,643	.8	219	1.0	299	25	1.0	244	24
27. Kansas	2,249	.7	208	.8	230	27	1.6	393	18
28. Colorado	2,207	.6	162	.7	218	29	2.3	565	13
29. Iowa	2,825	.5	153	.8	228	28	.7	179	27
30. Utah	1,059	.5	136	.5	162	31	1.2	299	20
31. Hawaii	769	.4	122	.4	109	34	.1	32	46
32. Oklahoma	2,559	.4	118	.5	152	32	.5	136	31
33. South Carolina	2,590	.4	115	.4	124	33	.3	65	37
34. Alaska	302	.4	105	.3	76	39	.3	63	38
35. New Mexico	1,016	.3	87	.3	88	38	.3	61	39
36. New Hampshire	738	.3	87	.3	99	35	.2	59	40
37. Nebraska	1,483	.3	78	.2	73	40	.2	53	42
38. Rhode Island	949	.3	74	.3	94	36	.2	58	41
39. Oregon	2,091	.2	63	.3	90	37	.2	46	43
40. North Dakota	618	.2	60	.6	188	30	.4	100	33
41. Kentucky	3,219	.2	55	.2	56	42	.2	44	44
42. Arkansas	1,932	.2	48	.2	69	41	.3	85	35
43. Delaware	548	.2	42	.1	22	47	.1	37	45
44. Maine	994	.2	42	.1	56	43	.3	80	36
45. Vermont	445	.1	41	.2	44	45	.1	16	50
46. West Virginia	1,744	.1	36	.2	46	44	.6	144	30
47. Montana	694	.1	22	.1	25	46	.1	31	47
48. Nevada	489	.1	16	.1	16	48	.1	8	51
49. Wyoming	332	.1	15	.1	14	49	.1	23	49
50. South Dakota	666	.1	14	.1	10	51	.5	113	32
51. Idaho	713	.1	8	.1	11	50	.1	26	48

TEXT OF U.S.-SOVIET INTERPRETATIONS OF MISSILE PACTS

NIXON MESSAGE

Following is the text, as made available by the White House, of President Nixon's June 13, 1972, message to Congress requesting ratification of the defensive arms treaty and offensive arms agreement signed in Moscow May 26. (Texts of accords, p. 109-111)

TO THE SENATE OF THE UNITED STATES:

I transmit herewith certified copies of the Treaty on the Limitation of Anti-Ballistic Missile Systems and the Interim Agreement on Certain Measures with respect to the Limitation of Strategic Offensive Arms signed in Moscow on May 26, 1972. Copies of these agreements are also being forwarded to the Speaker of the House of Representatives. I ask the Senate's advice and consent to ratification of the Treaty, and an expression of support from both Houses of the Congress for the Interim Agreement on Strategic Offensive Arms.

These agreements, the product of a major effort of this administration, are a significant step into a new era of mutually agreed restraint and arms limitation between the two principal nuclear powers.

The provisions of the agreements are explained in detail in the Report of the Secretary of State, which I attach. Their main effect is this: The ABM Treaty limits the deployment of anti-ballistic missile systems to two designated areas, and at a low level. The Interim Agreement limits the overall level of strategic offensive missile forces. Together the two agreements provide for a more stable strategic balance in the next several years than would be possible if strategic arms competition continued unchecked. This benefits not only the United States and the Soviet Union, but all the nations of the world.

The agreements are an important first step in checking the arms race, but only a first step; they do not close off all avenues of strategic competition. Just as the maintenance of a strong strategic posture was an essential element in the success of these negotiations, it is now equally essential that we carry forward a sound strategic modernization program to maintain our security and to ensure that more permanent and comprehensive arms limitation agreements can be reached.

The defense capabilities of the United States are second to none in the world today. I am determined that they shall remain so. The terms of the ABM Treaty and Interim Agreement will permit the United States to take the steps we deem necessary to maintain a strategic posture which protects our vital interests and guarantees our continued security.

Besides enhancing our national security, these agreements open the opportunity for a new and more constructive U.S.-Soviet relationship, characterized by negotiated settlement of differences, rather than by the hostility and confrontation of decades past.

These accords offer tangible evidence that mankind need not live forever in the dark shadow of nuclear war. They provide renewed hope that men and nations working together can succeed in building a lasting peace.

Because these agreements effectively serve one of this Nation's most cherished purposes—a more secure and peaceful world in which America's security is fully protected—I strongly recommend that the Senate support them, and that its deliberations be conducted without delay. RICHARD NIXON

AGREED INTERPRETATIONS

Following is the text, as made available by the White House June 13, of the agreed interpretations by the United States and the Soviet Union on the defensive arms treaty and the offensive arms agreement signed in Moscow May 26.

1. Agreed Interpretations.

(a) *Initialed Statements.*

The texts of the statements set out below were agreed upon and initialed by the Heads of the Delegations on May 26, 1972.

ABM Treaty

(A)

The Parties understand that, in addition to the ABM radars which may be deployed in accordance with subparagraph (a) of Article III of the Treaty, those non-phased-array ABM radars operational on the date of signature of the Treaty within the ABM system deployment area for defense of the national capital may be retained.

(B)

The Parties understand that the potential (the product of mean emitted power in watts and antenna area in square meters) of the smaller of the two large phased-array ABM radars referred to in subparagraph (b) of Article III of the Treaty is considered for purposes of the Treaty to be three million.

(C)

The Parties understand that the center of the ABM system deployment area centered on the national capital and the center of the ABM system deployment area containing ICBM silo launchers for each Party shall be separated by no less than thirteen hundred kilometers.

(D)

The Parties agree not to deploy phased-array radars having a potential (the product of mean emitted power in watts and antenna area in square meters) exceeding three million, except as provided for in Articles III, IV and VI of the Treaty, or except for the purposes of tracking objects in outer space or for use as national technical means of verification.

(E)

In order to insure fulfillment of the obligation not to deploy ABM systems and their components except as provided in Article III of the Treaty, the Parties agree that in the event ABM systems based on other physical principles and including components capable of substituting for ABM interceptor missiles, ABM launchers, or ABM radars are created in the future, specific limitations on such systems and their components would be subject to discussion in accordance with Article XIII and agreement in accordance with Article XIV of the Treaty.

(F)

The Parties understand that Article V of the Treaty includes obligations not to develop, test or deploy ABM interceptor missiles for the delivery by each ABM interceptor missile of more than one independently guided warhead.

(G)

The Parties understand that Article IX of the Treaty includes the obligation of the US and the USSR not to provide to other States technical descriptions or blueprints specially worked out for the construction of ABM systems and their components limited by the Treaty.

Interim Agreement

(H)

The Parties understand that land-based ICBM launchers referred to in the Interim Agreement are understood to be launchers for strategic ballistic missiles capable of ranges in excess of the shortest distance between the northeastern border of the continental U.S. and the northwestern border of the continental USSR.

(I)

The Parties understand that fixed land-based ICBM launchers under active construction as of the date of signature of the Interim Agreement may be completed.

(J)

The Parties understand that in the process of modernization and replacement the dimensions of land-based ICBM silo launchers will not be significantly increased.

(K)

The Parties understand that dismantling or destruction of ICBM launchers of older types deployed prior to 1964 and ballistic missile launchers on older submarines being replaced by new SLBM launchers on modern submarines will be initiated at the time of the beginning of sea trials of a replacement submarine, and will be completed in the shortest possible agreed period of time. Such dismantling or destruction, and timely notification thereof, will be accomplished under procedures to be agreed in the Standing Consultative Commission.

(L)

The Parties understand that during the period of the Interim Agreement there shall be no significant increase in the number of ICBM or SLBM test and training launchers, or in the number of such launchers for modern land-based heavy ICBMs. The Parties further understand that construction or conversion of ICBM launchers at test ranges shall be undertaken only for purposes of testing and training.

(b) *Common Understandings.*

Common understanding of the Parties on the following matters was reached during the negotiations:

A. Increase in ICBM Silo Dimensions

Ambassador Smith made the following statement on May 26, 1972: "The Parties agree that the term 'significantly increased' means that an increase will not be greater than 10-15 percent of the present dimensions of land-based ICBM silo launchers."

Minister Semenov replied that this statement corresponded to the Soviet understanding.

B. Location of ICBM Defenses

The U.S. Delegation made the following statement on May 26, 1972: "Article III of the ABM Treaty provides for each side one ABM system deployment area centered on its national capital and one ABM system deployment area containing ICBM silo launchers. The two sides have registered agreement on the following statement: 'The Parties understand that the center of the ABM system deployment area centered on the national capital and the center of the ABM system deployment area containing ICBM silo launchers for each Party shall be separated by no less than thirteen hundred kilometers.' In this connection, the U.S. side notes that its ABM system deployment area for defense of ICBM silo launchers, located west of the Mississippi River, will be centered in the Grand Forks ICBM silo launcher deployment area." (See Initialed Statement (C).)

C. ABM Test Ranges

The U.S. Delegation made the following statement on April 26, 1972: "Article IV of the ABM Treaty provides that 'the limitations provided for in Article III shall not apply to ABM systems or their components used for development or testing, and located within current or additionally agreed test ranges.' We believe it would be useful to assure that there is no misunderstanding as to current ABM test ranges. It is our understanding that ABM test ranges encompass the area within which ABM components are located for test purposes. The current U.S. ABM test ranges are at White Sands, New Mexico, and at Kwajalein Atoll, and the current Soviet ABM test range is near Sary Shagan in Kazakhstan. We consider that non-phased array radars of types used for range safety or instrumentation purposes may be located outside of ABM test ranges. We interpret the reference in Article IV to 'additionally agreed test ranges' to mean that ABM components will not be located at any other

test ranges without prior agreement between our Governments that there will be such additional ABM test ranges."

On May 5, 1972, the Soviet Delegation stated that there was a common understanding on what ABM test ranges were, that the use of the types of non-ABM radars for range safety or instrumentation was not limited under the Treaty, that the reference in Article IV to "additionally agreed" test ranges was sufficiently clear, and that national means permitted identifying current test ranges.

D. Mobile ABM Systems

On January 28, 1972, the U.S. Delegation made the following statement: "Article V(1) of the Joint Draft Text of the ABM Treaty includes an undertaking not to develop, test, or deploy mobile land-based ABM systems and their components. On May 5, 1971, the U.S. side indicated that, in its view, a prohibition on deployment of mobile ABM systems and components would rule out the deployment of ABM launchers and radars which were not permanent fixed types. At that time, we asked for the Soviet view of this interpretation. Does the Soviet side agree with the U.S. side's interpretation put forward on May 5, 1971?"

On April 13, 1972, the Soviet Delegation said there is a general common understanding on this matter.

E. Standing Consultative Commission

Ambassador Smith made the following statement on May 23, 1972: "The United States proposes that the sides agree that, with regard to initial implementation of the ABM Treaty's Article XIII on the Standing Consultative Commission (SCC) and of the consultation Articles to the Interim Agreement an offensive arms and the Accidents Agreement, agreement establishing the SCC will be worked out early in the follow-on SALT negotiations; until that is completed, the following arrangements will prevail: when SALT is in session, any consultation desired by either side under these articles can be carried out by the two SALT Delegations; when SALT is not in session, *ad hoc* arrangements for any desired consultations under these Articles may be made through diplomatic channels."

Minister Semenov replied that, on an *ad referendum* basis, he could agree that the U.S. statement corresponded to the Soviet understanding.

F. Standstill

On May 6, 1972, Minister Semenov made the following statement: "In an effort to accommodate the wishes of the U.S. side, the Soviet Delegation is prepared to proceed on the basis that the two sides will in fact observe the obligations of both the Interim Agreement and the ABM Treaty beginning from the date of signature of these two documents."

In reply, the U.S. Delegation made the following statement on May 20, 1972: "The U.S. agrees in principle with the Soviet statement made on May 6 concerning observance of obligations beginning from date of signature but we would like to make clear our understanding that this means that, pending ratification and acceptance, neither side would take any action prohibited by the agreements after they had entered into force. This understanding would continue to apply in the absence of notification by either signatory of its intention not to proceed with ratification or approval."

The Soviet Delegation indicated agreement with the U.S. statement.

2. Unilateral Statements.

(a) The following noteworthy unilateral statements were made during the negotiations by the United States Delegation:—

A. Withdrawal from the ABM Treaty

On May 9, 1972, Ambassador Smith made the following statement: "The U.S. Delegation has stressed the importance the U.S. Government attaches to achieving agreement on more complete limitations on strategic offensive arms, following agreement on an ABM-Treaty and on an Interim Agreement on certain measures with respect to the limitation of strategic offensive arms. The U.S. Delegation believes that an objective of the follow-on negotiations should be to constrain and reduce on a long-term basis threats to the survivability of our respective strategic retaliatory forces. The USSR Delegation has also indicated that the objectives of SALT would remain unfulfilled without the achievement of an agreement providing for more complete limitations on strategic offensive arms. Both sides recognize that the initial agreements would be steps toward the achievement of more complete limitations on strategic arms. If an agreement providing for more complete strategic offensive arms limitations were not achieved within five years, U.S. supreme interests could be jeopardized. Should that occur, it would constitute a basis for withdrawal from the ABM Treaty. The U.S. does not wish to see such a situation occur, nor do we believe that the USSR does. It is because we wish to prevent such a situation that we emphasize the importance the U.S. Government attaches to achievement of more complete limitations on strategic offensive arms. The U.S. Executive will inform the Congress, in connection with Congressional consideration of the ABM Treaty and the Interim Agreement of this statement of the U.S. position."

B. Land-Mobile ICBM Launchers

The U.S. Delegation made the following statement on May 20, 1972: "In connection with the important subject of land-mobile ICBM launchers, in the interest of concluding the Interim Agreement the U.S. Delegation now withdraws its proposal that Article I or an agreed statement explicitly prohibit the deployment of mobile land-based ICBM launchers. I have been instructed to inform you that, while agreeing to defer the question of limitation of operational land-mobile ICBM launchers to the subsequent negotiations on more complete limitations on strategic offensive arms, the U.S. would consider the deployment of operational land-mobile ICBM launchers during the period of the Interim Agreement as inconsistent with the objectives of that Agreement."

C. Covered Facilities.

The U.S. Delegation made the following statement on May 20, 1972: "I wish to emphasize the importance that the United States attaches to the provisions of Article V, including in particular their application to fitting out or berthing submarines."

D. "Heavy" ICBMs

The U.S. Delegation made the following statement on May 26, 1972: "The U.S. Delegation regrets that the Soviet Delegation has not been willing to agree on a common definition of a heavy missile. Under these circumstances, the U.S. Delegation believes it necessary to state the following: The United States would consider any ICBM having a volume significantly greater than that of the largest light ICBM now operational on either side to be a heavy ICBM. The U.S. proceeds on the premise that the Soviet side will give due account to this consideration."

E. Tested in ABM Mode

On April 7, 1972, the U.S. Delegation made the following statement: "Article II of the Joint Draft Text uses the term 'tested in an ABM mode,' in defining ABM components, and Article VI includes certain obligations concerning such testing. We believe that the sides should have a common understanding of this phrase. First, we would note that the testing provisions of the ABM Treaty are intended to apply to testing which occurs after the date of signature of the Treaty, and not to any testing which may have occurred in the past. Next, we would amplify the remarks we have made on this subject during the previous Helsinki phase by setting forth the objectives which govern the U.S. view on the subject, namely, while prohibiting testing of non-ABM components for ABM purposes: not to prevent testing of ABM components, and not to prevent testing of non-ABM components for non-ABM purposes. To clarify our inter-

pretation of 'tested in an ABM mode,' we note that we would consider a launcher, missile or radar to be 'tested in an ABM mode' if, for example, any of the following events occur: (1) a launcher is used to launch an ABM interceptor missile, (2) an interceptor missile is flight tested against a target vehicle which has a flight trajectory with characteristics of a strategic ballistic missile flight trajectory, or is flight tested in conjunction with the test of an ABM interceptor missile or an ABM radar at the same test range, or is flight tested to an altitude inconsistent with interception of targets against which air defenses are deployed, (3) a radar makes measurements on a cooperative target vehicle of the kind referred to in item (2) above during the re-entry portion of its trajectory or makes measurements in conjunction with the test of an ABM interceptor missile or an ABM radar at the same test range. Radars used for purposes such as range safety or instrumentation would be exempt from application of these criteria."

F. No-Transfer Article of ABM Treaty

On April 18, 1972, the U.S. Delegation made the following statement: "In regard to this Article (IX), I have a brief and I believe self-explanatory statement to make. The U.S. side wishes to make clear that the provisions of this Article do not set a precedent for whatever provision may be considered for a Treaty on Limiting Strategic Offensive Arms. The question of transfer of strategic offensive arms is a far more complex issue, which may require a different solution."

G. No Increase in Defense of Early Warning Radars

On July 28, 1970, the U.S. Delegation made the following statement: "Since Hen House radars (Soviet ballistic missile early warning radars) can detect and track ballistic missile warheads at great distances, they have a significant ABM potential. Accordingly, the U.S. would regard any increase in the defenses of such radars by surface-to-air missiles as inconsistent with an agreement."

(b) The following noteworthy unilateral statement was made by the Delegation of the U.S.S.R. and is shown here with the U.S. reply:—

On May 17, 1972, Minister Semenov made the following unilateral "Statement of the Soviet Side": "Taking into account that modern ballistic missile submarines are presently in the possession of not only the U.S., but also of its NATO allies, the Soviet Union agrees that for the period of effectiveness of the Interim 'Freeze' Agreement the U.S. and its NATO allies have up to 50 such submarines with a total of up to 800 ballistic missile launchers thereon (including 41 U.S. submarines with 656 ballistic missile launchers). However, if during the period of effectiveness of the Agreement U.S. allies in NATO should increase the number of their modern submarines to exceed the numbers of submarines they would have operational or under construction on the date of signature of the Agreement, the Soviet Union will have the right to a corresponding increase in the number of its submarines. In the opinion of the Soviet side, the solution of the question of modern ballistic missile submarines provided for in the Interim Agreement only partially compensates for the strategic imbalance in the deployment of the nuclear-powered missile submarines of the USSR and the U.S. Therefore, the Soviet side believes that this whole question, and above all the question of liquidating the American missile submarine bases outside the U.S., will be appropriately resolved in the course of follow-on negotiations."

On May 24, Ambassador Smith made the following reply to Minister Semenov: "The United States has studied the 'statement made by the Soviet side' of May 17 concerning compensation for submarine basing and SLBM submarines belonging to third countries. The United States does not accept the validity of the considerations in that statement."

On May 26 Minister Semenov repeated the unilateral statement made on May 24. Ambassador Smith also repeated the U.S. rejection on May 26.

TEXT OF U.S.-SOVIET ANTIBALLISTIC MISSILE TREATY

Following is the text, as made available by the White House, of the treaty between the United States of America and the Union of Soviet Socialist Republics on the limitations of anti-ballistic missile systems:

The United States of America and the Union of Soviet Socialist Republics, hereinafter referred to as the Parties,

Proceeding from the premise that nuclear war would have devastating consequences for all mankind,

Considering that effective measures to limit anti-ballistic missile systems would be a substantial factor in curbing the race in strategic offensive arms and would lead to a decrease in the risk of outbreak of war involving nuclear weapons,

Proceeding from the premise that the limitation of anti-ballistic missile systems, as well as certain agreed measures with respect to the limitation of strategic offensive arms, would contribute to the creation of more favorable conditions for further negotiations on limiting strategic arms,

Mindful of their obligations under Article VI of the Treaty on the Non-Proliferation of Nuclear Weapons,

Declaring their intention to achieve at the earliest possible date the cessation of the nuclear arms race and to take effective measures toward reductions in strategic arms, nuclear disarmament, and general and complete disarmament,

Desiring to contribute to the relaxation of international tension and the strengthening of trust between States,

Have agreed as follows:

Article I

1. Each Party undertakes to limit anti-ballistic missile (ABM) systems and to adopt other measures in accordance with the provisions of this Treaty.

2. Each Party undertakes not to deploy ABM systems for a defense of the territory of its country and not to provide a base for such a defense, and not to deploy ABM systems for defense of an individual region except as provided for in Article III of this Treaty.

Article II

1. For the purpose of this Treaty an ABM system is a system to counter strategic ballistic missiles or their elements in flight trajectory, currently consisting of:

(a) ABM interceptor missiles, which are interceptor missiles constructed and deployed for an ABM role, or of a type tested in an ABM mode:

(b) ABM launchers, which are launchers constructed and deployed for launching ABM interceptor missiles; and

(c) ABM radars, which are radars constructed and deployed for an ABM role, or of a type tested in an ABM mode.

2. The ABM system components listed in paragraph 1 of this Article include those which are:

(a) operational;
(b) under construction;
(c) undergoing testing;
(d) undergoing overhaul, repair or conversion; or
(e) mothballed.

Article III

Each Party undertakes not to deploy ABM systems or their components except that:

(a) within one ABM system deployment area having a radius of one hundred and fifty kilometers and centered on the Party's national capital, a Party may deploy: (1) no more than one hundred ABM launchers and no more than one hundred ABM interceptor missiles at launch sites, and (2) ABM radars within no more than six ABM radar complexes, the area of each complex being circular and having a diameter of no more than three kilometers; and

(b) within one ABM system deployment area having a radius of one hundred and fifty kilometers and containing ICBM silo launchers, a Party may deploy: (1) no more than one hundred ABM launchers and no more than one hundred ABM interceptor missiles at launch sites; (2) two large phased-array ABM radars comparable in potential to corresponding ABM radars operational or under construction on the date of signature of the Treaty in an ABM system deployment area containing ICBM silo launchers, and (3) no more than eighteen ABM radars each having a potential less than the potential of the smaller of the above-mentioned two large phased-array ABM radars.

Article IV

The limitations provided for in Article III shall not apply to ABM systems or their components used for development or testing, and located within current or additionally agreed test ranges. Each Party may have no more than a total of fifteen ABM launchers at test ranges.

Article V

1. Each Party undertakes not to develop, test, or deploy ABM systems or components which are sea-based, air-based, space-based, or mobile land-based.

2. Each Party undertakes not to develop, test, or deploy ABM launchers for launching more than one ABM interceptor missile at a time from each launcher, nor to modify deployed launchers to provide them with such a capability, nor to develop, test, or deploy automatic or semi-automatic or other similar systems for rapid reload of ABM launchers.

Article VI

To enhance assurance of the effectiveness of the limitations on ABM systems and their components provided by this Treaty, each Party undertakes:

(a) not to give missiles, launchers, or radars, other than ABM interceptor missiles, ABM launchers, or ABM radars, capabilities to counter strategic ballistic missiles or their elements in flight trajectory, and not to test them in an ABM mode; and

(b) not to deploy in the future radars for early warning of strategic ballistic missile attack except at locations along the periphery of its national territory and oriented outward.

Article VII

Subject to the provisions of this Treaty, modernization and replacement of ABM systems or their components may be carried out.

Article VIII

ABM systems or their components in excess of the numbers or outside the areas specified in this Treaty, as well as ABM systems or their components prohibited by this Treaty, shall be destroyed or dismantled under agreed procedures within the shortest possible agreed period of time.

Article IX

To assure the viability and effectiveness of this Treaty, each Party undertakes not transfer to other States, and not to deploy outside its national territory, ABM systems or their components limited by this Treaty.

Article X

Each Party undertakes not to assume any international obligations which would conflict with this Treaty.

Article XI

The Parties undertake to continue active negotiations for limitations on strategic offensive arms.

Article XII

1. For the purpose of providing assurance of compliance with the provisions of this Treaty, each Party shall use national technical means of verification at its disposal in a manner consistent with generally recognized principles of international law.

2. Each Party undertakes not to interfere with the national technical means of verification of the other Party operating in accordance with paragraph 1 of this Article.

3. Each Party undertakes not to use deliberate concealment measures which impede verification by national technical means of compliance with the provisions of this Treaty. This obligation shall not require changes in current construction, assembly, conversion, or overhaul practices.

Article XIII

1. To promote the objectives and implementation of the provisions of this Treaty, the Parties shall establish promptly a Standing Consultative Commission, within the framework of which they will:

(a) consider questions concerning compliance with the obligations assumed and related situations which may be considered ambiguous;

(b) provide on a voluntary basis such information as either Party considers necessary to assure confidence in compliance with the obligations assumed;

(c) consider questions involving unintended interference with national technical means of verification;

(d) consider possible changes in the strategic situation which have a bearing on the provisions of this Treaty;

(e) agree upon procedures and dates for destruction or dismantling of ABM systems or their components in cases provided for by the provisions of this Treaty;

(f) consider, as appropriate, possible proposals for further increasing the viability of this Treaty, including proposals for amendments in accordance with the provisions of this Treaty;

(g) consider, as appropriate, proposals for further measures aimed at limiting strategic arms.

2. The Parties through consultation shall establish, and may amend as appropriate, Regulations for the Standing Consultative Commission governing procedures, composition and other relevant matters.

Article XIV

1. Each Party may propose amendments to this Treaty. Agreed amendments shall enter into force in accordance with the procedures governing the entry into force of this Treaty.

2. Five years after entry into force of this Treaty, and at five-year intervals thereafter, the Parties shall together conduct a review of this Treaty.

Article XV

1. This Treaty shall be of unlimited duration.

2. Each Party shall, in exercising its national sovereignty, have the right to withdraw from this Treaty if it decides that extraordinary events related to the subject matter of this Treaty have jeopardized its supreme interests. It shall give notice of its decision to the other Party six months prior to withdrawal from the Treaty. Such notice shall include a statement of the extraordinary events the notifying Party regards as having jeopardized its supreme interests.

Article XVI

1. This Treaty shall be subject to ratification in accordance with the constitutional procedures of each Party. The Treaty shall enter into force on the day of the exchange of instruments of ratification.

2. This Treaty shall be registered pursuant to Article 102 of the Charter of the United Nations.

Done at Moscow on May 26, 1972, in two copies, each in the English and Russian languages, both texts being equally authentic.

FOR THE UNITED STATES   FOR THE UNION OF SOVIET
OF AMERICA   SOCIALIST REPUBLICS

RICHARD NIXON   LEONID I. BREZHNEV
President of the United   General Secretary of the Central
States of America   Committee of the CPSU

TEXT OF U.S.-SOVIET AGREEMENTS ON OFFENSIVE MISSILES

THE PROTOCOL

Following is the text, as made available by the White House, of the protocol to the interim agreement between the United States of America and the Union of Soviet Socialist Republics on certain measures with respect to the limitation of strategic offensive arms: (Agreement p. 111)

The United States of America and the Union of Soviet Socialist Republics, hereinafter referred to as the Parties,

Having agreed on certain limitations relating to submarine-launched ballistic missile launchers and modern ballistic missile submarines, and to replacement procedures, in the Interim Agreement,

Have agreed as follows:

The Parties understand that, under Article III of the Interim Agreement, for the period during which that Agreement remains in force:

The US may have no more than 710 ballistic missile launchers on submarines (SLBMs) and no more than 44 modern ballistic missile submarines. The Soviet Union may have no more than 950 ballistic missile launchers on submarines and no more than 62 modern ballistic missile submarines.

Additional ballistic missile launchers on submarines up to the above-mentioned levels, in the U.S. - over 656 ballistic missile launchers on nuclear-powered submarines, and in the

U.S.S.R. - over 740 ballistic missile launchers on nuclear-powered submarines, operational and under construction, may become operational as replacements for equal numbers of ballistic missile launchers of older types deployed prior to 1964 or of ballistic missile launchers on older submarines.

The deployment of modern SLBMs on any submarine, regardless of type, will be counted against the total level of SLBMs permitted for the U.S. and the U.S.S.R.

This Protocol shall be considered an integral part of the Interim Agreement.

FOR THE UNITED STATES OF AMERICA	FOR THE UNION OF SOVIET SOCIALIST REPUBLICS
RICHARD NIXON The President of the United States of America	LEONID I. BREZHNEV The General Secretary of the Central Committee of the CPSU

INTERIM AGREEMENT

Following is the text, as made available by the White House, of the Interim Agreement between the Union of Soviet Socialist Republics and the United States of America on certain measures with respect to the limitation of strategic offensive arms:

The Union of Soviet Socialist Republics and the United States of America hereinafter referred to as the Parties,

Convinced that the Treaty on the Limitation of Anti-Ballistic Missile Systems and this Interim Agreement on Certain Measures with Respect to the Limitation of Strategic Offensive Arms will contribute to the creation of more favorable conditions for active negotiations on limiting strategic arms as well as to the relaxation of international tension and the strengthening of trust between States,

Taking into account the relationship between strategic offensive and defensive arms,

Mindful of their obligations under Article VI of the Treaty on the Non-Proliferation of Nuclear Weapons,

Have agreed as follows:

Article I

The Parties undertake not to start construction of additional fixed land-based intercontinental ballistic missile (ICBM) launchers after July 1, 1972.

Article II

The Parties undertake not to convert land-based launchers for light ICBMs, or for ICBMs of older types deployed prior to 1964, into land-based launchers for heavy ICBMs of types deployed after that time.

Article III

The Parties undertake to limit submarine-launched ballistic missile (SLBM) launchers and modern ballistic missile submarines to the numbers operational and under construction on the date of signature of this Interim Agreement, and in addition launchers and submarines constructed under procedures established by the Parties as replacements for an equal number of ICBM launchers of older types deployed prior to 1964 or for launchers on older submarines.

Article IV

Subject to the provisions of this Interim Agreement, modernization and replacement of strategic offensive ballistic missiles and launchers covered by this Interim Agreement may be undertaken.

Article V

1. For the purpose of providing assurance of compliance with the provisions of this Interim Agreement, each Party shall use national technical means of verification at its disposal in a manner consistent with generally recognized principles of international law.

2. Each Party undertakes not to interfere with the national technical means of verification of the other Party operating in accordance with paragraph 1 of this Article.

3. Each Party undertakes not to use deliberate concealment measures which impede verification by national technical means of compliance with the provisions of this Interim Agreement. This obligation shall not require changes in current construction, assembly, conversion, or overhaul practices.

Article VI

To promote the objectives and implementation of the provisions of this Interim Agreement, the Parties shall use the Standing Consultative Commission established under Article XIII of the Treaty on the Limitation of Anti-Ballistic Missile Systems in accordance with the provisions of that Article.

Article VII

The Parties undertake to continue active negotiations for limitations on strategic offensive arms. The obligations provided for in this Interim Agreement shall not prejudice the scope or terms of the limitations on strategic offensive arms which may be worked out in the course of further negotiations.

Article VIII

1. This Interim Agreement shall enter into force upon exchange of written notices of acceptance by each Party, which exchange shall take place simultaneously with the exchange of instruments of ratification of the Treaty on the Limitation of Anti-Ballistic Missile Systems.

2. This Interim Agreement shall remain in force for a period of five years unless replaced earlier by an agreement on more complete measures limiting strategic offensive arms. It is the objective of the Parties to conduct active follow-on negotiations with the aim of concluding such an agreement as soon as possible.

3. Each Party shall, in exercising its national sovereignty, have the right to withdraw from this Interim Agreement if it decides that extraordinary events related to the subject matter of this Interim Agreement have jeopardized its supreme interests. It shall give notice of its decision to the other Party six months prior to withdrawal from this Interim Agreement. Such notice shall include a statement of the extraordinary events the notifying Party regards as having jeopardized its supreme interests.

Done at Moscow on May 26, 1972, in two copies, each in the Russian and English languages, both texts being equally authentic.

FOR THE UNION OF SOVIET SOCIALIST REPUBLICS	FOR THE UNITED STATES OF AMERICA
LEONID I. BREZHNEV General Secretary of the Central Committee of the CPSU	RICHARD NIXON The President of the United States

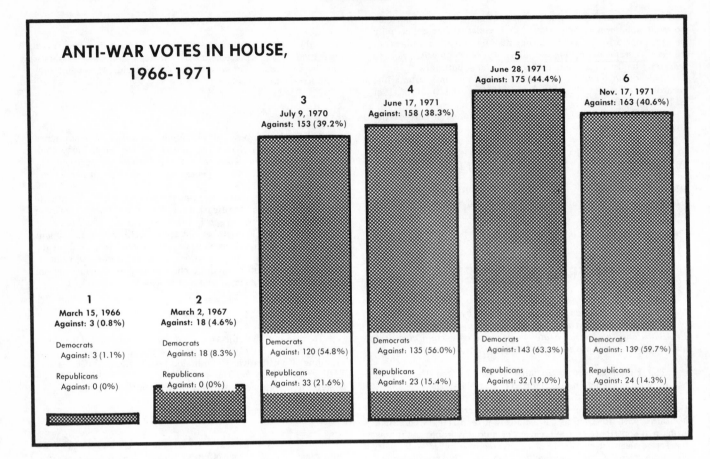

ANTI-WAR VOTES IN HOUSE, 1966-1971

3
July 9, 1970
Against: 153 (39.2%)

4
June 17, 1971
Against: 158 (38.3%)

5
June 28, 1971
Against: 175 (44.4%)

6
Nov. 17, 1971
Against: 163 (40.6%)

1
March 15, 1966
Against: 3 (0.8%)

Democrats
Against: 3 (1.1%)

Republicans
Against: 0 (0%)

2
March 2, 1967
Against: 18 (4.6%)

Democrats
Against: 18 (8.3%)

Republicans
Against: 0 (0%)

Democrats
Against: 120 (54.8%)

Republicans
Against: 33 (21.6%)

Democrats
Against: 135 (56.0%)

Republicans
Against: 23 (15.4%)

Democrats
Against: 143 (63.3%)

Republicans
Against: 32 (19.0%)

Democrats
Against: 139 (59.7%)

Republicans
Against: 24 (14.3%)

The Vietnam War: Growing Congressional Opposition

HOUSE

1. Supplemental Funds. (March 15, 1966). Bill appropriating $13.1-billion in supplemental funds for the Defense Department, primarily for support of U.S. operations in Southeast Asia. Passed 389-3: R 122-0; D 267-3. *(HR 13546; 1966 CQ Almanac p. 153, 88)*

2. Supplemental Funds. (March 2, 1967). Amendment stating that no funds authorized by the bill were to be used to carry out military operations in or over North Vietnam. Rejected 18-372: R 0-173; D 18-199. *(HR 4515; 1967 CQ Almanac p. 100, 207)*

3. Cambodia. (July 9, 1970). Motion opposing the Cooper-Church amendment barring funds for U.S. military operations in Cambodia after July 1, 1970. Motion adopted 237-153: R 138-33; D 99-120. *(HR 15628; 1970 CQ Almanac p. 927, 42-H)*

4. Withdrawal. (June 17, 1971). Nedzi-Whalen amendment barring use of funds to carry out military operations in Indochina after Dec. 31, 1971, without congressional approval. Rejected 158-255: R 23-149; D 135-106. *(HR 8687; 1971 CQ Almanac p. 305, 32-H)*

5. Withdrawal. (June 28, 1971). Motion opposing instruction of House conferees to support the Mansfield amendment declaring it U.S. policy to withdraw all troops from Indochina within 9 months of enactment. Motion adopted 219-175: R 136-32; D 83-143. *(HR 6531; 1971 CQ Almanac p. 257, 36-H)*

6. Withdrawal. (Nov. 17, 1971). Amendment setting July 1, 1972, cutoff for funds used in support of U.S. military operations in Indochina, calling for withdrawal of all troops by a specified date, subject to release of all U.S. POWs. Rejected 163-238: R 24-144; D 139-94. *(HR 11731; 1971 CQ Almanac p. 330, 90-H)*

SENATE

1. Gulf of Tonkin. (Aug. 7, 1964). Passage of the resolution. Passed 88-2: R 32-0; D 56-2. *(H J Res 1145, 1964 CQ Almanac p. 331, 710)*

2. Gulf of Tonkin. (March 1, 1966). Motion to kill an amendment to repeal the Gulf of Tonkin Resolution. Motion adopted 92-5: R 32-0; D 60-5. *(S 2791; 1966 CQ Almanac p. 390, 943)*

3. Cambodia. (June 30, 1970). Cooper-Church amendment barring funds for U.S. military operations in Cambodia after July 1, 1970, unless authorized by Congress. Adopted 58-37: R 16-26; D 42-11. *(HR 15628; 1970 CQ Almanac p. 927, 33-S)*

4. Withdrawal. (Sept. 1, 1970). McGovern-Hatfield amendment limiting troop strength to 280,000 men after April 30, 1971, and providing complete withdrawal by Dec. 31, 1971, but authorizing the President to delay the withdrawal deadline up to 60 days. Rejected 39-55: R 7-34; D 32-21. *(HR 17123; 1970 CQ Almanac p. 380, 46-S)*

5. Withdrawal. (Sept. 30, 1971). Mansfield amendment declaring it U.S. policy that withdrawal of troops from Indochina would be completed within 6 months of enactment, dependent only on the release of American POWs. Adopted 57-38: R 15-27; D 42-11. *(HR 8687; 1971 CQ Almanac p. 305, 37-S)*

6. Withdrawal. (Oct. 28, 1971). Scott amendment deleting Cooper-Church provisions barring use of funds authorized for U.S. forces in Indochina for any purpose except withdrawal or protection of troops as they withdrew. Adopted 47-44: R 30-11; D 17-33. *(HR 9910; 1971 CQ Almanac p. 387, 42-S)*

ANTI-WAR VOTES IN SENATE, 1964-1971

(For descriptions of votes, see preceding page.)

3
June 30, 1970
Against: 58
(D 42, R 16)

Aiken (R Vt.)
Anderson (D N.M.)
Bayh (D Ind.)
Bible (D Nev.)
Brooke (R Mass.)
Burdick (D N.D.)
Byrd (D W.Va.)
Cannon (D Nev.)
Case (R N.J.)
Church (D Idaho)
Cooper (R Ky.)
Cranston (D Calif.)
Dole (R Kan.)
Eagleton (D Mo.)
Fulbright (D Ark.)
Goodell (R N.Y.)
Gore (D Tenn.)
Gravel (D Alaska)
Harris (D Okla.)
Hart (D Mich.)
Hartke (D Ind.)
Hatfield (R Ore.)
Hollings (D S.C.)
Hughes (D Iowa)
Inouye (D Hawaii)
Jackson (D Wash.)
Javits (R N.Y.)
Jordan (D N.C.)
Kennedy (D Mass.)
Magnuson (D Wash.)
Mansfield (D Mont.)
Mathias (R Md.)
McCarthy (D Minn.)
McGovern (D S.D.)
McIntyre (D N.H.)
Metcalf (D Mont.)
Mondale (D Minn.)
Montoya (D N.M.)
Moss (D Utah)
Muskie (D Maine)
Packwood (R Ore.)
Pastore (D R.I.)
Pearson (R Kan.)
Pell (D R.I.)
Percy (R Ill.)
Proxmire (D Wis.)
Randolph (D W.Va.)
Ribicoff (D Conn.)
Saxbe (R Ohio)
Schweiker (R Pa.)
Smith (R Ill.)
Spong (D Va.)
Stevens (R Alaska)
Symington (D Mo.)
Tydings (D Md.)
Williams (D N.J.)
Yarborough (D Texas)
Young (D Ohio)

5
Sept. 30, 1971
Against: 57
(D 42, R 15)

Aiken (R Vt.)
Anderson (D N.M.)
Bayh (D Ind.)
Bentsen (D Texas)
Bible (D Nev.)
Brooke (R Mass.)
Burdick (D N.D.)
Byrd (D W.Va.)
Cannon (D Nev.)
Case (R N.J.)
Chiles (D Fla.)
Church (D Idaho)
Cook (R Ky.)
Cooper (R Ky.)
Cotton (R N.H.)
Cranston (D Calif.)
Eagleton (D Mo.)
Fulbright (D Ark.)
Gambrell (D Ga.)
Gravel (D Alaska)
Harris (D Okla.)
Hart (D Mich.)
Hartke (D Ind.)
Hatfield (R Ore.)
Hollings (D S.C.)
Hughes (D Iowa)
Humphrey (D Minn.)
Javits (R N.Y.)
Jordan (D N.C.)
Jordan (R Idaho)
Kennedy (D Mass.)
Magnuson (D Wash.)
Mansfield (D Mont.)
Mathias (R Md.)
McClellan (D Ark.)
McGovern (D S.D.)
McIntyre (D N.H.)
Metcalf (D Mont.)
Mondale (D Minn.)
Moss (D Utah)
Muskie (D Maine)
Nelson (D Wis.)
Packwood (R Ore.)
Pastore (D R.I.)
Pearson (R Kan.)
Pell (D R.I.)
Proxmire (D Wis.)
Randolph (D W.Va.)
Ribicoff (D Conn.)
Schweiker (R Pa.)
Spong (D Va.)
Stafford (R Vt.)
Stevenson (D Ill.)
Symington (D Mo.)
Tunney (D Calif.)
Williams (D N.J.)
Young (R N.D.)

6
Oct. 28, 1971
Against: 44
(D 33, R 11)

Aiken (R Vt.)
Anderson (D N.M.)
Bayh (D Ind.)
Brooke (R Mass.)
Burdick (D N.D.)
Case (R N.J.)
Church (D Idaho)
Cooper (R Ky.)
Cranston (D Calif.)
Eagleton (D Mo.)
Gravel (D Alaska)
Hart (D Mich.)
Hartke (D Ind.)
Hatfield (R Ore.)
Hughes (D Iowa)
Humphrey (D Minn.)
Javits (R N.Y.)
Jordan (D N.C.)
Kennedy (D Mass.)
Magnuson (D Wash.)
Mansfield (D Mont.)
Mathias (R Md.)
McIntyre (D N.H.)
Metcalf (D Mont.)
Mondale (D Minn.)
Montoya (D N.M.)
Moss (D Utah)
Muskie (D Maine)
Nelson (D Wis.)
Pastore (D R.I.)
Pell (D R.I.)
Percy (R Ill.)
Proxmire (D Wis.)
Randolph (D W.Va.)
Ribicoff (D Conn.)
Schweiker (R Pa.)
Spong (D Va.)
Stafford (R Vt.)
Stevenson (D Ill.)
Symington (D Mo.)
Talmadge (D Ga.)
Tunney (D Calif.)
Weicker (R Conn.)
Williams (D N.J.)

4
Sept. 1, 1970
Against: 39
(D 32, R 7)

Bayh (D Ind.)
Brooke (R Mass.)
Burdick (D N.D.)
Case (R N.J.)
Church (D Idaho)
Cranston (D Calif.)
Eagleton (D Mo.)
Fulbright (D Ark.)
Goodell (R N.Y.)
Gravel (D Alaska)
Harris (D Okla.)
Hart (D Mich.)
Hartke (D Ind.)
Hatfield (R Ore.)
Hughes (D Iowa)
Inouye (D Hawaii)
Javits (R N.Y.)
Kennedy (D Mass.)
Magnuson (D Wash.)
Mansfield (D Mont.)
Mathias (R Md.)
McCarthy (D Minn.)
McGovern (D S.D.)
McIntyre (D N.H.)
Metcalf (D Mont.)
Mondale (D Minn.)
Montoya (D N.M.)
Muskie (D Maine)
Nelson (D Wis.)
Pastore (D R.I.)
Pell (D R.I.)
Proxmire (D Wis.)
Ribicoff (D Conn.)
Schweiker (R Pa.)
Symington (D Mo.)
Tydings (D Md.)
Williams (D N.J.)
Yarborough (D Texas)
Young (D Ohio)

2
March 1, 1966
Against: 5
(D 5, R 0)

Fulbright (D Ark.)
Gruening (D Alaska)
McCarthy (D Minn.)
Morse (D Ore.)
Young (D Ohio)

1
Aug. 7, 1964
Against: 2
(D 2, R 0)

Gruening (D Alaska)
Morse (D Ore.)

PROVISIONS OF 1971 SELECTIVE SERVICE EXTENSION ACT

As signed Sept. 28, 1971, by the President, HR 6531:

Draft Extension

• Extended the President's authority to induct men into the armed forces for two years, to June 30, 1973.

Manpower Limitations

• Imposed an average manpower ceiling on active duty strength of 2,553,409 men in each of fiscal 1972 and 1973 (Army 974,309; Navy, 613,619; Marine Corps, 209,846; Air Force, 755,635) which the President could exceed only with the consent of Congress; provided that the President could call up the National Guard and the Reserves to cope with civil disturbances without regard to personnel limitations contained in the bill.

• Ceilings on the number of men who could be drafted annually were set at 130,000 for fiscal 1972 and 140,000 for fiscal 1973; the President could exceed the ceiling only with the consent of Congress.

Vietnam Withdrawal

• Provided that it was the sense of Congress that the United States terminate "at the earliest practicable date" all U.S. military operations in Indochina and that the withdrawal of U.S. troops be completed by a certain date, not specified, subject to the release of all American prisoners of war and an accounting of those missing in action; urged the President to begin negotiations for a cease-fire immediately and to establish a definite date for withdrawal of U.S. forces.

Compensation

(The total cost of itemized pay package listed below was $2,384,600,000.)

• Provided a basic pay increase weighted heavily toward first-term enlistees and low-ranking officers at a cost estimated at $1,825,400,000 in fiscal 1972.

• Increased a bachelor's quarters allowance at an estimated cost of $409,800,000 in fiscal 1972.

• Increased dependents' allowances at an estimated cost of $105,900,000 in fiscal 1972.

• Provided a maximum enlistment bonus of $3,000 per enlistee to be allocated at the discretion of the armed forces at an estimated cost of $20,000,000 in fiscal 1972.

• Increased dependents' allowances for reservists at an estimated cost of $20,000,000 in fiscal 1972.

• Increased expenses for recruiters in carrying out their duties at an estimated cost of $2,900,000 in fiscal 1972.

• Increased optometrists' pay at an estimated cost of $600,000 in fiscal 1972.

• Provided for an increase in travel pay for uncompensated Selective Service employees to $500 per year from $50.

Conscientious Objector

• Required that a conscientious objector serve a two-year term of alternate service subject to recall for an additional year of service during a national emergency declared by the President.

• Provided that a CO's alternate service program would be placed under the jurisdiction of the director of Selective Service.

Deferments and Exemptions

• Provided that a divinity student would have a statutory deferment from the draft, rather than an exemption, and that he would be eligible for induction until age 35; if the student should either drop out of divinity school or fail to become an ordained minister, he would be subject to induction.

• Provided the President with discretionary authority over student deferments; stipulated that students who entered college prior to the summer of 1971 would maintain their deferments until graduation or to age 24.

• Provided that, if drafted, a high school senior who reached the age of 20 during his senior year would be permitted to graduate before induction.

• Provided that no person could be inducted against his will who had lost a member of his immediate family through service in the armed forces or in which a member had subsequently died as a result of injuries or disease incurred in the line of duty; provided immediate discharge to those already in the service who were eligible for the exemption. The exemption pertained to family members lost after Dec. 31, 1959, and who were of "the whole blood" of the person exempted.

• Provided that a college student could finish the semester, term or, in the case of a senior, the academic year, after receiving his induction notice.

Procedural Rights

• Granted to the potential draftee the right to appear in person before any local or appeal board.

• Provided the right to present witnesses before a local draft board.

• Required the attendance of a quorum of any local or appeal board during a registrant's personal appearance.

• Required the local and appeal board to provide, upon request, a written report when the board had made a decision adverse to the claim of a registrant.

• Provided that no person could enlist in the armed forces after an induction notice had been issued for him.

Draft Boards and Draft

• Provided that members of a local draft board could not serve for more than 20 years.

• Provided that in making future appointments to local boards, the President should see to the "maximum extent possible" that the boards reflected proportionately the racial and religious breakdowns of the community in which the board served.

• Provided that for a state to have joint headquarters for draft boards the governor must give his approval.

• Provided that the Selective Service System would remain as an active standby organization if manpower needs were being met by volunteers intead of by draftees.

• Specified that no regulation contained in the bill could become effective until 30 days after the regulation had been published in the *Federal Register*.

• Provided for a uniform national lottery call of draftees eliminating the local board quota system.

• Provided that a state director of Selective Service could not serve concurrent terms in an elected or appointed position in state or local government without the approval of the director of Selective Service.

• Specified a minimum age for draft board members of 19 years and a maximum of 65.

• Extended the statute of limitations for prosecution until age 31 for those persons who failed to register for the draft.

Drug and Alcohol Control
• Provided an interim measure whereby all practical methods for treating, identifying and rehabilitating drug addicts and alcoholics would be implemented immediately for both men already in the service and those taking pre-induction physicals. The Secretary of Defense was ordered to report to Congress 60 days after enactment of the bill on the department's programs and plans for drug and alcohol problems.

Studies
• Provided for a study of the Defense Department's and the Health, Education and Welfare Department's use of civilian medical facilities.
• Provided for a study of the effectiveness of the program for increasing voluntary enlistments.

Discrimination and Aliens
• Prohibited job discrimination against American citizens and their dependents in hiring on U.S. military bases in foreign countries.

• Exempted from service in the U.S. armed forces any alien who served at least 12 months of active duty in the armed forces of a nation which was associated with mutual defense activities of the United States.
• Provided that aliens who held foreign-affairs-oriented jobs, such as those in a diplomatic or counselor capacity or with official international organizations, were exempted from the draft.
• Provided that an alien who had lived in the United States for a period up to one year was exempted from the draft.
• Provided that an alien who was in the country as a temporary worker, treaty trader, investor, fiance of an American citizen or a temporary visitor was exempted from the draft.

Reserve Officers
• Provided that promotions to the grade of lieutenant colonel/commander and above, in both the reserves and the regular armed forces, would require Senate confirmation.

Index: Charts, Tables, Summaries

OTHER CQ PUBLICATIONS

HARD COVER BOOKS

Congress and the Nation
Volume I: 1945-1964   **$27.50**
Volume II: 1965-1968   **$35.00**

This 3,100 page, two-volume resource brings detail and perspective to the important issues and events in national affairs since World War II, spanning five Presidencies and twenty-four years. Carefully organized and indexed for reference. Volume I: 1945-1964 (1965) 2,000 pages, 8½" x 11", hard cover; Volume II: 1965-1968 (1969) 1,100 pages, 8½" x 11", hard cover.

Congressional Quarterly's   **$35.00** Guide to the Congress of the United States
The definitive reference on Congress— its origins, history and development. Explains how Congress works, its powers, the pressures upon it, and prospects for change. Carefully organized and indexed for reference. September 1971. 984 pages, 8½" x 11", hard cover.

American Votes 9   **$22.50**
A handbook of American election statistics. Official results for the 1970 vote in each state for Senator, Representative and Governor, with vote totals, percentages and pluralities. Compiled and edited by Richard M. Scammon, Director, Elections Research Center. July 1972. 470 pages, 8½" x 11", hard cover. Also available: American Votes 2, 4, 5 ($12.50); 6, 7 ($17.50); 8 ($20.00).

CQ PAPERBACKS

China and U.S. Foreign Policy   **$4.00**
Current and historical background on President Nixon's efforts to normalize relations with China. Nixon Doctrine, Far East trade, U.S.—Asian allies, China lobbies, Congress and Politics. January 1972. 96 pages, 8½" x 11", paper.

Civil Rights Progress Report 1970   **$4.00**
Public and private actions in the field of civil rights during 1968-1970. Civil Rights Commission report, Supreme Court decisions, the Black Movement, Nixon administration policy. January 1971. 92 pages, 8½" x 11", paper.

Congressional Roll Call 1971   **$8.00**
A chronology and analysis of votes in the House and Senate, 92nd Congress, 1st Session. Reports the vote of each Representative and Senator for every roll call vote taken during 1971. Indexed. April 1972. 224 pages, 8½" x 11", paper. Also available: Congressional Roll Call 1970 ($8.00) and Congressional Roll Call 1969 ($8.00).

Crime and the Law   **$4.00**
The fight by federal forces to control public problem number one in America. Crime facts and figures, urban crime, organized crime and white collar crime, penal and court reform, political response of the administration, Congress and the courts. July 1971. 96 pages, 8½" x 11", paper.

Current American Government (CQ Guide)   **$3.00**
Updated and published twice each year, in January and August, to serve as an up-to-date handbook on recent significan developments in the legislative, executive and judicial branchs of American government. Spring edition (January) and Fall edition (August). About 150 pages, 8½" x 11", paper. Annual subscription for both Spring and Fall editions is $6.00

Dollar Politics   **$4.00**
The issue of campaign spending. How funds are raised and spent; wealthy candidates and richest givers; Campaign Spending Act of 1971; 1972 spending data. January 1972. 96 pages, 8½" x 11" paper.

Standing order. Includes future paperback titles which will be mailed upon publication.

Global Defense: U.S. Military Commitments Abroad   **$2.95**
Growth of commitments, history of involvement, congressional concern, and presidential war power. September 1969. 92 pages, 8½" x 11", paper.

Man's Control of the Environment   **$4.00**
Ecological problems facing America: population explosion, land use, air and water pollution, solid waste disposal, pesticides, electric power problems, coastal pollution, noise pollution, politics of pollution, state actions, international vs. national interests. August 1970. 96 pages, 8½" x 11", paper.

Members of Congress 1789-1970   **$4.00**
A complete list of Members of Congress, party affiliation and dates of service, 1st through 91st Congress. September 1971. 187 pages, 8½" x 11", paper.

National Diplomacy 1965-1970   **$5.00**
Foreign policy under President Johnson and under the Nixon administration. Includes chronology of events in 1965-1970 and texts of Nixon statements on foreign policy. Military commitments, arms sales, Middle East policy, relations with China, and Indochina. May 1970. 156 pages, 8½" x 11", paper.

Nixon: The Third Year of his Presidency   **$4.00**
Reviews 1971 administration actions on the economy, China, the budget, nominations and appointment, regulatory agencies. Texts of Presidential messages, statements and news conferences. April 1972. 236 pages, 8½" x 11", paper. Also available: Nixon: The Second Year of his Presidency ($4.00) and Nixon: The First Year of his Presidency ($4.00).

Politics in America 1946-1970   **$4.00**
The politics and issues of the years since World War II including the 91st Congress and 1970 elections. Results of 6 presidential and 13 congressional elections. Fourth edition: September 1971. 160 pages, 8½" x 11", paper.

The Washington Lobby   **$4.00**
A continuing struggle to influence government policy. Lobbying and the law, lobbying and elections, lobby coalitions, case studies, appended documents. July 1971. 128 pages, 8½" x 11", paper.